A Theology
of Love

"I literally cannot think of another scholar who could reasonably attempt what Richard Smoley not only attempts but succeeds in doing in *A Theology of Love*. Smoley constructs a new, mysterious, utterly practical, and broadly gnostic Christian-based approach to life; it is one of mysticism, questioning, critical belief, and personal change. Some contemporary scholars possess the intellect, some possess the inner experience—but none, other than Smoley, possess both, and in sufficient amounts, to achieve this unprecedented task. When you read *A Theology of Love* you will understand why Richard is our generation's premier independent scholar of spirituality."

MITCH HOROWITZ, PEN AWARD–WINNING
AUTHOR OF *OCCULT AMERICA* AND *THE MIRACLE CLUB*

"In our increasingly secular world, people hunger for a way of harmonizing their actual spiritual experiences and their inner knowing with religious traditions that no longer affirm them. In *A Theology of Love,* Richard Smoley shows how this is possible. This is a powerful contribution, powerful because it is also simple and uncomplicated. To those who grieve that Christianity has lost its way because of its sellout to tawdry, unprincipled politicians, Smoley's message is CPR for the soul."

LARRY DOSSEY, M.D., AUTHOR OF
*ONE MIND: HOW OUR INDIVIDUAL MIND IS PART OF A GREATER
CONSCIOUSNESS AND WHY IT MATTERS*

A Theology of Love

of Love

Reimagining
Christianity through
A Course in Miracles

A Spirituality Based on
Love, Not Fear

Richard Smoley

Inner Traditions
Rochester, Vermont

Inner Traditions
One Park Street
Rochester, Vermont 05767
www.InnerTraditions.com

Text stock is SFI certified

Cataloging-in-Publication Data for this title is available from the Library of Congress

ISBN 978-1-62055-925-3 (print)
ISBN 978-1-62055-926-0 (ebook)

Printed and bound in the United States by Lake Book Manufacturing, Inc.
The text stock is SFI certified. The Sustainable Forestry Initiative® program
promotes sustainable forest management.

10 9 8 7 6 5 4 3 2 1

Text design and layout by Priscilla Baker
This book was typeset in Garamond Premier Pro with Cinzel, Columbia Serial,
and Gill Sans used as display typefaces

Because hyperlinks do not always remain viable, we are no longer including URLs
in our resources, notes, or bibliographic entries. Instead, we are providing the
name of the website where this information may be found.

To send correspondence to the author of this book, mail a first-class letter to the
author c/o Inner Traditions • Bear & Company, One Park Street, Rochester, VT
05767, and we will forward the communication, or contact the author directly at
www.innerchristianity.com.

For my family

Contents

Acknowledgments   ix

Note on Citations from *A Course in Miracles*   x

Introduction   1

Part 1

Fall

ONE   What Is God?   12

TWO   The Five-Dimensional Box   21

THREE   The Cloud of Oblivion   32

FOUR   The Reign of Number   38

FIVE   Of Mirrors and Madness   46

SIX   A Suppositional Moment   57

Part 2

Regeneration

SEVEN   The Law on Two Levels   70

EIGHT   Meaning for a Meaningless World   78

NINE   From the Unreal to the Real   88

TEN   Creating, Making, and the Qualia   97

ELEVEN   The Scandal of Particularity   106

TWELVE   Being toward Death   120

THIRTEEN   Relationships, Special and Holy   130

FOURTEEN   Church and Sacraments   139

FIFTEEN   The Ladder of Prayer   149

SIXTEEN   Dispensations   160

SEVENTEEN   The Age of the Holy Spirit   172

EIGHTEEN   *Summa Theologiae*   185

APPENDIX   Studying *A Course in Miracles*   197

Notes   199

Selected Bibliography   212

Index   221

ACKNOWLEDGMENTS

Of course there are innumerable people I would like to thank for contributing to the making of this book. Most immediately, I am indebted to my agent, John Loudon, and to Jon Graham and Meghan MacLean at Inner Traditions for their help in turning this book into a printed reality. I am also grateful to the Foundation for Inner Peace for their generosity in granting me permission to quote from *A Course in Miracles.*

And I certainly am grateful for the support and affection of my loving family: my wife, Nicole, and my sons, Robert and William.

Note on Citations from *A Course in Miracles*

Quotations from *A Course in Miracles* are taken from the third edition, published by the Foundation for Inner Peace in 2007. In-text references are to the three volumes of the Course: the Text (T), the Workbook (W), and the Teacher's Manual (M), along with page numbers. Thus a reference to page 1 of the Text will be (T, 1), etc.

Also see the Appendix, "Studying *A Course in Miracles*," for additional information about these three cited texts.

INTRODUCTION

She was a queen, and her reign was long, imperious, and cruel. She held up high ideals and inspired a great civilization, but she could be arrogant and capricious. She demanded full agreement to everything she said; dissent was not tolerated. She could change her mind, and sometimes did, but it was forbidden for anyone to point out that she had done so or to claim that she had ever said anything than what she was saying now.

Physical submission and tribute were not enough for her. She demanded the allegiance of the heart and the mind, and those who did not give it could and did have their tongues torn out, their hands cut off, or their bodies burned at the stake. She was the mother of totalitarianism.

Her reign came to an end, as all reigns must, and she was cast off her throne. The strain was too much for her, and she broke down. She now sits ignored and doddering, muttering scraps of jargon to which few pay attention.

She is theology. She was once called Queen of the Sciences, but now she is no longer called a science at all.

I find it hard to read or hear anything of contemporary theology without being assailed by images like these. Theology is a fallen despot, and its pronouncements are now ignored, even, perhaps, by those who utter them. Many of the great minds of twentieth-century theology—

1

Barth, Bultmann, Bonhoeffer, Niebuhr—leave me with the overwhelming impression that they are grasping for faith and that the pillars of conventional Christian belief—the divinity of Christ, the vicarious atonement, the final judgment—make no sense to them, whether or not they can admit this. They seem to be asking, "What do we believe now that we no longer believe?"

You may want an example of what I am talking about. Very well. Here is a passage from *The Symbolism of Evil*, a classic work of twentieth-century theology by Paul Ricoeur, in regard to the loss of faith in the literal meaning of Christian doctrine:

> Does that mean that we can go back to a primitive naïveté? Not at all. In every way, something has been lost, irremediably lost: immediacy of belief. But if we can no longer live the symbolisms of the sacred in accordance with the original belief in them, we can, we modern men, aim at a second naïveté in and through criticism. In short, it is by *interpreting* that we can *hear* again. Thus it is in hermeneutics that the symbol's gift of meaning and the endeavor to understand it by deciphering are knotted together.
>
> How does hermeneutics meet the problem?
>
> What we have just called a knot—the knot where the symbol gives and criticism interprets—appears in hermeneutics as a circle. The circle can be stated bluntly: "We must understand in order to believe, but we must believe in order to understand."[1]

Ricoeur adds that this circle is "not vicious . . . ; it is a living and stimulating circle." But in the half century since this passage was written, it has not proved so. Such hermeneutics has proved to be so contrived and artificial that it now seems neither worthwhile nor possible to try to sort its ideas out—except as questions. But then we are back to "What do we believe now that we no longer believe?"

Moreover, those forms of Christianity—notably liberal and mainstream Protestantism—that have taken such hermeneutics most to heart have been the ones that have suffered the severest hemorrhages in membership. Sheer numbers only mean so much, of course; but in this case they are telling us that some basic spiritual need is not being met by such hermeneutical athletics.

Why take my word for it? Here are the views of the late Huston Smith, one of the twentieth century's most admired scholars of religion:

> The problem with the mainline churches is their seminaries. Those seminaries surround the major universities and look up to the universities, which have more prestige and more money. And the universities are secular to the core, so their secularism rubs off on the seminaries. I've heard mainline seminaries described as institutions for inventing new religions—hybrids of the religions the seminaries were created to serve and of the reigning secular styles of thought in the universities nearby. . . . Of course the seminaries continue to say "God," but what is the cash value of that word when it is injected into a world created by Darwin, Marx, Freud, and the Big Bang?[2]

James T. Charlesworth of Princeton Theological Seminary adds another perspective. He explains why scholarly findings about the literal truth of the Bible have barely made their way into the public eye:

> Seminary students study for three years at the major seminaries such as the Princeton Theological Seminary. They are taught what scholars have learned about the composition of the books selected as "the Bible"; they often do extremely well in our classes, and then they leave us to serve a local church. Within a few years, their interest has shifted to the needs of the congregation, and often as young pastors they are no longer dedicated to struggling against the ignorance of those who pick up the Bible and read it as if it were this morning's newspaper. Fearing that the local church leaders may not be supportive, they frequently forget our teachings and proceed to preach

and teach, far too often, as if the uneducated have the final word on the composition of the biblical books.[3]

Blunt as he is, Charlesworth fails to point out that the clergy yield to "the uneducated" because they have no coherent theology to put in place of the old one.

It may be time to rethink theology along completely different lines. We now know that the current dominant worldview, that of materialistic science, does not have the range or depth to sustain the human need for meaning. To begin with, science does not have, and cannot have, any genuine ethical component. Science per se has no relation to ethics. A scientist can conduct a valid experiment even if it requires him to commit atrocities. And scientists frequently hire themselves out to cook up new recipes—all of them scientifically correct—for environmental desecration and mass destruction.

Nor is science a reliable guide to truths—not, at any rate, to ultimate truths. It is merely a method, and its findings are provisional and open to correction. Once it was scientific to believe in phlogiston and the luminiferous ether; it no longer is. This is as it should be. But we need more solid ground than theories and hypotheses in order to build complete and integrated lives.

So it may be time to revisit theology.

Of course it is constantly being revisited. Plenty of banners have been hoisted proclaiming new theologies; they are proffered to us as regularly as detergent manufacturers stamp "New and improved!" on products that are no different from their predecessors. But these revolutionary theologies are finding fewer and fewer hearers. They are no longer even preaching to the converted, because the converted too have lost interest.

So one could well be suspicious of something that claims to be a fresh look at theology. All the same, there may be reason to risk this venture.

Conceivably, one element that needs to be added is *experience*—that is, religious experience. Many believe that religious experience occurs only to the few and favored. But this is clearly not the case.

Because theology has refused to admit this fact, it is being left at the wayside. Instead, in some neurotic fashion, much of present-day theology preoccupies itself with anything but religious experience. Your minister may be eager to tell you what to think about abortion, or gay marriage, or immigration, or the current presidential candidates. But if you go to him and ask why you saw your deceased mother at the foot of your bed, he will probably be clueless. He never learned how to deal with such issues. I have often heard from people that they have gone to a cleric to ask about some unusual experience, some apparition, some intuition of a higher world, and gone away empty-handed.

This is one aspect of the problem of religious experience: having such experience, but finding no one who can give any guidance about it. Then there is the other side: people who *want* to have spiritual experience but have received no guidance for that either. Often they seek out some form of meditation, and while this can be valuable and powerful, it is limited if one's meditative experience does not also fit into a meaningful and complete worldview.

There is another aspect still. Consider this item from *The Economist*:

> In the summer of 1974, a 26-year-old Mayan villager lay drunk in a town square in the Guatemalan highlands. Suddenly he heard a voice that was to change the course of his life and that of his home town, Almolonga. "I was lying there and I saw Jesus saying, 'I love you and I want you to serve me,'" says the man, Mariano Riscajche. He dusted himself down, sobered up and soon started preaching, establishing a small Protestant organization in a room not far from the town's ancient Catholic church.[4]

The article provides no further details about Mariano Riscajche, but we can still draw some conclusions. Without evidence to the contrary, we have to assume that Riscajche had this vision of Jesus, that it appeared to him as he said it did. That is, we need to take these experiences seriously from a phenomenological point of view. This does not mean, of course, that we need to take them at face value ontologically or theologically: we do not have to conclude that this vision was really of the historical Jesus Christ—a matter about which there can be no proof one way or the other. But it is intellectually treacherous—and logically circular—to write such experiences off as mere hallucinations.

Furthermore, if this was the totality of Riscajche's experience—that is, Jesus appeared to him and told him to serve him—then it was more or less devoid of theological content. Riscajche evidently took it to mean that he should embrace evangelical Protestantism, because Protestantism is spreading rapidly in Latin America, but if he had had the same experience a hundred years ago, he would have had to turn to Catholicism, because there was no alternative at that time and place.

Religious experience tends to be free of conceptual content.* With some exceptions, visions do not as a rule lay down doctrines or posit theses: they are what they are. They call the individual to awaken; they may even give him some instructions. But he will decide what he makes of that theologically in the light of his own situation and beliefs.

Could this have happened in the earliest times of Christianity? Could the many diverse Christian faith communities have arisen almost immediately because the disciples, although they had a common experience, drew extremely different conclusions from that experience?[5] We see this in the New Testament: evidently both Paul and James the brother of Jesus had visions of the risen Jesus, but as a result one decided that this meant he no longer needed to observe the Jewish Law, while the other decided that he must continue to observe it rigorously.

Thus spiritual experience is not enough. It operates, perhaps, on all levels of the mind, but most intensely on the emotions. Thus we get what G. I. Gurdjieff calls "an emotional religion, sometimes very pure

---

*I am not drawing any rigid distinction between religious experience and spiritual experience; I am using the terms more or less synonymously.

but without force, sometimes full of bloodshed and horror leading to the Inquisition, to religious wars."[6]

Gurdjieff is speaking about collective madness, but unbalanced spiritual experience produces individual madness as well. How many people are wandering around, broken and homeless, because they had some religious experience that, however genuine, hit the mind the wrong way and threw it off balance? Psychiatry begrudgingly admits the reality of religious and spiritual issues in mental dysfunction, but that does not mean that psychiatrists know how to deal with them.[7]

Guidance in spiritual matters implies theology. You will handle a vision of Jesus Christ very differently if you believe he was the Son of God than if you believe he did not exist. But theology has not been stripped of her crown for arbitrary reasons. As Christian theology developed, it mutated into various doctrines that are, viewed objectively, bizarre and self-contradictory. The most glaring example is unfortunately also the centerpiece of Christianity as it exists today: the doctrine of atonement through the sacrifice of Christ.[8] Another example is the paradox that is the atheist's delight: how an all-good and all-powerful God can permit evil.

E. M. Forster said it in the epigraph to his novel *Howards End*: "Only connect." It was the connection between the mind and the emotions—or, if you prefer, the heart—that he meant. A religion that cannot do this, or one that permits one side to hypertrophy while the other side withers, is not a healthy religion at all. And it will bring forth fruit like itself.

The most obvious example is the degeneration of a large sector of American evangelical Christianity into a lobby for political extremism and reaction. Miguel de la Torre, a professor of social ethics at Denver's Iliff School of Theology, states the case bluntly when he writes on the Baptist News Global website:

Christianity has died in the hands of Evangelicals. Evangelicalism ceased being a religious faith tradition following Jesus' teachings concerning justice for the betterment of humanity when it made a Faustian bargain for the sake of political influence. The beauty of the gospel message—of love, of peace and of fraternity—has been murdered by the ambitions of Trumpish flimflammers who have sold their souls for expediency.[9]

Liberal and mainstream Protestantism has by and large avoided this mistake, but because its theological core has eroded so completely, it too is grasping at politics—for example, advocacy (admittedly more benign) for social justice. Its theological content has become extraordinarily skimpy—a cause of bewilderment to clergy and laity alike.

So where can we look for theology today? It should take into account spiritual experience, not only the raptures and stigmata of saints, but spiritual experience as it occurs to ordinary people (meaning practically all of us), and it should be able to deal with such experience intelligently, articulately, and open-mindedly. It should be able to point someone toward religious experience. It should also provide a doctrine that possesses inner consistency and does not beg us to merely have faith the minute we start pointing out internal contradictions. This doctrine should be convincing in and of itself, and should not need threats and punishments (in this world or the next) to beat down objections. And it should take the discoveries of recent centuries—including those of science—into account without creating another form of dogmatism, as present-day scientistic materialism has done. (I am using the term *scientistic* to indicate the attitudes of many current secularists, who invoke science as a kind of resurrected goddess of reason while ignoring the limits of the scientific method.)

Am I personally a Christian, then? Let me define what, in my view, a Christian is. A Christian is someone who tries to live by the teachings of Jesus Christ. That's it. Most of the rest is doctrinal cant. The creeds and dogmas came centuries later than Christ and his disciples, and often contradict what the disciples evidently believed themselves.

By the terms stated above, I am a Christian. But I have no connection with any church or denomination, or for that matter with any religious organization. Some may regard this as a minus; others, as a plus.

Nor do I believe that Christianity is superior to the other great religions. Hinduism and Buddhism in particular offer any number of insights that are absent from Western thought. But I do think there is a universal core underlying all the traditions. This core can be expressed in many different modes, each of which needs to be considered without trying to boil them all down together in the same pot or, on the other hand, turning all others into straw men to be kicked over in favor of one's own pet. These modes of expression can be viewed as religious languages. No one goes around trying to prove that one language is truer than the others.

In that case, why bother with Christianity in particular? Because Christianity is our background, our heritage, our thrownness.[10] Christianity is not software. You can't clear it out of your head as you clear a program from your computer. It sinks in deep, and it stays. And it is hard to install another system on top of it.

I discovered this in the 1980s. For several years I studied Tibetan Buddhism, and even came to think of myself as a Buddhist. But in the end I couldn't become one. There was nothing wrong with Buddhism, but, especially in the Tibetan form, it seemed to require me to install another, equally elaborate but completely alien, theological contraption in my head besides the one I had gotten from Christianity. There was no point in that: one contraption was quite enough.

So I went back to exploring the Western esoteric traditions. With my book *Inner Christianity,* I attempted to encapsulate some of the central ideas of these traditions in the language that comes most naturally to them—Christianity.

Yet it would be unwise, I think, to reject the spiritual insights that we have gotten from other traditions. They tell us too much for us to turn them away.

Thus it would be useful if this new theology were able to make use of insights from all the world's religions. In this book, sources of inspiration will include the Bible; Hinduism and Buddhism; esoteric and mystical strands of thought, including the Kabbalah; individual visionaries such as William Blake and C. G. Jung; insights from Kant, William James, Heidegger, Gurdjieff, and Karl Jaspers, and fiction writers such as Dostoevsky and Philip K. Dick. In the first part, I will sketch out an outline of the problematic reality we inhabit. In the second part, I will focus on the twentieth-century text *A Course in Miracles,* possibly the greatest reformulation of Christianity in recent times, to suggest some answers to questions posed in the first part.

This mishmash may open me up to the charge of bricolage. You can certainly mix and match all of these texts and traditions, but aren't you just cooking up a thick gray mess? Possibly, but as Jacques Derrida famously observed, every discourse is a kind of bricolage.[11] So, for that matter, is cognition. Right this moment your mind is pulling together an adventitious collection of data—your sense impressions—and using them to fashion a world. There is no avoiding bricolage. When constructing a worldview, you have to employ the materials at hand.

With all this said, we may as well begin at the best place to begin. With nothing.

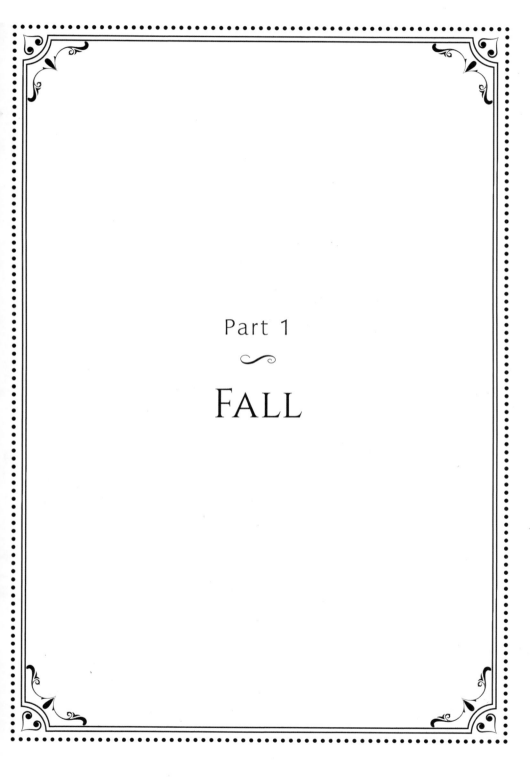

Part 1

FALL

ONE

WHAT IS GOD?

It is daunting to ask who or what God is. Each time I face the question, my mind has to stretch itself beyond capacity. As soon as it has done so, another dimension, another vista, opens up, and my mind has to stretch itself still further.

Some say God is ineffable, beyond all thought or conception; therefore it is impossible to say anything about God. This sounds reasonable until you realize that this is a self-refuting statement akin to "This sentence is false." If it is impossible to say anything about God, then it is also impossible to say that it is impossible to say anything about God.

Usurping permission in this way, we can begin.

Perhaps the question of who God is is too difficult a place to start. So let's begin with something easier—like creating the universe.

To create the universe, you have to start with *nothing*. Literally. So let's start with nothing, symbolized by a patch of black (see figure 1.1).

This Ground of Being (as one may call it; it has been called many things) is mentioned in many of the world's sacred texts. In the Kabbalah, it is called *Ain Sof*, literally, "no limit," or the "infinite." Here is a description by a thirteenth-century Kabbalist named Azriel of Gerona:

Figure 1.1

The boundless is called Ein Sof,* Infinite. It is absolute undiffer-
entiation in perfect, changeless oneness. Since it is boundless, there
is nothing outside of it. Since it transcends and conceals itself, it is
the essence of everything hidden and revealed. . . . The philosophers
acknowledge that we comprehend it only by the way of no.[1]

The "way of no" is sometimes called the *via negativa,* the "negative
way." It means that you can only characterize the Ain Sof by saying
what it is *not*.

The Kabbalah also speaks of three *veils of negative existence*. They
are these:

> Ain ("Nothing")
> Ain Sof ("No limit" = the infinite)
> Ain Sof Aur ("Limitless light")

In some odd way, something is described both as infinite darkness
and infinite light. How could that be?

---

*Ein Sof is an alternate transliteration of *Ain Sof.*

If there is nothing to see, all is darkness. But what if light were limit-less? Everything would be light. There would *still* be nothing to see.

The only difference is that infinite light creates a situation in which *seeing is possible*. Let's represent it by this white dot against the black patch (see figure 1.2).

In fact the point may be the most common symbol for this primor-dial beginning. Another thirteenth-century Kabbalistic text, the *Zohar* ("Splendor"), describes it ornately:

> At the head of the potency of the King, He engraved engravings in luster on high. A spark of impenetrable darkness flashed within the concealed of the concealed, from the head of Infinity [the Ain Sof]—a cluster of vapor forming in formlessness, thrust in a ring, not white, not black, not red, not green, no color at all. . . . Deep within the spark gushed a flow, splaying colors below, concealed within the concealed of the mystery of *Ein Sof*. It split and did not split its aura, was not known at all, until under the impact of splitting, a single, concealed supernal point shone. Beyond that point, nothing is known, so it is called *Reshit, Beginning*, first command of all.[2]

Figure 1.2

It would take a long commentary to explicate this passage. But let us put it plainly and baldly: now we have something, even if we don't know what it is. In fact we now have two things: *something* and *nothing*.

It is partly explained by the word *reshit,* "beginning," which is in the first word in the Bible, *bereshit,* usually translated as "in the beginning."

Much attention has been paid to this word. To begin with, the first letter is bet (ב), the equivalent of the English B, and, like it, the second letter of the alphabet. Sages have often asked why the Bible should begin with the second letter of the alphabet rather than alef (א), the first.

The answer often goes along these lines. *Bet* was originally an ideogram meaning "house"—in fact, *bet* is the word for "house" in Hebrew. A house defines an *inside* and an *outside.* Without some distinction between these two, a house is simply not a house at all. Furthermore, the letter bet at the beginning of a word signifies a preposition that is usually translated as "in."

In and out: this is the most elementary distinction that can be made. Having said this, let us go back to the idea that this primordial nothing is absolute—that, as Azriel of Gerona said, "There is nothing outside of it." If this is so, the universe is something that cannot be created, as it were, from a distance, but must be created from within. This requires us to take a certain stance at a certain place—*somewhere,* even if we know nothing further about what this *somewhere* is.

Now we have two things: where we are—or, better, where *I am*— and everywhere else. (This would suggest why many mystics have said that the ultimate name of God is "I am.")

These things can be called, respectively, *self* and *other.*

In the image of the diagram, the white dot is the self, the black space the other—at least initially. But from the other side, the black space is the self, the white dot the other. These two entities now exist in relation to each other. Note, however, that this is an arbitrary and suppositional distinction. It could have been so, but it could just as well have *not* been so. This introduces a dissonance: the distinction between *self* and *other* is real from a certain point of view, but from the point of view of the Absolute, it is not. This helps explain a number of esoteric teachings, such as why the world is so often characterized as an illusion and why Buddhism says that everything is ultimately void or empty or open.

Because this distinction between *self* and *other* is both true and not true, it can and does appear to vacillate back and forth between the two—between existing and not existing. This vacillation assumes a certain regularity and even rhythm. Hence the idea of *vibration,* which has also been said to underlie all of existence at all levels.

This idea of a primordial distinction between *self* and *other* appears fairly often in esoteric literature. Here it is, as stated by Papus (Gérard Encausse), one of the leaders of the French occult revival of the late nineteenth century:

> The Ego cannot be realized except through its opposition to the Non-Ego. The assertion of the Ego is scarcely established, when we must instantly realize a reaction of the Ego, or Absolute, upon itself, from which the conception of its existence will be drawn, by a kind of division of the Unity. . . . But the opposition between the Ego and the Non-Ego immediately gives rise to another factor, which is the Affinity existing between this Ego and this Non-Ego.[3]

What Papus (or his translator) calls *Ego* I am calling *self.* What Papus calls *Non-Ego* I am calling *other.* What Papus calls *Affinity,* I will call *relation.*

There are now three things: *self, other,* and the *relation* between self and other. We can represent them as shown in figure 1.3.

They are all purely relative stances: no one of these is *absolutely* self or other or relation.

Each of the three sees itself as *self* and the remaining two as *other.* The remaining two, from the point of view of the third, are an *other,* an additional entity. But this *other* too, from its own point of view, is *self,*

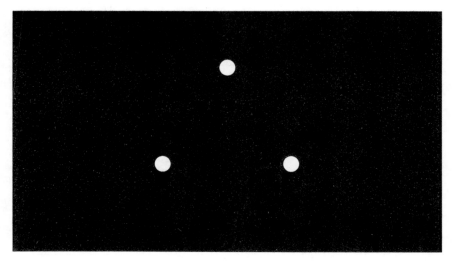

Figure 1.3

and it beholds its counterparts as *other*. The process can, and does, continue indefinitely, with iterations of increasing complexity. These ideas help us understand this verse from the *Tao Te Ching*:

> *Tao gave birth to One;*
> *One gave birth to Two;*
> *Two gave birth to Three;*
> *Three gave birth to the ten thousand things.*

What Lao-tzu calls the Tao is conceivably equivalent to the Ain Sof. The Tao, which, as he emphasizes, is undefinable ("The Tao that can be stated is not the Eternal Tao"), thus seems to be the source, or the background, for manifest existence, whose primary characteristic is that of *self versus other*. As the *Tao Te Ching* also says, "These two come out from the same source, / But are different in name."[4]

Is this Ain Sof God? It may be, or, as we shall see, it may not be. At any rate the fourteenth-century German mystic Meister Eckhart describes it as the ultimate God, the "Godhead," which lies behind the Christian Trinity:

The soul enters the Trinity but it may become even more blessed by going further, to the barren Godhead, of which the Trinity is a revelation. In this barren Godhead, activity has ceased and therefore the soul will be most perfect when it is thrown into the desert of the Godhead, where both activity and forms are no more.[5]

For Eckhart, the personal God—in fact, the three persons of the Trinity—is merely a manifestation of the impersonal Ground of Being. (Meister Eckhart's name for this is the Godhead.) In light of what I have just laid out above, the Godhead is the Ain Sof, while the Trinity is the primordial sacred ternary, which I have characterized as self, other, and the relation between the two.

The idea of the sacred ternary appears virtually everywhere. Table 1.1 lists some of the names given to it.

TABLE 1.1. THE SACRED TERNARY IN VARIOUS TRADITIONS

Tradition	Self	Other	Relation
Christianity	Father	Son	Holy Spirit
Judaism (symbolized in the three letters of YHWH, the Tetragrammaton, the name of God)	Yod (׳; y)	Heh (ה; h)	Waw or vav (ו; w)
Hindu gods	Brahma	Shiva	Vishnu
Hindu primordial elements	Rajas	Tamas	Sattva
Taoism	Heaven	Earth	Man
Buddhism: The Three Poisons	Desire	Anger	Ignorance or obliviousness
G. I. Gurdjieff's system	Holy Affirming	Holy Denying	Holy Reconciling

It would take a long time to go through this table and discuss exactly how all these systems relate to one another: as usual, there is a clear general pattern, but one must be careful about rushing to conclusions and simplistically deciding that they are all saying exactly the same thing. René Guénon discusses this issue at length in his book *The Great Triad*.[6] For the time being, it will be enough simply to keep the idea of the sacred ternary in mind.

So is there no personal aspect to the divine? Much of Hindu and Buddhist thought appears to reach this conclusion. Here is one statement of such a position, by one of the hidden Masters who allegedly instructed the nineteenth-century Russian occultist H. P. Blavatsky. (The existence and identity of these Masters has been much debated, but I think it is safe to assume that these personages existed and were not made up by Blavatsky.) One of them, known as Koot Hoomi, writes in 1882:

Neither our philosophy nor ourselves believe in a God, least of all in one whose pronoun necessitates a capital H. . . . We know there is in our system no such thing as God, either personal or impersonal. Parabrahm [the Ground of Being] is not a God, but absolute immutable law, and Iswar [the personal God] is the effect of Avidya [ignorance] and Maya [illusion], ignorance based upon the great delusion.[7]

Rarely have I read such a categorical statement about a subject about which so little is known. In any event, this position is not satisfying. "Absolute immutable law"? Very well—but where did this law come from? Who decreed it? In this worldview, this law, known in Sanskrit as *dharma,* appears out of nowhere, for no discernible reason.

In any case, even in this short space, we see an impressive collection of witnesses saying that the source of manifestation as we know it is ultimately *impersonal.* Today it's much easier to believe this than it was in the past, because we have an expanded idea of the magnitude of the physical universe. According to a recent news item, there are now known to be two trillion galaxies, ten times more than astronomers believed.[8] It becomes rather hard to say that the source of this infinitude is a person like us who can be irked and flattered and placated.

This is not the end of the question, of course. But before we can explore it further, we need to say a little more about the nature and process of manifestation.

TWO

THE FIVE-DIMENSIONAL BOX

Before we return to theology per se, we may need to take another few steps in the creation of the universe.

Each of us creates a universe every second. Our cognition takes in the data of the senses and uses them to create a reality. This reality is (usually) enough like those of other humans so that we can communicate with them about it. So it must be based on some more or less universal coordinates.

Consider: you are here now. There is something in front of you. There is something in back of you. There is something above, something beneath, something to your right, and something to your left.

Let's count them:

1. Front
2. Back
3. Above
4. Below
5. Left
6. Right

If we add you sitting in the center of all these, we have a total of seven. These seven are always with you. They are the coordinates of your reality and mine. It is practically impossible to envisage a world without them. This suggests why seven is universally regarded as a sacred number.*

Taken on its own, this sevenfold world is static. If it is not to stay frozen in place forever, it must include movement. Movement, in the world as we know it, is unidirectional. You cannot move in two directions at once.

The question then arises: why move at all? Why not stay right exactly where you are? You must have a motivation: you must have a reason to move toward something or away from something else. You would not even get up and go into the next room unless you thought that somehow you would benefit from it.

What you move toward is what you perceive as *good*. What you move away from is *evil*. If you do not regard something as either good or evil, you have no reason to move in either direction. Even if you think of something as bad in the long run, you will move toward it if your desires pull you that way. Cigarette smoking is one example. A teenager takes up smoking because the immediate benefits (looking cool, yielding to social pressure) outweigh the disadvantages of disease decades later. (It could be the epitaph of humanity: "It seemed like a good idea at the time.")

We now have a curious development. We not only have a dimension of movement in the universe, but we have a *moral* dimension: good and evil.

Movement necessarily involves another factor: change. If you move toward something, your relation to it immediately changes. It is closer. The opposite is true if you move away from something.

So finally there is the dimension of change. Like movement, it is

---

*The Self as center is sometimes counted in esoteric enumeration, sometimes left out. The most obvious example is the creation account in Genesis, with six days of creation and one day of rest, symbolizing the timeless, unmoving, and eternal Self in the center. The ten-directional concept below, as described in the *Sefer Yetzirah*, does not include this central point.

unidirectional: it goes, or appears to go, in one direction only. We can consider this the dimension of time. In fact time is sometimes defined as the measurement of change.

We end up with ten directions:

1. Front
2. Back
3. Above
4. Below
5. Left
6. Right
7. Toward (Good)
8. Away from (Evil)
9. Past
10. Future

With the self as the center of them all.

I am speaking phenomenologically: this is the way the world appears to us. It would appear to be universally true for all humans. It has nothing to do with religious dogmas or scientific formulations. A thousand years from now our religion may be forgotten and our science may have mutated into something beyond recognition, but people will still have fronts and backs, lefts and rights.

This schema inspires some striking realizations. For one, we now know why there is evil in the universe. Evil is one of the primary dimensions of the universe. The universe—*our* universe, as experienced by us moment by moment—could not exist without it.

We see evidence for this fact in people's conceptions of heaven. People often complain that heaven would be extremely boring. Who wants to stand around on a cloud, strumming a harp and praising the Almighty forever? Even more hedonic views—heaven as a pleasure garden with lots of fruit and lions and tigers to pet—do not improve the picture much.

Not that heaven is anything like these images. But it is true that if we try to conceive of a realm without evil, it looks extremely flat and flavorless. Evil is so much a part of the fabric of our reality that it is hard to imagine a world without it.

We now also can answer the question of whether the universe, or rather *our* universe, is fundamentally good or evil. It is *both* good and evil. It is not fundamentally one or the other. One seems to be preponderant at a certain time and place; the other, at other times and places. There even seems to be some alternation between the two, an action producing an equal and opposite reaction.

This ten-directional schema is a remarkably clear, concise, yet comprehensive outline of the structure of reality as we know it. I did not invent it. I found it in the *Sefer Yetzirah* ("Book of Formation"), the oldest of the Kabbalistic texts, dated to sometime between the third and sixth centuries AD:

> Ten Sefiroth alone: they are measured by ten without end: the depth of the first and the depth of the last, the depth of good and the depth of evil, the depth above and the depth below, the depth of the east and the depth of the west, the depth of the north and the depth of the south.[1]

This text, in a couple of thousand words, provides a schema for fashioning a world. The Infinite, the Ain Sof, gives rise to three primary forces, *self, other,* and *relation* (or, if you prefer, ו ה י, yod, heh, and waw, the three letters in the Tetragrammaton, the Hebrew name of God par excellence). These in turn, through their own combinations, fashion a realm of dimensions that is more familiar than we are to ourselves.

To see this world from a wider perspective, we can turn to the literature of near-death experiences (NDEs). C. G. Jung had such an experience after he had a heart attack in the spring of 1944. It took the form of several visions. In the first, he wrote, "it seemed to me that I was high up in space. Far below I saw the globe of the earth, bathed in a gloriously blue light. . . . I knew I was on the point of departing from the earth." But, he added, "the sight of the earth from this height was the most glorious thing I had ever seen."

He also had a vision of a temple carved from a rock, of the sort he had seen on the coast of the Bay of Bengal. "As I approached . . . I had the feeling that everything was being sloughed away; everything I aimed at or wished for or thought, the whole phantasmagoria of earthly existence, fell away or was stripped from me—an extremely painful process."

Jung was not allowed to enter the temple. He encountered Dr. H., the physician who was treating him in real life, here in the guise of an ancient Greek healer-king. "As he stood before me, a mute exchange of thought took place between us. Dr. H. had been delegated by the earth to deliver a message to me, to tell me that there was a protest against my going away. I had no right to leave the earth and must return."

The image of the doctor vanished, and Jung returned to earth and his physical body. "In reality," he went on, "a good three weeks were still to pass before I could truly make up my mind to live again. I could not eat because all food repelled me. The view of city and mountains from my sickbed seemed to me like a painted curtain with black holes in it, or a tattered sheet of newspaper full of photographs that meant nothing. Disappointed, I thought, *Now I must return to the "box system" again.*" Afterward, "although my belief in the world returned to me, I have never since entirely freed myself of the impression that this life is a segment of existence which is enacted in *a three-dimensional boxlike universe especially set up for it*" (emphasis added).[2]

So this sublime dimensional structure, viewed from a distance, turns out to be a narrow and confining box.

Many of those who experience NDEs say they did not want to come back to physical life. (Obviously we only hear from the ones who have.) Jung's case is typical: the subject is reminded of some commitment or obligation that he has on earth, and he returns, but with irritation and disappointment—a strange response to a life to which we cling so desperately.

A more recent NDE is described by Natalie Sudman in her book *Application of Impossible Things*. Sudman was a civilian contractor with the U.S. Army in Iraq. In 2007 she was in a vehicle that was blown up by a roadside bomb. Badly hurt, she lost consciousness for a few seconds.

In that time she was transported to another reality. She found herself in an auditorium, lecturing to a gathering of beings from other dimensions, who were fascinated to hear about her unusual experience. Evidently getting blown up is not a frequent occurrence in other realms.

> I was aware that I deliberately offered the . . . data in fulfillment of a request that had been made by this Gathering of personalities prior to my taking on this body for this physical lifetime. . . . They then requested that I return to my physical body to accomplish some further work. I was given to understand that my particular skills with energy were needed at this time and would be effective only were I actually present.

Sudman agreed, but, she adds, "I requested that particular assistance be provided within that continued physical existence." After all, her body had been badly damaged by the explosion. She was then taken to a healing dimension, where her body was repaired—up to a point. "The injuries weren't entirely healed, as some were to be of use in situating me for tasks I had agreed to perform or things that I wanted to experience as a whole infinite Self."[3] Among other disabilities, she was left blind in one eye.

Sudman's view of physical life as seen through her NDE resembles Jung's at some points. In the first place, she believes that her entire life experience—including the explosion—was the result of some decision on her part, determined before she had been born. According to her, humans do have free will, but not in the way we usually imagine. We have the free will, *before* incarnation, to choose our existence and the events, good and bad, that will take place in it. Once we are born, the script plays out as planned. Jung is silent about these questions, but here too his return is the result of a decision on his own part—even though he was pressured to do so. ("There was a protest against my going away. I had no right to leave the earth and must return.")

I am reminded of the myth of Er, an NDE account in the last book of Plato's *Republic*.[4] Er, a soldier, is slain, or nearly slain, on a battlefield. Journeying through the land of the dead, he comes to the point where souls choose to take on their next lives, in which "there was every kind of mixture and combination." They draw lots to find the order in which they will choose their lives. "The drawer of the first lot at once sprang to seize the greatest tyranny, and . . . in his folly and greed . . . failed to observe that it involved the fate of eating his own children." The soul of Odysseus, the shrewdest of men, draws the lowest lot and has the last choice. He chooses the life of an ordinary citizen who minds his own business, and says that he would have done the same if he had drawn the first lot.

In Plato's account, as in Sudman's, the soul chooses in advance its whole life and the baggage that comes with it, good and bad—the joy of tyranny, the horror of eating one's children. But Plato does not explain why. Sudman gives this explanation:

> From expanded awareness *every* action is understood to express creativity, have meaning, and influence the balance and order of the whole of All That Is. From my experiences in expanded awareness, it appears to me that *no being* is considered evil or bad. *Actions* of a being may be understood to be disruptive, inharmonious, or detrimental to the creative flow within any one reality, but the *creativity* of an action could be understood as valid—perhaps even necessary or useful—regardless of the overall disruption.[5]

Thus all life choices, good and evil, from the perspective of the whole self, have an integral place within the whole.

Such an attitude detaches one from conventional moral judgments. Sudman writes: "Instead of thinking, *Whoa, that person is seriously f*ed up!* I could think, *Whoa! That experience took guts,* or *That one gets high* *points for drama,* or *Huh—very subtle,* or *Shit—they're really piling it on,* or *Hmm—they're like a microcosm of the macrocosm of what's going on in the world,* or *I wonder what I'm/they're doing with this? I wonder how it fits into the cooperative whole of creation?"*[6]

This perspective has something to be said for it. The present-day world gives us endless opportunities to become upset or angry or exasperated—attitudes that do no good whatsoever, as we should have learned long ago. Viewing them with detachment may not always prevent evil, but it could keep us from compounding it.

Sudman's view resonates with what I believe to be the inner meaning of the myth of the Fall in Genesis. The primordial man and woman eat of the fruit of the Tree of Knowledge of Good and Evil: they wish to know what good and evil are like. As a result they are cast into a realm where it hurts to have babies and you have to work hard for a living: "In sorrow thou shalt bring forth children. . . . In the sweat of thy face shalt thou eat bread" (Genesis 4:16, 19). That is *this* realm—earthly life. Notice that it says nothing about hell.

Undoubtedly the Genesis myth is not literally true and was never meant to be. Even so, I wonder what tiny chip of truth might be preserved in the amber of this legend. In 1955 the author Laurens van der Post explored the Kalahari Desert, close to the cradle of the human race in East Africa. One of his companions was a healer and prophet named Samutchoso. At one point they encountered what Samutchoso called the "tree of true knowledge."[7] Van der Post describes it: "From the branches hung round, green fruit like large navel oranges. Samutchoso announced that they were still too green for eating. . . . The fruit, when ripe, he said, was more delicious than honey." Van der Post wanted to pick one to bring it back to civilization to be identified, but Samutchoso begged him not to. Here we have a literal tree of knowledge.

In Sudman's view, the human task, or desire, is to experience the total range of possibilities, good and evil, in this realm. This is the only plausible explanation for the whole course of history: the human race has collectively chosen to explore all possible combinations and all possible outcomes at this level of reality, however pleasant or painful. This would include all types of behavior, from the most admirable to the most abominable. If you can think of it, and it is physically feasible (and sometimes even if it isn't), someone will have tried it.

The admiration that the Gathering express for Sudman casts light on this issue. They admire her because it takes a certain specialized skill to function on this physical level of reality: not all beings can do it. But every human who has a physical body can and does. She observes, "That it isn't exactly easy from an energy standpoint seems to me, conversely and paradoxically, one reason why it can be difficult to remember who we are as Whole Selves while we're in the physical. But the point is this: *all of us* are sharing a unique experience that takes real and amazing skill. We have absolutely no idea how amazing and totally cool we are, really, each of us, and how totally amazing and cool it is that we can maintain a physical body and comprehend experience from within time and space as we do."[8]

Sudman's view resembles many New Age views of earthly life as viewed from other dimensions. We are here living a great experiment, and from an ultimate point of view, our sufferings and moral failures don't matter, because they have no relevance beyond this level. Even those who die horrible deaths remain essentially eternal, immortal, and unstained.

This perspective makes me think of the Sarajevo War Hostel—a hostel that attempts to recreate the experience of the Bosnian civil war in the 1990s. One visitor writes, "The ambience of this hostel might resemble how people were living under siege +20 years ago in this city: you sleep in mattresses on the floor, you get a military blanket as a pillow, there is no electrical light in the rooms and bathrooms, so you can use candles or flashlights (some of them are very old, as the ones that might have been used during the siege). But no worries, sleeping in confy [sic], and you get power sources for your smart phones."[9]

From a cosmic perspective, your whole life on earth may well look like a night spent in the War Hostel. Only sleeping is not always comfy and your smartphone doesn't always work. If there is some reassurance in the fact that this existence is highly finite and your Self is a whole being on a much larger scale (what Sudman calls the "Whole Self"), it can be hard to have access to that reassurance. Life on earth can be, and often is, dreadful and excruciating, and seems to offer no recourse. Admittedly Sudman does grapple with the problems with this view:

> I don't mean to diminish the reality of pain and anguish: it exists, it is real, and it matters. Personally, being in the throes of a migraine or nerve pain or falling down the stairs because having only one fully functioning eye doesn't afford the best depth of field, I'm not wondering how I created this torment and leafing through my beliefs to find the source. I am often, however, aware of and at least slightly amused by my perception of these events as flaws in my life. I'm also perpetually sure that I created the experience, so after the cussing has run its course a quick trip through my beliefs or a little chat with my Whole Self *is* sometimes in order. The differences between the intentions of the Whole Self and the intentions of our conscious physical minds can be a yawning gulf, which can seem confounding if not downright outrageous.[10]

Sudman's is one of the most nuanced, subtle, and astute accounts of an NDE that I have read. Yet even if we accept her view, we are still left with the fact that life seems problematic at the core. For many, it feels like incarceration. We have already seen Jung's response to his return to earth from his cosmic awakening. There is also the adage of the Greek mystery religions, *sōma sēma* ("The body is a tomb"),[11] as well as the words that Plato puts in Socrates's mouth when he is about to die: "We humans are put in a sort of guardhouse, from which one must not free oneself or run away."[12] Indeed "freeing oneself"—committing suicide— is prima facie evidence that the individual is seeking to escape from this life in the hope that the aftermath (if any) will be better, or at any rate no worse.

So we are forced to bracket this present immensity, with its ten boundless directions, as a narrow and cramped and uncomfortable box for the Self. We need to take another step to see where all this leads us.

THREE

THE CLOUD OF OBLIVION

We now have to go back to the beginning.

Or rather to *a* beginning.

In chapter 1, I pointed out that the first word of Genesis is *bereshith,* "in the beginning." Actually, this translation—the most common one in English versions of the Bible—is not quite accurate.

The *b,* as noted earlier, stands for the Hebrew letter ‭ב‬ (bet). Used as a prefix to a word, it represents a preposition most often translated as *in.* Hence "*in* the beginning." The first *e* in *bereshith* is a schwa, an indefinite vowel, equivalent to the *a* in *another.* This is important, because if the word really meant "in *the* beginning," the vowel would be a long *a* like the *a* in *father.* This vowel would indicate that the definite article is to be read here. The fact that this long *a* is absent means that the first word of Genesis would be better translated as "in *a* beginning."

The opening verse of the Gospel of John—usually translated as "In the beginning was the Word"—echoes the opening verse of Genesis, but it too is mistranslated, and in exactly the same way. The Greek words translated as "in the beginning" are *en arkhē. En* is "in," and *arkhē* is "beginning." But again the definite article is missing. The Greek equivalent for "in the beginning" would be *en tē arkhē,* which is not what the text has. The ancient Greek language has the definite article, but, unlike English, no indefinite article. Thus *en arkhē* should also be translated as "In a beginning."[1]

Many scholars who have discussed these verses have often overlooked this point. Yet it reveals that the "beginning" that the Bible speaks of is not *the* beginning, but *a* beginning—one of many possible beginnings, which would suggest that the Ain Sof, the Infinite, would be only a *relative* infinity.

This sounds nonsensical. For something to be relative, it has to be limited in some way, and infinity is, by definition, limitless. Isn't it? Not necessarily. An analogy comes to mind from mathematics. In the nineteenth century Georg Cantor, creator of set theory, found that the infinity of real (i.e., both rational and irrational) numbers was larger than the infinity of rational numbers.[2] Thus there at least two infinities, one of which is twice as long as the other. Clearly not all infinities are the same.

I don't want to push the mathematical analogy any further, but it suggests that we should not take the Ain Sof, as described above, as an absolute in a simplistic sense. So we may press on and inquire into the nature of this supposed absolute. It is a darkness. Why? Remember the passage from the *Zohar* that I quoted in chapter 1, which says that manifestation began when "a spark of impenetrable darkness flashed within the concealed of the concealed." Other mystics also use the image of darkness: Pseudo-Dionysius the Areopagite speaks of "a ray of divine darkness"; Gregory of Nyssa, of the "luminous darkness." The Iranian Sufis use the term "black light."[3]

To speak of a dark, or black, light is to invoke paradox. Earlier I said that this is a darkness in which seeing becomes possible. But it is seeing of a very particular and restricted kind. It is our seeing of the physical universe, which constrains our thinking. It is almost impossible, for example, to think of anything that is not rooted in images of things we have already seen with our physical eyes. Some say that all visualization is based on memory, which is very likely the case, as you can discover from trying to imagine a color that you have never seen. (I am unable to do this.)

This is the seeing of the three-dimensional world—or, better, the five-dimensional world. Some physicists argue that matter ultimately consists of ten-dimensional strings. But these strings are not part of our experience, and we cannot even conceive of them, except as abstract, quasimathematical entities posited so that certain equations can work out. Moment by moment, we live in a five-dimensional world; we could not eat or breathe apart from it; and there seems to be no escape. Even the most brilliant physicist has to stand in line and park his car like the rest of us.

Why should this be a problem? The answer is, quite simply, that it *is* a problem. Man is the animal that believes something is wrong. This sense of something wrong pervades our entire existence. We may equate it with personal grievances and unmet needs or with global issues such as poverty or environmental deterioration. No matter: this sense of a problem is persistent and unending. As soon as one problem is solved, another rises up to take its place.

This sense of something wrong underlies the human sense of isolation and existential anxiety. And to all appearances it is unique to humans. Our species seems to be out of joint with the world in a way that other creatures are not.

Several years ago, my wife and I took our small sons to a petting farm. There was a black-and-white calf, only a few hours old. It was still unsteady on its legs, but it seemed to be content. It did not seem to mind where it was. Compare this to a human newborn, who writhes and bawls horribly, possibly because it is coming to a world that is not suited for it.

So this darkness, out of which everything appears to arise, is problematic for us. It seems to be keeping us from something, and it does this so well that we conceive of it as an absolute. But its real nature may be disclosed in a famous passage from the fourteenth-century work *The Cloud of Unknowing.* I will quote it in the original Middle English:

> *For when I sey derknes, I mene a lackyng of knowyng;* as alle that thing that thou knowest not, or elles that thou hast forgetyn, it is

derk to thee, for thou seest it not with thi goostly [mental] ighe.
And for this skile it is not clepid a cloude of the eire, bot a cloude of
unknowyng, that is bitwix thee and thi God.[4]

Here is a description from a slightly different angle, by the Sufi
sheikh Lahiri:

I saw myself present in a world of light. Mountains and deserts
were iridescent with lights of all colors: red, yellow, white, blue. I
was experiencing a consuming nostalgia for them; I was as though
stricken with madness and snatched out of myself by the violence
of the intimate emotion and feeling of the presence. Suddenly I saw
that the *black light* was invading the entire universe. Heaven and
earth and everything that was there had wholly become black light,
and, behold, I was totally absorbed in this light, losing consciousness. Then I came back to myself.[5]

The black light again. So this darkness is "unknowing," a loss of consciousness. We might call it a cloud of oblivion. We go into this darkness
at certain points—such as deep sleep—but we do not go past it.

Meditation, at least of certain types, may involve entering this
cloud of oblivion, and, ideally, piercing through to what is beyond. This
may be what much of Buddhist practice is attempting to do. After all,
according to Buddhism, the main problem of man and the cosmos, the
cause of *dukkha* or "suffering," is *avidya,* "not knowing." All relative,
limited existence is rooted in it. Ending this cycle of suffering means
piercing through this ignorance—or, as I prefer to put it, obliviousness.

These considerations bring to mind an idea in the Hindu tradition:
that deep, dreamless sleep—the state that, above all others, is closest to
oblivion—is, paradoxically, also the closest to illumination. Compare
this verse from the *Chāndogya Upanishad*: "Now, when one is sound
asleep, composed, serene, and knows no dream—that is the Self
(Ātman). . . . That is the immortal, the fearless."[6]

Yogis have a practice called *yoga nidra* that works with this idea. Here is a description from Swami Jnaneshvara Bharati:

> It is a state of conscious Deep Sleep. In Meditation, you *remain* in the Waking state of consciousness, and gently focus the mind, while allowing thought patterns, emotions, sensations, and images to arise and go on. However, in Yoga Nidra, you *leave* the Waking state, go *past* the Dreaming state, and go to Deep Sleep, yet remain awake. While Yoga Nidra is a state that is very relaxing, it is also used by Yogis to purify the Samskaras, the deep impressions that are the driving force behind Karma.[7]

Yoga nidra, at an advanced level, would seem to be entering the state of deep sleep while retaining at least a degree of consciousness. Of course this is not easy.

The Cloud of Unknowing describes a different technique. It urges the use of a meditation word, such as *God* or *love,* as a means of focus: "With this worde thou schalt bete on this cloude and this derknes aboven thee. With this worde thou schalt smite doun al maner thought under the cloude of forgeting."[8]

In this scheme, within the seeker's consciousness, there is the level of "thought"; beyond that, "the cloude of forgeting" or "unknowing," which the seeker should "bete on" and "smite doun."

Brain-wave levels can illuminate the picture from a scientific point of view. At present, five levels of brain-wave activity have been defined:

Gamma: 40–100 hertz (Hz): associated with high arousal and cognitive activity

Beta: 12–40 Hz: more or less equivalent to the ordinary state of waking consciousness

Alpha: 8–12 Hz: relaxation, light reverie

Theta: 4–8 Hz: sleep

Delta: 0–4 Hz: extremely deep sleep

It is possible that the lower levels of brain-wave frequency are the ones closest to higher states of being. But precisely for this reason, they are hard to reach. We could thus understand meditation, as well as less familiar practices such as dream yoga and yoga nidra, as ways of gaining access to these levels while preserving some measure of consciousness. It is striking that the first verse of Patañjali's *Yoga Sutras* is *yoga citta vritti nirodha,* which could be translated, "Yoga is the cessation of the oscillation of the mental substance."

So very likely the closer you come to the flatline state—0 Hz of brain-wave activity—the closer you come to primordial states of being. Of course the flatline state is also associated with brain death. This would explain near-death experiences: those who have had them may have had very low levels of brain-wave activity—or even none—for a brief period before they returned to normal states. We also have new insight into why mystical initiations are sometimes described as "journeying to the gates of death," and into the biblical verse in which the Lord says: "Thou canst not see my face: for there shall no man see me, and live" (Exodus 33:20). You can only flatline up to a certain point before you will not come back.

We only have a dim idea of what lies beyond these gates of death. Perhaps we could call it enlightenment. Perhaps we could call it God.

FOUR

THE REIGN OF NUMBER

To recapitulate, this is what we have so far:

1. The five-dimensional box, which includes all of physical and psychological reality as we know it.
2. The cloud of oblivion, a blank space in cognition, possibly equivalent to deep sleep and certain meditative states.
3. Something beyond the cloud.

Before we go on to what may be lying behind the cloud, it may be valuable to see a bit more into the five-dimensional box. There is, then:

The cognizing self: the *one*;
The primordial ternary: the *three*;
Six directions that comprise the combinations of this ternary.

Let's take this one step further. Each of these six can be regarded as a separate, independent entity—a *self*. It would, then, have to take a stance against the rest of existence, which would then be *other* for it. This would produce a second *other*—a *fourth* entity.

Although this is an *other,* it is not reckoned as a new force, for the very simple reason that the *other,* the passive or denying force, is already posited in the primal ternary.

This idea surfaces over and over in esoteric philosophy. Here is one version, from Maria Prophetissa, sometimes called Maria the Jewess, a mysterious figure from around the third century AD who is regarded as one of the founders of Western alchemy. It is called the axiom of Maria: "One becomes two, two becomes three, and out of the Third comes the One as the Fourth."[1]

Many—including many alchemists—have pondered over this dark utterance, but in light of our discussion, it seems fairly clear. Making the ternary into a quaternary has long exercised philosophers. Plato may be alluding to it at the beginning of his *Timaeus,* where Socrates says, "One, two, three, but where, my dear Timaeus, is the fourth of those who were yesterday my guests and are to be my entertainers today?"[2]

C. G. Jung occupied himself with this problem in the last years of his career. He set out his discoveries in his late works *Aeon* and *Mysterium Coniunctionis* ("The Mystery of the Conjunction"). For Jung, there are four basic psychological functions: thinking, feeling, sensation, and intuition, which he placed in a quaternary schema as in figure 4.1 on page 40.

For Jung, the absent fourth, the fourth that is not a fourth, is connected to the *inferior function.* He believed that in each individual, one (it may be any) of these functions is discernibly weaker than the others—"the darkest and most uncomfortable of all." Jung adds, "The fourth function has its seat in the unconscious."[3] As such, it is also the gateway to the unconscious—to which, in his view, one must gain access in order to become a full and complete, or "individuated," being.

Going beyond psychology, Jung believed that the papal proclamation of the dogma of the Assumption of the Virgin (made in 1950) marked a significant acknowledgment of the quaternity in Catholic theology: the Virgin Mary had been added, in a way, to the three of the Trinity. She was the missing fourth, but she was not a fourth person of the Trinity. Catholic dogma says that, unlike the persons of the Trinity,

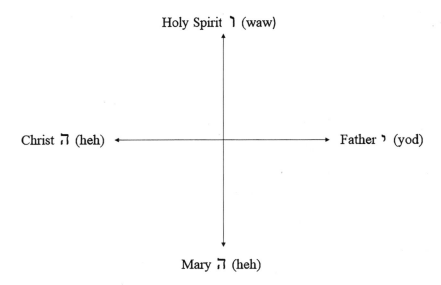

Figure 4.1. Jung's quaternity: the Christian Trinity with Mary added. I have added the corresponding letters of the Tetragrammaton.
After Jung, *Mysterium Coniunctionis,* 186.

she transmits grace but does not generate it.[4] A fourth is added—but, again, not *a fourth force.*

The most famous symbol of this process is the Hebrew name of God, known as the Tetragrammaton: YHWH: יהוה. How many letters are there in the Tetragrammaton? Four, clearly: the word comes from the Greek prefix *tetra-,* "four." But they are not four different letters. The heh (ה), *H,* is repeated. Heh symbolizes the passive, feminine force, partly because this letter at the end of a Hebrew noun generally indicates that it is in the feminine gender. So there is a fourth, but it is not a primordial force: there are only three of those. Rather the fourth is the result of the interactions among the three. This is one of the mysteries of the Tetragrammaton.

If you permute these letters into all their possible combinations, you will get twelve (the transliteration reflects the fact that Hebrew is written from right to left):

YHWH	יהוה
YWHH	יוהה
YHHW	יההו
WYHH	ויהה
WHYH	והיה
WHHY	וההי
HYWH	היוה
HWYH	הויה
HHYW	ההיו
HHWY	ההוי
HYHW	היהו
HWHY	הוהי

We now have these, each of which we can view as levels of manifestation:

1

3

6

12

The level of the twelve takes us to the twelve signs of the zodiac, which are practically universal. Western astrology has the familiar ones: Aries, Taurus, Gemini, and so forth. Curiously, Chinese astrology also has twelve signs, although these are associated with different creatures, and each is assigned to a whole year, rather than to a month, as in the Western system. (You often see this system on place mats in Chinese restaurants.) The twelve tribes of Israel, the twelve apostles, and the twelve Knights of the Round Table reflect other aspects of the same symbolism.

The *Sefer Yetzirah* also associates the twelve signs of the zodiac with the twelve tribes, as well as to twelve organs of the body. Again this only makes sense if you view things from the primal center, which, in the words of the *Sefer Yetzirah,* is to "make the Creator sit on his throne."

Extending outward from this primal point, there are the three forces: *self, other,* and *relation,* with their associated letters and symbols.

The next level is formed of the interactions of these three, which fall into six unique patterns, equated with the six spatial directions.

The third level is the twelve, consisting of the six patterns, each combined with a fourth element—represented by the ה or heh. This level is depicted in the signs of the zodiac, the twelve tribes, the twelve apostles, and so on. The fourth level is the manifestation of these twelve in the organs of the body.

The upshot of all this is that manifestation, as viewed by the *Sefer Yetzirah,* is not a matter of something coming down, as it were, from heaven, but of something proceeding from *within,* from a primal center with its primordial forces.

This perspective sheds a great deal of light on the Kabbalah as well as on many other systems. Without wanting to push the connection too far, I find it interesting that Kant's categories—the fundamental means by which, according to him, the mind structures experience a priori— also number twelve, arranged in four sections:

1. Of quantity
   Unity
   Plurality
   Totality

2. Of quality
   Reality
   Negation
   Limitation

3. Of relation
   Of inherence and subsistence (substance and accident)
   Of causality and dependency (cause and effect)
   Of community (reciprocity between agent and patient)

4. Of modality
   Possibility—impossibility
   Existence—nonexistence
   Necessity—contingency[5]

Many of Kant's categories resemble things that have featured in our discussion. *Identity* could be related to *self; negation* and *limitation,* to *other; community* or *reciprocity,* to *relation.* When one tries to boil down the fundamental structures by which we experience the world, some basic features will invariably appear.

There is another curious feature in the symbolism of the twelve. Consider the twelve apostles: one, Judas, betrays Jesus. Compare this with the twelve sons of Jacob: one, Joseph, is betrayed by his other brothers. We can even connect this pattern with King Arthur and the (traditionally twelve) Knights of the Round Table. Again, Arthur is betrayed by one of them, Lancelot, who commits adultery with Arthur's queen, Guinevere. In each instance, one of the twelve is either betrayed or a betrayer.

I believe this has to do with the symbolism of astrology. Say the spirit enters manifest reality through one of the twelve signs of the zodiac. This is the sun sign, which astrologically characterizes the individual's essence. It shapes her being. But each of these signs sees things in its own particular way, which is accurate if integrated with the other eleven perspectives, but which, taken on its own, is distorted. Thus the Gemini may be inclined to put too much trust in surfaces, whereas Scorpio, always drawn to the depths, may find hidden motives and machinations that do not exist. This distortion, although inevitable, is a betrayal in the sense that it causes one to see things from a limited and faulty perspective.

So, esoterically, your sun sign is your Judas, your betrayer.

It is possible to go further with these calculations, as the *Sefer Yetzirah* does. But it would be best to stop here. In the first place, the ramifications grow more and more complex beyond this point. In the second place, the low counting numbers are by far the most important from a symbolic point of view: 1, 3, 6, 7, 12 appear in all sorts of schemas, including those we take completely for granted, such as the days of the week and the months of the year. They are also the most important in terms of the way our minds structure the world. C. G. Jung observed:

> There is something peculiar, one might even say mysterious, about numbers. They have never been entirely robbed of their numinous aura. . . . The sequence of natural numbers turns out to be unexpectedly more than a mere stringing together of mathematical units: it contains the whole of mathematics and everything to be discovered in this field. Number, therefore, is in one sense an unpredictable entity. . . .
>
> I must confess that I incline to the view that numbers were as much found as invented, and that in consequence they possess a relative autonomy analogous to that of the archetypes. They would then have, in common with the latter, the quality of being pre-existent in consciousness, and hence, on occasion, of conditioning it rather than being conditioned by it.[6]

Jungian author Robin Robertson comments:

> Through his study of the patients' "number" dreams, Jung came to believe that the smaller *natural numbers* [e.g., the integers 1, 2, 3, etc.] are symbols. . . . The integers seemed to correspond to progressive stages of development within the psyche. In brief, one corresponds to a stage of non-differentiation; two—polarity or opposition; three—movement toward resolution, as expressed in the Christian trinity; four—stability, wholeness, as in a quaternary, or a mandala, which is most commonly four-sided.[7]

Strikingly, Jung characterized the lower integers much as I have done above, even though he started from the raw material of his patients' dreams rather than from mystical texts. For Jung, the numbers are archetypes; conversely, the archetypes may be numbers. So it would seem that the numbers—particularly the low counting numbers—and their interrelations form a structure that undergirds existence *as we know it*. These interrelations are represented, not only by mathematical operations, but by symbolic systems including the sacred ternary, the seven traditional planets, the twelve signs of the zodiac. I underscore *as we know it* because there is no reason to assume that this structure is unique or absolute, or perhaps ultimately correct.

Scientists constantly say they are amazed that mathematics should account for the structure of the universe so precisely. More likely it does no such thing. Science, using mathematics, pays attention only to the part of the world that can be quantified. What science can measure and express in mathematical equations, it takes as reality. Whatever eludes these descriptions is dismissed or ignored. It is as if a man had a mountaintop house with a window that presented him with an enormous and lovely vista but insisted that, despite all evidence to the contrary, anything he could not see out of this window did not exist.

FIVE

OF MIRRORS AND MADNESS

I t is a theme that goes back to the earliest Greek philosophers, but only recently has it surfaced in popular culture.

The idea takes many forms. In the Netflix TV series *The OA,* Hap, a villainous anesthesiologist, speaks of the life we are in as a "coma." The 1999 film *The Matrix* portrays life as a perceptual simulation to which humans—again comatose—are subjected so that their energy may be siphoned off to sustain a race of androids.

Going beyond fiction, we sometimes hear scientists wonder whether the entire universe is a simulation, of the sort that our computers run to calculate climate change or the outcomes of nuclear war. At the 2016 Isaac Asimov Memorial Debate at the American Museum of Natural History, the speakers debated this question. The astrophysicist Neil deGrasse Tyson, who hosted the debate, argued that indeed the universe was very likely a simulation.[1]

Paranoid conclusions are near at hand. If we are in a simulation, who or what created it? Tyson speculates about a race of beings that are as far superior to us as we are to other animals. "What would we look like to them? We would be drooling, blithering idiots in their presence," he suggests. Drawing out the implications, we would have no reason to imagine that these beings are benevolently disposed toward us, or that they would not exploit us as viciously as humans exploit the earthly world.

The Gnostic worldview returns.* The Gnostics of the early centuries of the Christian era believed that this universe was created by a stupid inferior deity called the Demiurge (from the Greek *dēmiourgós,* "craftsman") and not by the true, good God, who is almost irretrievably remote from us. A hundred years ago, Gnosticism was a quaint, mostly forgotten heresy, of interest chiefly to specialists. Today it supplies an endless number of tropes for a world that, for all its freedoms, is starting to feel more and more like a vast prison without walls.

To pursue these ideas, we can go back to the image of the box and take it further. Suppose that a man builds a box and puts mirrors in it on all sides. He sits in the box and closes the lid upon himself. Wherever the man looks—up, down, side to side—he sees countless iterated reflections of himself. He sees nothing else and forgets that there is anything else.

The man goes mad. He imagines that each of these reflections is another man, and he thinks their facial expressions are their personalities. He makes an angry face and imagines that this face is another man, angry at him. He smiles and finds a friend. He cries and feels pity for the suffering being he sees.

Soon he becomes so absorbed in these images that he forgets he is himself. He no longer remembers his own individuality. He is submerged in the mirror's reflections and thinks that he is these persons. He becomes what he beholds.

His condition deteriorates further. His mind fixates on one of these images, happy or sad, and identifies with it. He becomes this face. He imagines that he is this face looking at all the other faces, whom he arbitrarily sees as friends or enemies, strangers or lovers. He becomes so lost in these fancies that he loses all function and thrashes around in the wildest ways.

"Strange beings, but very much like us," as Plato said about the people in his cave.[2]

---

*For a fuller discussion of Gnosticism and its influence, see my *Forbidden Faith: The Secret History of Gnosticism.*

We are this man in the mirror-lined box. Each of us and all of us together. But that is not who we think we are. We each think we are one of these faces, and we take his thrashings, reflected in all the mirrors, for our own actions and indeed for the history of humanity and the universe.

Schopenhauer expresses a similar idea: "It is a vast dream, dreamed by a single being; but in such a way that all the dream characters dream too. Hence, everything interlocks and harmonizes with everything else."[3]

Like Schopenhauer, many spiritual teachers tell us that the world is an illusion and life is a dream. Shankara, the eighth-century formulator of the Advaita Vedanta, made one often-quoted analogy: "You see a rope and think it is a snake. As soon as you realize that the rope is a rope, your false perception of a snake ceases, and you are no longer distracted by the fear which it inspired. Therefore, the man who wishes to break his bondage must know the Reality."[4]

To put it in contemporary language: Remember all the times you have heard about "the search for the self" or have felt that you have no idea of who you are. As long as you think you are one of these faces, you certainly have no idea of who you are. You may search for the self, but it is not where you believe it is.

As for the man in the box, his condition lasts only a short time, but to him it is eternity. The confusion and suffering, punctuated by intermittent joys, seem endless. Finally someone takes pity on him. This person does not force open the box, which would drive the man still further into madness, but begins speaking to him. It tells him, "Remember. You are not these crazy reflections that are flashing around. You are who you are."

At first it does no good. The man hears this message and confuses it with his own ravings. Later he realizes that this voice is not his own, but he believes that it is the maddest thing of all. The voice repeats its message, soothingly but persistently. Sometimes the man hears it as sounds mysteriously coming out of another dimension; sometimes he thinks it is emitted by one of the faces in the mirrors. Eventually he starts to trust the voice. He calms down and begins to remember something—at first he does not even know what. As he settles down, the images begin to stabilize. They move around less. The world becomes quieter. He starts to see the faces in the mirrors, not as delusory individuals, but as reflections of himself. He even remembers that he himself built the box. Finally he is quiet and sane enough to open the box and step out of it into a reality he had forgotten.

This weird fable is probably a reasonable approximation of the condition we are in. Now we see who the Gnostic Demiurge is. He is not an evil, inferior god out there. He is ourselves. We are the Demiurge who has forged this world. We have forgotten this fact, but that makes it no less true.

Some may wonder why in the previous chapters I have paid so much attention to the schema of the *Sefer Yetzirah*. It is for this reason: the *Sefer Yetzirah*, cryptically and yet clearly, gives the schema for the box we have cognitively built for ourselves: three spatial dimensions, one dimension of time, and one dimension of good and evil. In order to escape from this box, we need to go into its structure.

The box we inhabit was built from the inside out. In fact it started with the distinction between inside and out—between self and other. The box was elaborated by the interactions and subinteractions of these forces. It ended with five-dimensional reality—the reality that we accept as true for practically all of our waking lives.

In chapter 4, I mentioned that the external (and apparently final) manifestation of this process of cognitive world construction is the physical body. The *Sefer Yetzirah* expresses this truth by correlating the seven planets (as known at the time) with the openings in the skull: "Seven stars in the cosmos, Saturn, Jupiter, Mars, Sun, Mercury, Moon. Seven days in the week, seven gates in the human body, two eyes, two ears, two nostrils, and the mouth."[5]

The twelve signs of the zodiac, and the twelve months of the year, are associated with the organs.

The twelve signs are, Aries, Taurus, Gemini, Cancer, Leo, Virgo, Libra, Scorpio, Sagittarius, Capricorn, Aquarius, Pisces. The twelve months of the year are Nisan, Iyar, Sivan, Tammuz, Av, Elul, Tishrei, Cheshvan, Kislev and Tevat, Shvat and Adar. The twelve organs of the psyche of male and female are two hands, two legs, two kidneys, gall, small intestine, liver, gullet, stomach, spleen.[6]

There are further associations. The Kabbalah speaks of ten *sefirot* (probably best translated roughly as "principles"). If you take these and add them to the twenty-two, you have a total of thirty-two "paths." Kabbalists relate these to the thirty-one nerves that emanate from the spinal cord, plus the complex of cranial nerves (of which there are twelve) taken as a single path.[7]

Above I use the verbs *correlate* and *associate* to describe these connections. These words lead to the doctrine of correspondences, one of the main axioms of occult philosophy. One of its classic expressions is in Henry Cornelius Agrippa's *Occult Philosophy,* published in 1533, which states: "There is no cause of the necessity of effects other than the connection of all things to the First Cause and their correspondence to the divine exemplars and eternal form. From these each thing has its particular determined place in the archetypal world, from which it lives and takes its origin. And all the powers of herbs, stones, metals, animals, words, and prayers—and of all things—have been instilled by God."[8]

Agrippa speaks of a *correspondentia*—correspondence: the heavens above are mirrored by the parts of the body below. But perhaps it would be better to use verbs such as *express* or *manifest* to characterize these relations. By the view I am proposing, the organs of the body are the outermost manifestations of the energies of the twelve. We associate these with the planets and the zodiac, which are apparently external, but which are, esoterically speaking, inside us. The idea is echoed in the title of the first book by the best-selling author Thomas Moore: *The Planets Within.**

---

*For a guided meditation intended to illuminate this idea, see pages 115–18 of my book *Inner Christianity.*

Sometimes the planets are associated with the organs. The illustration on page 52, from an eighteenth-century work by the Christian theosopher Johann Georg Gichtel, shows these associations, along with those of the four traditional elements. Again, the organs are the outermost manifestations of these forces. The title of the diagram, referring to the "dark" human nature, emphasizes that we are dealing here with the world of the Fall.

Systems like that of the *Sefer Yetzirah* are a way of retracing the mind's steps: we go back through the primordial principles—which we perceive first as our own bodily organs, then as planets and constellations, then, at a deeper level, as numbers, geometric figures, and abstract patterns—in order to return to the Ain Sof, the Unconditioned, and thence beyond. This may explain why Pythagoras and Plato laid such emphasis on geometry. Plato's Academy in Athens is said to have had an inscription over it that said, "Let no one enter who is ignorant of geometry."[9]

To look at things from another angle, psychedelics often generate abstract, geometrical, moving patterns in the mind.[10] If we assume that these drugs do remove some of the mind's customary barriers, we may suppose that these abstract geometrical images reflect a contact with a more primordial experience.

Meditation can take the mind still further—to the level of the unconditioned itself. This may explain why many meditative practices produce states of blank or dark consciousness—sometimes called *samadhi,* sometimes called *consciousness without an object.*

I don't, incidentally, mean to imply that the system outlined in the *Sefer Yetzirah* is the single correct way of analyzing these deeper levels of our cognition. Other, similar systems seem to cover the same ground from somewhat different perspectives. The most famous is the one in the *I Ching.* Like the *Sefer Yetzirah,* it traces primordial reality to the small counting numbers and their interchanges, but it posits two forces (yang and yin) and three possible places (in the trigrams), which give a total of eight possible combinations. Thus we have an

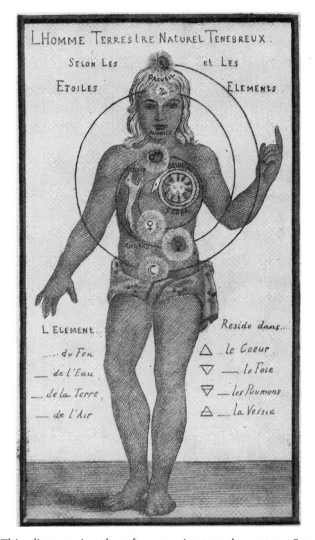

Figure 5.1. This diagram is taken from a nineteenth-century French edition of Johann Georg Gichtel's *Theosophia practica* (originally published in 1701), as reproduced in C. W. Leadbeater's book *The Chakras* (1927). It shows the planets and elements manifested externally in certain organs and centers of the body. They are also connected to the deadly sins (e.g., Saturn, at the crown, with *orgueil*, "pride"; Jupiter, in the forehead, with avarice). The text on the bottom half of the chart reads: "The element of fire resides in the heart; the element of water, in the liver; earth, in the lungs; and air, in the bladder." Its title, translated as "The Dark, Natural, Terrestrial Human according to the Stars and the Elements," emphasizes that it represents the fallen aspect of the human entity.

initial sequence of 1–2–3–8 rather than 1–3–6–12. I find the parallels fascinating, but I would be cautious about saying which one was more correct, and equally cautious about trying to reduce both systems to a single ur-system underneath. Each is, I suspect, equally valid from its own point of view. I have used the Kabbalistic system here because I believe it resonates more with the Western psyche and its familiar symbols.

But to say that *we* have engendered the five-dimensional box is not in itself very informative. Who is this *we*?

The use of the first-person pronoun is apt here, but it may be better stated in the singular number: who is this *I*? The most common name for it is in fact the first-person singular pronoun—in Latin, not in English: the *ego*. Some argue that what the Gnostics called the Demiurge is today often called the *ego*. Stephan A. Hoeller, one of the most prominent advocates of a revived modern Gnosticism, elaborates on this idea in the context of Jung's thought:

> The primary demiurge in the Jungian system is, so it would seem, none other than the alienated human ego. This conscious selfhood, having pulled itself away from the original wholeness of the unconscious, has become a blind and foolish being, unaware of its roots in the unconscious, yet desperately attempting to re-create a semblance of the over-world by effecting unconscious projections. . . . Like the Gnostic demiurge, the ego in its alienated, blind arrogance boldly but falsely proclaims that "there is no other God" before it—that it alone is the true determinant of existence. . . . The ego-demiurge creates its own *kosmos,* but it is a flawed and distorted one, inasmuch as in it the light of the deeper selfhood is obscured and polluted by unconscious projections and compulsions. It is thus that the ego becomes a demiurge, the foolish architect of a foolish world.[11]

At this point we have no way of knowing how or why God created the world, because we do not see the world that God created. We do not see it because we only see the world of the Fall. Indeed everything I have said in the previous chapters has been about the world of the Fall—the world generated by a cosmic loss of awareness, known to the Hindus and Buddhists as *avidya* or *maya*—"ignorance" or "illusion." Genesis says that "a deep sleep fell upon Adam," but nowhere does it say that he woke up.[12]

Some may want a more poetic account of this process. If so, they can go to William Blake's *Book of Urizen*, created in 1794. Like much of Blake's work, it takes the form of an illuminated book, melding poetry and graphic art into a sublime and overwhelming whole. Although only a few copies of Blake's original survive, it is fairly easy to find editions that reproduce the color art in full.

Urizen, in the poem, is "unknown, unprolific, self-clos'd, all repelling, . . . a soul-shudd'ring vacuum." He is the force of cosmic limitation. His name probably comes from a multilingual pun of the sort that James Joyce would later employ: it connotes "horizon," "your eyes," "your reason," and the Greek verb *orízein*, "to limit." And limitation is what he does: "Times on times he divided and measur'd / Space by space in his ninefold darkness" (*The Book of Urizen*, 1.1).

> *And a roof vast, petrific, around*
> *On all sides he fram'd, like a womb,*
> *Where thousands of rivers in veins*
> *Of blood pour down the mountains to cool*
> *The eternal fires, beating without*
> *From Eternals; & like a black globe*
> *View'd by sons of Eternity, . . .*
> *Like a human heart, strugling* [sic] *and*
>   *beating,*
> *The vast world of Urizen appear'd.* (3.7)

The words "womb," "veins," "blood," and "heart" tell us what vast world is appearing. The process continues:

In a horrible, dreamful slumber,
Like the linked infernal chain,
A vast Spine writh'd in torment
Upon the winds, shooting pain'd
Ribs, like a bending cavern;
And bones of solidness Froze
Over all his nerves of joy. (4.6)

And, further,

In harrowing fear rolling round,
His nervous brain shot branches
Round the branches of his heart
On high into two little orbs;
And fixed in two little caves
Hiding carefully from the wind,
His Eyes beheld the deep. (4.8)

Like the man in the box of mirrors, Urizen has imprisoned himself—but in a human body. Here are the consequences:

All the myriads of Eternity,
All the wisdom & joy of life
Roll like a sea around him,
Except what his little orbs
Of sight by degrees unfold.

And now his eternal life
Like a dream was obliterated. (5.2–3)

He has entombed himself in a vault called the human body.

Out of this a woman, Enitharmon, is generated; she in turn conceives and generates "a Worm within her womb," which grows into a serpent and finally into "an infant form / Where there was a Worm before" (6.3, 6).

I will not pursue the story further here, but it is easy to see the parallels within the cosmic imprisonment I have sketched out above. It is the horror of being locked into the physical body, with eternal life "obliterated." It is the horror of falling into the realm of good and evil, incarcerated within coats of skin.

Such is the cosmic sleep of man.

SIX

A SUPPOSITIONAL MOMENT

Once, when I was editor of *Gnosis,* a journal of the Western mystical traditions, we received an unusual submission. It was neatly typed, single-spaced, ten or fifteen pages long, and, in its way, quite literate. Its author gave an elaborate account of a conspiracy that was being waged against him by a cabal including Jimmy Carter and the *Detroit Free Press.* Messages were being transmitted to him telepathically through signals coming through his TV set. The document included an alphabetic key to this conspiracy (J = Jimmy Carter, etc.).

Although it had a certain resonance (after all, I remember it twenty-five years later), we did not publish it. It went into a special drawer, which Jay Kinney, the magazine's founder, had set aside for items like this, which were too far out but still held a certain allure. In any case, even a layman could see that some psychiatric disorder was at work here.

To understand this writer's condition, we could no doubt take many routes. But they would probably not include trying to discover how Jimmy Carter and the *Detroit Free Press* and the TV networks were conspiring against him.

You cannot explain madness within the framework of the madness itself.

The schema described in the previous chapters explains our situation *phenomenologically*—how the five-dimensional box appears to us—but not *ontologically*: it does not say what is really going on. We do not know what is going on because we are in the box ourselves and entrapped in its madness.

Thus it would be difficult for us to see, from within our perspective, how the Fall came about. Genesis tells us that it happened because the primordial man and woman wished to know good and evil. That is profound and compelling, but it remains a myth—that is, it is using figurative language to describe something that cannot really be described at all.

From our point of view within the box, we can only see up to the cloud of oblivion—the primal loss of consciousness. Beyond that, it is a blank. And it must remain so as long as we are in this condition. For this reason I believe it is important to tread cautiously when attempting to speak of the cause of the Fall.

To return to the long-deferred question of Christian theology, there is only one system of Christian theology that has ever made sense to me—that did not seem to create contradictions that it attempted to paper over, thus creating more contradictions. This is the theology of *A Course in Miracles*.

The Course, as it is called, is a stone that the builders rejected. It certainly appears to be a curiosity. I remember buying the first edition, which came in three volumes, hardbound, with dark blue covers stamped with gold, and showing it to a friend of mine, who burst out laughing. A *course* in *miracles*?

Such has been its reception by the intelligentsia. I have almost never seen it discussed in the intellectual press, and when it is, the discussions are so shallow and misinformed that it is beyond any doubt that the writers put almost no effort into understanding it. Nor have I ever seen it treated in mainstream theological circles. If anything, it has been consigned to the purgatory known as the study of new religious movements.

Despite this official indifference, the Course has sold over three million copies in twenty-seven languages since its publication in 1975. It has won widespread admiration in the human-potential movement.

Willis Harman, the late president of California's Institute of Noetic Sciences, wrote, "The set of books comprising *A Course in Miracles* comprise perhaps the most important writing in the English language since the translation of the Bible."[1]

The theology of the Course, as we will see, is very different from that of mainstream Christianity, but it has the same core spirit. Psychologist Frances Vaughan, raised as an Episcopalian, observes, "The core message that I got as an Episcopalian was that Jesus taught 'God is love.' The good news of the Gospel of the New Testament was that sins are forgiven. The rest of the message was 'Know the truth and the truth shall make you free.' That was it. And that's totally consistent with the Course."[2]

The history of the Course has often been told, so I will only recount some basic facts here.[3] Helen Schucman, the Course's "scribe," was a psychologist and statistician at Columbia University's College of Physicians and Surgeons. She was a self-professed atheist. In response to an appeal for help from her colleague and boss, Bill Thetford, Schucman began to experience a series of powerful visions that culminated in October 1965, when she heard a clear inner voice that said, "This is a course in miracles. Please take notes."

Schucman feared for her own sanity and told Thetford what was going on. Because she was not displaying any signs of clinical madness (she remained completely functional and capably carried out her duties in the Columbia psychology department), he suggested that she simply take the voice's advice and write down what it was saying. Thetford helped her transcribe the notes.

Over the next few years Schucman produced a 1,200-page document consisting of a Text, a Workbook, and a Manual for Teachers, setting out a program for personal redemption through forgiveness. (Although the books were initially published in three volumes, most editions now have the volumes collected under a single cover.) The voice that dictated this work spoke in the first person as Jesus Christ.

The material circulated privately for several years and was finally published in 1975. Its astonishing popularity since then attests to its power. I began working with it in 1981. I still find myself picking it up and thinking, "Yes. This is the only way out."

To put it bluntly, if Christian theology has a future, it probably lies with *A Course in Miracles*. Whether it was really dictated by Jesus Christ is impossible to prove one way or another. What would you judge it against? The teachings of the churches? They were invented often centuries later. The Gospels? The most esteemed scholars cannot agree about what in these texts goes back to Jesus and what was put in his mouth afterward.

My own view of the authorship of the Course is like Helen Schucman's:

> I do not understand the real authorship of the writing, but the particular combination of certainty, wisdom, gentleness, clarity and patience that characterized the Voice make that form of reference [i.e., as "the Voice"] seem perfectly appropriate.
>
> At several points in the writing the Voice itself speaks in no uncertain terms about the Author. My own reactions to these references, which literally stunned me at the time, decreased in intensity until they reached a level of mere indecision. I do not understand the events that led up to the writing. I do not understand the process and I certainly do not understand the authorship. It would be pointless for me to attempt an explanation.[4]

Is the Course Christian? It cannot be reconciled with the doctrine of the Christian church as it evolved over the centuries. The Course's theology, theodicy, soteriology, Christology, eschatology, and all the rest differ irreconcilably from the doctrines of this mainstream Christianity. If you are satisfied with this familiar Christianity, you may as well stay with it. But if many of the central teachings of Christian theology make no sense to you, you may find the Course to be of interest. In any event, the Course has to be taken on its own terms, and from that point of view, I find it not only persuasive but profound.

The Course's theology begins with God the Father. God is infinite love and light: "God is the light in which I see," says one lesson in the Workbook (W, 69).* As infinite love, the nature of God is to extend himself. In so doing, God has created the Son, who is a primordial unity, although the Sonship is also expressed in the plural form: "God has only *one* Son. If all His creations are His Sons, everyone must be an integral part of the whole Sonship. The Sonship in its Oneness transcends the sum of its parts" (T, 33; emphasis in the original). In short, the Son is each of us, individually and collectively. One Workbook lesson says, "My mind is part of God's. I am very holy" (W, 53); another says, "I am one Self, united with my Creator" (W, 166). Thus the Course does not equate the Son of God, also known as Christ, with the historical Jesus exclusively. "Is he the Christ?" it says at one point. "O yes, along with you" (M, 87).

The Son of God shares all of the Father's characteristics except one: the Father created the Son, but the Son did not create the Father. Otherwise the two are identical in all respects. The nature of the Son, then, is also infinite love and light. The Son creates in his turn, as God does: "As God's creative Thought proceeds from Him to you, so must your creative thought proceed from you to your creations. . . . Your creations belong in you, as you belong in God. You are part of God, as your sons are part of His Sons" (T, 112).

God has decreed this to be so, and it is immutable. Because only what God creates is real, our only reality as Sons of God is light and love and happiness. This cannot be reversed. Thus there is no danger, no pain, no sorrow. This is heaven. We have never left it. "Heaven is now. There is no other time. Heaven is here. There is no other place" (M, 61).

Yet the opposite seems to be the case. Heaven often seems remote, as do infinite light and love and power. What happened?

---

*Please see "Note on Citations from *A Course in Miracles*" at the beginning of this book.

The Course also speaks of the Fall, which it usually calls the *separation*. The separation never happened, because God did not will it, and, because his Son shares all his characteristics, the Son does not will it either. Nonetheless, "into eternity, where all is one, there crept a tiny, mad idea, at which the Son of God remembered not to laugh" (T, 586).*

This "tiny, mad idea" is the idea of separation—the idea that the Son could be isolated from God. In a sense this idea is suppositional only: it is as if the Son wondered, in a brief moment, "What if I could exist apart from God?" The Course calls this "the detour into fear."

If you were to take a minute to imagine the worst things that could happen to you—death, degradation, pain, torture, the loss of loved ones—you could make them all seem quite real in your mind. (It is probably not a good idea to try this for very long.) While you were imagining it, it would feel as if it were real. You would, for a moment, suffer almost as if you were going through these terrible things.

Such a suppositional moment, as it were, is the interval that constitutes the world as we know it, throughout all of time and space. (Indeed time and space are part of this specious world.) It is an imaginary reality; it could not have any actual substance, because God has not willed it. God loves his Son, and contrary to certain theologies, will never make his Son suffer. But his Son can *imagine* he is suffering. And because the Son has all the power of God himself, he can make this imaginary world seem powerfully real. He can even forget his own reality. "In his forgetting did the thought become a serious idea, and possible of both accomplishment and real effects" (T, 586–87). This is the world we see. It was made by the *ego*. The ego is the "tiny, mad idea."

This idea is echoed in one of the most famous passages in American literature: the scene in *Moby-Dick* in which Ahab tells his astonished crew the real goal of their voyage—to strike at the monstrous white

---

*There is a semantic ambiguity here. The Course is written in a high literary style (although it is in prose, much of it scans as blank verse). Here "the Son remembered not to laugh," stated in a more ordinary fashion, means "the Son of God did not remember to laugh."

whale to which he lost his leg. Ahab does not think of Moby-Dick as a whale only. Behind it lies something else. He says:

All visible objects, man, are but as pasteboard masks. But in each event—in the living act, the undoubted deed—there, some unknown but still reasoning thing puts forth the mouldings of its features from behind the unreasoning mask. If man will strike, strike at the mask! How can the prisoner reach outside except by thrusting through the wall? To me, the white whale is that wall, shoved near to me. Sometimes I think there's naught beyond. But 'tis enough. He tasks me; he heaps me; I see in him outrageous strength, with an inscrutable malice sinewing it. That inscrutable thing is chiefly what I hate; and be the white whale agent, or be the white whale principal, I will wreak that hate upon him.[5]

Ahab is crazy. Even so, he does see something behind the masks of palpable reality. It is the ego—the furious, unreasoning force of separation. Ahab is insane because he mistakes the mask for the force behind it, or believes he cannot hit at this force otherwise. Ahab does not see less than the ordinary person, but more. Nonetheless, he is unable to get to this deeper agent, because he fails to see it within. He projects it onto the whale, and that is the root of his tragedy. It is as if the man in the box of mirrors were trying to smash the images he sees, which would lead him only further into madness. Melville may be suggesting that the same craziness lies within us and structures the world we see.

In short, the Son of God—which is all of us—is the man who has built the box of mirrors and climbed into it. The ego is the madness that arises from his forgetting of where and who he is. It projects its own madness onto the figures on the glass, imagining that their ravings and twistings are his identity.

We could ask why this suppositional moment should last, or appear to last, so long—and why it should be so painful. After all, you watch a horror movie and are taken into its reality enough to be frightened, but there is a limit to this fright. In the background you know that you are sitting in a comfortable theater, and although you let the movie thrill you, ultimately you are not fooled.

That is not the way the world appears to us now. The Course is saying that we have a similar background of safety—indeed a much greater one—but we have lost awareness of it.

How did all of this happen? Part of the answer has already been given. The Son has all the power of the Father. Thus even his "miscreations" have vigor and force. The power and ingenuity of this particular miscreation (like the "inscrutable malice" that Ahab sees) is not to be discounted. Consider the natural world as we experience it. In his classic *Meditations on the Tarot,* the twentieth-century esotericist Valentin Tomberg writes:

> The world of evolution . . . is . . . a matter . . . of a really vast intelligence and a very resolute will pursuing a definite aim determined by the method of "trial and error." One could say that it is a matter more of a great scientific intellect and the will of an experimenter which is revealed in natural evolution (the existence of which one can no longer deny), rather than divine wisdom and goodness. The tableau of evolution that the natural sciences—above all biology—have at last obtained as the result of prodigious work reveals to us *without any doubt* the work of a very subtle, but imperfect, intellect and a very determined, but imperfect, will. It is therefore the serpent, "the most artful animal of the fields," who is the "prince of this world," and who is the author and director of the purely biological evolution following the Fall.[6]

I am not saying exactly what Tomberg is saying. I do not believe that evolution is guided by the "serpent," otherwise known as the ego. I am saying that the ego structures the way we cognize the world, and that the process that science terms *evolution* is, like many other theories, the product of the ego. What goes on in the real world is opaque to us:

the scientific perspective is that of the man inside the box, who is controlled by his delusions. Hence the savagery of the natural world that we perceive all around us, and which, in imitating, we surpass. From this perspective, "the whole creation groaneth and travaileth in pain" (Romans 8:22). What it is like in reality we will not know until we have gone past the delusions of the ego.

In short, I am not suggesting that the ego dictates the process of biological evolution, as Tomberg is. I am saying that it is the ego that causes us to posit this hypothesis—along with all the other hypotheses, scientific, religious, and otherwise—and causes us to see the world this way.

Some will be irritated to see that I am bracketing the grandiose edifice of science as nothing more than the projections of the ego onto a natural world that is undoubtedly quite different. Heresy, to present-day thought. But consider at least this fact: This worldview has prevailed in the West for the last two centuries. It coincides precisely with the rise of the environmental degradation that continues to this day. This fact suggests something quite different from what we usually believe: that the scientific perspective, which we worship like a golden calf, so distorts our view that we cannot help responding to the world cruelly and exploitatively. And in our state of delusion, we cannot evade the results.

I am not saying that we should revert to a naive creationism (I have already said that the story in Genesis was not meant to be taken literally). The creation account of conventional Christianity is also dictated by the ego. Some say that the attitudes of many indigenous peoples, which see the human race as much more integrated into a living natural world, are closer to reality. Maybe, but these views are probably not so accurate that we should return to them wholesale. How we will sort out this quandary over the next few generations is far from clear.

Our existential situation is more complicated still. The ego is motivated by fear—or rather, the ego *is* fear. Having posited itself as existing separately from God, it perceives God as a threat. Because the ego is vindictive—it is the source of all vindictiveness—it imagines that God is vindictive too. It sees its separation as "sin," and, imagining that God is seeking it out to kill, it tries to hide from God as Adam and Eve hid in the Garden. Although the Course's schema does not exactly replicate the myth of Genesis, it evokes the same mood—the bizarre fear that the man and woman feel after they have eaten the fruit, even the haunted anxiety of the murderous Cain.

The Course does not, incidentally, teach the existence of a personal devil as conceived by mainstream Christianity. The only "devil" is the ego:

> The mind can make the belief in separation very real and very fearful, and this belief *is* the "devil." It is powerful, active, destructive and clearly in opposition to God, because it literally denies His Fatherhood. Look at your life and see what the devil has made. But realize that this making will surely dissolve in the light of truth, because its foundation is a lie. Your creation by God is the only Foundation that cannot be shaken, because the light is in it. (T, 50–51)

Thus there was, in the beginning, a "tiny, mad idea, at which the Son of God remembered not to laugh" (T, 586). This idea, the ego, gained power from the Son's belief in it. It grew in fear, gave rise to guilt, and imagined that a cruel God was hunting it down to punish it. But there is nothing to punish. The ego does not need to be punished, or saved. It must simply be acknowledged for what it is—as nothing.

This "tiny, mad idea" sends the Son of God into amnesiac shock. This shock gives rise to the cloud of oblivion—which could be identified as the "circle of fear."

> The circle of fear lies just below the level the body sees, and seems to be the foundation on which the world is based. Here are all the illusions, all the twisted thoughts, all the insane attacks, the fury, the vengeance and betrayal that were made to keep the guilt in place, so that the world could rise from it [guilt] and keep it [guilt] hidden.

Its [guilt's] shadow rises to the surface, enough to hold its [guilt's] most external manifestations in darkness, and to bring despair and loneliness to it [the shadow, i.e., the world] and keep it joyless. Yet its [guilt's] intensity is veiled by its [guilt's] heavy coverings, and kept apart from what was made to keep it [guilt] hidden. The body cannot see this [guilt], for the body arose from this [guilt] for its protection, which depends upon keeping it [guilt] not seen. The body's eyes will never look on it [guilt]. Yet they will see what it [guilt] dictates (T, 394).*

The ego, imagining that God is angry and in pursuit of it, hides in the body. The body, according to the Course, is the product of the ego, as the passage above indicates.

We would seem to be returning to the old Christian demonization of the physical body. Actually, this is not the case. The Course says that the body is not evil; it is completely neutral. It only reflects what the mind makes of it. If it is used for vengeance, it suffers. If it is used to express love, it will remain healthy and serviceable.

Given all this, it must be true that we do not experience the world correctly either. The Course stresses that the world we see is the product of the ego: one of its lessons is "What I see is a form of vengeance." It explains: "Today's idea accurately describes the way anyone who holds attack thoughts in his mind must see the world. Having projected his anger onto the world, he sees vengeance about to strike at him. His own attack is thus perceived as self defense. This becomes an increasingly vicious circle until he is willing to change how he sees. Otherwise, thoughts of attack and counterattack will preoccupy him and people his entire world. What peace of mind is possible to him then?" (W, 33).

The Course characterizes this world ruthlessly:

---

*This passage is difficult because of the text's rather confusing use of pronouns. Bracketed insertions are adopted from Wapnick, *Love Does Not Condemn*, 432. Chapters 11 through 19 of Wapnick's book are an excellent introduction to the Course's theology.

The world you see is the delusional system of those made mad by guilt. Look carefully at this world, and you will realize that this is so. For this world is the symbol of punishment, and all the goals that seem to govern it are the laws of death. Children are born into it in pain and through pain. Their growth is attended by suffering, and they learn of sorrow and separation and death. Their minds seem to be trapped in their brain, and its powers to decline if their bodies are hurt. They seem to love, yet they desert and are deserted. They appear to lose what they love, perhaps the most insane belief of all. And their bodies wither and gasp and are laid in the ground, and are no more. Not one of them but has the thought that God is cruel.

If this were the real world, God *would* be cruel (T, 236; emphasis in the original).

Christian theologians generally balk at such conclusions. They scoff at the "world-denying nihilism," real and imagined, of the Eastern religions. Similarly, they often write off the Course itself as nothing more than the old Gnostic heresy revived. (Theology has its own version of the naming fallacy: a view is identified with some past heresy, supposedly already refuted, and therefore dismissed.) The standard Christian formula has usually been *Natura vulnerata, non deleta:* "Nature has been wounded, but not destroyed" by the Fall. The world is fundamentally a good place.

But the world is not fundamentally a good place. We have seen why. The world is neither solely good nor solely evil. It is *both* good and evil. It is *constituted* of both good and evil. The evil comes from the ego. Because the ego is illusory, evil is illusory. Therefore a world constituted of good and evil is also illusory.

Hence the Course instructs the student to say, "The world I see holds nothing that I want" (W, 233). But because "I have invented the world I see" (W, 49), "there is another way of looking at the world" (W, 50). Indeed "I could see peace instead of this" (W, 51).

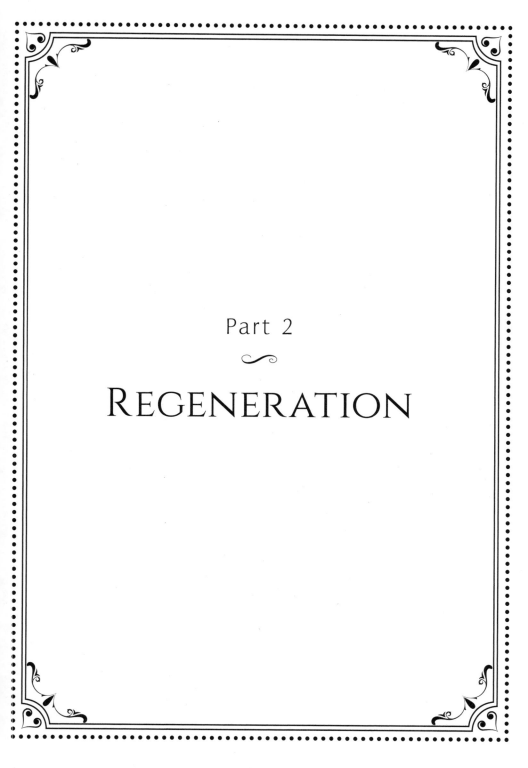

Part 2

REGENERATION

SEVEN

THE LAW ON TWO LEVELS

If we are in this predicament, what is the way out?

According to the Course, the way out is the *Atonement.* It was set into effect the instant the Fall, or the separation, began.

I should say something here about the Course's terminology. In this discussion, I am, to the best of my ability, using the Course's terms and with the meanings that it intends. Thus all of the concepts that we have encountered so far—the Father, the Son, the Fall, the Atonement—are used as the Course uses them. Many students of the Course have some difficulty with its terminology, which is essentially Christian. Others dislike the gender-specific language: the Father, the Son, and the constant use of the masculine pronouns to refer to them.

These objections are easy to understand, but the Course uses Christian terminology as a corrective to mainstream Christian theology (one of the main purposes of this book as well). As for the use of masculine pronouns to refer to both genders, that was the standard literary practice when the Course was written. (I suppose someone could take on the project of creating a gender-neutral version of the Course, but I am not going to.)

To resume: the Atonement is the means of healing the separation. "The escape is brought about by your acceptance of the Atonement, which enables you to realize that your errors never really occurred" (T, 18). The means of the Atonement is the Holy Spirit.

The Father, it must be remembered, is not aware of the separation. If he were, it would be real, for the Father only knows what is real: indeed that is what makes it real. Nonetheless, God has a response to the separation. The mediator, or Comforter (as he is sometimes called in conventional Christianity), is the Holy Spirit. The Holy Spirit is the aspect of God that can serve as a bridge between the eternal Father and the temporarily deluded Son. The Atonement did not exist before the separation; it was unneeded. But the *principle* of the Atonement—which is love—existed long before the separation, and there was no point at which it did not exist.

> The Thought of peace was given to God's Son the instant that his mind had thought of war. There was no need for such a Thought before, for peace was given without opposite, and merely was. But when the mind is split there is a need of healing. So the Thought that has the power to heal the split became a part of the mind that still was one, but failed to recognize its oneness. Now it did not know itself, and thought its own Identity was lost. (W, 407)

The man in the box of mirrors has gone mad and thinks he is all the crazy reflections he sees. A voice outside reminds him of the truth. It cannot open the box, because if it did, the man would be driven still further into madness and fear. The voice can only gently and persistently whisper, and wait for the man to hear it through the noise of his own ravings.

This voice is the Holy Spirit.

What is the truth? It is this:

> This is God's Final Judgment: "You are still my holy Son, forever innocent, forever loving and forever loved, as limitless as your Creator, and completely changeless and forever pure. Therefore awaken and return to Me. I am your Father and you are my Son." (W, 455)

This is the message that everyone must hear and ultimately will hear: "Tolerance for pain may be high, but it is not without limit. Eventually everyone comes to recognize, however dimly, that there *must* be a better way" (T, 22; emphasis in the original). The Course teaches predestination, but it is not predestination to hellfire. It is predestination to eternal, limitless, and unimaginable happiness. Because this is God's will, it cannot be reversed. It *can* be delayed in time, because the Son has the free will to refuse it—temporarily. But he cannot *ultimately* refuse it, because this truth is his very identity.

At this point it becomes necessary to discuss one concept underlying the Course: the concept of levels. The physical world, made by the ego, is unreal; the spiritual world, created by God, is real.

Initially such a claim seems easy to refute. The physical world is unreal? Go jump off a building and see if that's true. (Curiously, this is like how the Devil in the Gospels tempted Jesus: Matthew 4:4–5; Luke 4:9–10). The Course is not saying that. Indeed "the use of miracles as a spectacle to induce belief is a misunderstanding of their purpose" (T, 3). The physical world has its own reality to it, but it is an unstable and unsatisfactory one, as is proved by the fact that it is constantly changing and that this change itself is the source of limitless misery.

The world that God created is the opposite in every way. There is no change in it, no suffering, no loss, nothing but endless joy and love. (As I said, this is so inconceivable to the ego that we cannot imagine such a world that is not colossally boring.)

It is crucial to avoid confusing the two levels. The Course underscores this point semantically: the world of the ego is the world of "making," the world of God is the world of "creating": "Thoughts can represent the lower or bodily level of experience, or the higher or spiritual level of experience. One *makes* the physical, and the other *creates* the spiritual" (T, 3; emphasis added).

We are led to the question of miracles—obviously a central concern of the Course, in view of its title. G. I. Gurdjieff once said, "A 'miracle' is the manifestation in this world of the laws of another world."[1] The Course similarly observes: "Miracles transcend the body. They are sudden shifts into invisibility, away from the bodily level. That is why they heal" (T, 4).

To the ultimately unreal world of the physical, the miracle stands as a corrective: "A miracle is a correction introduced into false thinking by me [Jesus]. It acts as a catalyst, breaking up erroneous perception and reorganizing it properly. This places you under the Atonement principle, where perception is healed. Until this has occurred, knowledge of the Divine Order is impossible" (T, 5). Evidently, then, the miracle is a means of shifting the consciousness from one level—one that is false—to one that is true. Note too that the passage says we cannot know the Divine Order—reality in its true sense—until our perception is healed.

The Theosophist Annie Besant provides some insights into this matter in a discussion of dharma. Dharma, as used by the Hindus, is *law* in its ultimate sense: not only legislative and moral law, but the law of the divine order. The ancient Greeks made much of the distinction between *nómos* and *phúsis*, "convention" and "nature." The Hindus make no such distinction. Dharma, law, is the way the universe operates. Human law and morality operate through knowledge of this dharma, and in accordance with it; otherwise they are erroneous and unworkable. (This happens often in practice.)

Besant says, "Dharma may . . . be defined as the 'inner nature of a thing at any given stage of evolution, and the law of the next stage of its unfolding'—the nature at the point it has reached in its unfolding, and then the law which brings about the next stage of its unfolding."[2]

We can take this idea this way: the present "inner nature of a given stage of evolution" means, for us humans, the physical world as we know it. We are subject to its laws—not only to those of physics and biology, but of convention and human legality. This is what Heidegger called our "thrownness." We have no choice in the matter. As people often say, "I didn't ask to be born."

This law, this dharma, cannot be overcome *at its own level*. If you try to do so, you become subject, not to a higher law, but to a lower one. If you obey the laws of your country, you retain some freedom of movement. If you break them, you will be caught, and you will lose this freedom. You will no longer be subject to the laws of everyday life, but to the much harsher laws of the prison. This, incidentally, casts light on the problem of the superman as posed in the nineteenth century. Dostoevsky's Raskolnikov tries to prove that he is above the law by murdering the old woman pawnbroker and her sister. He tries to free himself from the laws of the ordinary level—but by using laws of a still lower level, those of brute violence. So he fails. The end of *Crime and Punishment* shows him on his way to penal service in Siberia.

The laws of the current level cannot be violated, but they can be transcended. How? By submitting to the laws of a higher level, what Besant calls "the law of the next stage of . . . unfolding." Goethe expresses the same idea: "From the power that binds all being / The man who masters himself is freed."[3]

In the present context, if you wish to transcend the laws of the physical—and open up the possibilities of the miraculous—you do so by following the laws of God rather than the laws of the world. One lesson in the Workbook says, "I am under no laws but God's" (W, 134).

Does this free you, say, from the laws of your country? In a way, no; in a way, yes. If you operate from a lower level, like Raskolnikov, you will get into trouble. If you operate from a higher level, of love and compassion, you will have more freedom. If you are trustworthy, you are more likely to be trusted. No one will need to use the law to enforce anything upon you.

The apostle Paul recognized this truth about the law: it is a central theme of his epistles. As a Jew, he conceives of law as the Mosaic Law, with all 613 of its commandments and prohibitions. The law of Christ frees one from the Mosaic Law. This is in large part why Paul takes such great pains to drive home the idea that Christians do not have to live by it. "Now we know that what things soever the law saith, it saith to them who are under the law" (Romans 3:19). But "Christ is the end of the law for righteousness to every one that believeth" (Romans 10:4).

All this is very well, you may say, but what exactly constitutes a miracle?

The Course's answer: "The miracle is an expression of an inner awareness of Christ and the acceptance of His Atonement" (T, 6; T 1.I.44).

The Atonement, "an interlocking chain of forgiveness" (T, 4; T 1.I.25), takes place in time, but it is not limited by time, because time ultimately does not exist. "The miracle is a learning device that lessens the need for time," says the Course. "It establishes an out-of-pattern time interval not under the usual laws of time. . . .This introduces an interval from which the giver and receiver both emerge farther along in time than they would otherwise have been. . . . The miracle substitutes for learning that might have taken thousands of years" (T, 6, 8).

The Course does not say that all miracles are physical healings, but the concepts are interwoven. The miracle corrects false thinking— a belief that the body controls the mind rather than being controlled, indeed made, by it. As such, the miracle can heal illness. "Miracles enable you to heal the sick and raise the dead because you made sickness and death yourself, and can therefore abolish both" (T, 4). (I do not know how to take the statement about raising the dead.)

Because only the mind is real, all healing is ultimately mental. "Since only the mind can be sick, only the mind can be healed. Only the mind is in need of healing."[4]

Does this work? I will answer with a story from my own experience. In December 1985, I was traveling in India. I drank some water that I should not have drunk and came down with a violent case of dysentery.

That night I was staying at a cheap hotel, which had no air conditioning. Consequently the windows had to stay open, giving free rein to any number of mosquitoes that were swarming around the room. The bed had a mosquito net, which protected me reasonably well, but every fifteen or twenty minutes I was faced with the choice of confronting the assaults of the mosquitoes or confronting even more terrible sufferings from my bowels. Of course my bowels won every time, so I would have to shuffle off to the bathroom, exposing myself to multiple insect attacks.

The next day I felt no better, but I did have a change of mind. I resolved with all the will power I could muster that *I would not be sick*. I simply refused to be sick. I met my traveling companion for lunch. All I could take were two large lassis—Indian yogurt drinks—but afterward I felt much better. The dysentery went away, and, except for a minor relapse on the plane home, it did not come back.

This is somewhat like a situation six years earlier, when I was traveling in Egypt and also came down with dysentery. My girlfriend called in an Egyptian doctor, who prescribed some Lomotil and an antibiotic. It made me feel better, but not entirely. When I got back to Oxford, where I was studying, I came down with a virulent infection that put me in the hospital for ten days and made me miss half a term of studies.

The episode in Egypt could be considered, from a quasiscientific point of view, as a control. After all, there was the same individual—me—starting off in more or less identical states of health. There was the same disease in similarly unfamiliar Third World settings. When I was in Egypt, I had the attentions of a doctor as well as prescription medication, while in India I had none. But in India the ailment passed in twenty-four hours, whereas the one in Egypt ended in the worst illness I have had so far in my life.

Unless you want to extol the magnificent healing properties of lassi, the only real difference was that in the second case I had resolved not to be sick. Whether I invoked the principles of the Course per se, I don't remember, but I had gone through the Workbook some four years earlier, and its principles were embedded in my mind.

You can decide for yourself whether this was a miracle. Skeptics could come up with the usual rational explanations, but many of these would no doubt be more far-fetched than the case itself. Or you could talk about willpower—but willpower is just as mysterious as miracles.

I could cite other instances, but this is one of the more dramatic ones.

It occurs to me to mention, as I write this in August 2018, that I have just received a package from the only friend I have who is a Christian Scientist. I met her in a *Course in Miracles* group some fifteen years ago. At this point she must be close to a hundred. The package contains her fifth book. Make of that what you like.

EIGHT

MEANING FOR A MEANINGLESS WORLD

If the world we see is defective and unreal, what is the meaning of life? For that matter, *is* there a meaning to life?

Life in this context almost always means human life (as opposed to, say, biological life as a whole). *Meaning,* in its customary sense, always points to something beyond, something *else*. In the language of twentieth-century critical theory, which harks back to Saussure, meaning necessarily involves a *signifier* and a *signified*. The signifier points to the signified. The word *dog* points to a certain familiar domestic animal; thus it means more or less the same thing as *chien* or *Hund* or *sobaka* to speakers of other languages. The word *nfaaraa* points to nothing and so has no meaning in English, or, so far as I know, in any language. To someone who does not know German, *Hund* does not mean anything either.

In that case, if there is such a thing as a meaning to life, life must point to something beyond itself. Not for all, perhaps. There are those for whom life has no meaning beyond itself; it presents itself simply and directly, with all its joy and suffering. One cannot help loving such people; literature has immortalized them in Falstaff, Sancho Panza, Zorba the Greek, and the characters in Aristophanes. They may well be happier than the common run of mortals, but theological or philosophical questions generally do not occur to them.

Others, after ransacking the schools of human thought and going away disappointed from all of them, come up with a similar answer. As FitzGerald's *Rubaiyat* puts it:

> *Myself when young did eagerly frequent*
> *Doctor and Saint, and heard great Argument*
> *About it and about: but evermore*
> *Came out by the same Door as in I went.*[1]

Sometimes people who have lost faith in explanation try to return to a primitive simplicity. This does not seem to work very well; the whiff of disappointment does not go away. I have this impression, for example, with Tolstoy, whose overbearing embrace of Christian humility and simplicity toward the end of his life often sounds forced.

For some, the meaning of life points to something *within* life. Frequently the answer is some form of excellence or dominance. For the Homeric heroes it was glory and future renown. They had nothing else, because the Homeric concept of the afterlife as a miserable evanescence did not give them much to look forward to. Other common answers are wealth or power. Certainly there are many who view life in these terms, but the emptiness and impermanence of these aims have been stressed by almost all of the wisest individuals in history—many of whom learned this truth from grim experience. Ecclesiastes is one of its greatest expressions.

If most people were asked what gives meaning and purpose to their lives, they would no doubt answer in terms of family: it is for my spouse and children and kin that I live. No one could condemn them, but like all attempts to find meaning within life, it is treacherous. Loved ones leave or die just like everyone else. Few families, no matter how solid, would not be convulsed by a desertion, an accident, a medical diagnosis. It is common to see people who have been irreparably damaged by the loss of a spouse, or especially a child. If you live for your child and your child is taken away, what do you have left?

Let us turn then to the next possibility: that life neither means itself nor anything contained within its own sphere; it has no meaning at all. Many have reached this conclusion, notably the existentialists. Because there is no God and man has no innate essence, they argue, life is meaningless and therefore man is totally free. But the consequences of this daring proclamation are not what you might expect. Discarding the Christian God with his double-entry moral accounting ought to be exhilarating: someone who does this should feel like a child who has been let out of school. But this is almost never the case. The existentialist sees the meaninglessness of life not as a permanent vacation, but as a curse that is more bitter than slavery.

Some say the desire for a meaning to life is merely wishful thinking, a belief in a Santa Claus that the mature adult has to set aside. But if there were no meaning to be desired, why would we desire it? Desire, like meaning, always refers to something beyond itself—the desire itself is evidence that the thing desired must exist. It is never directed toward a nonexistent object, even when this is far beyond reach. A man wants to be rich; he is lazy and stupid, so he has no chance of attaining his goal. But that does not make the goal nonexistent: it *is* possible to be rich. Similarly, you may desire world peace, even though world peace does not exist. And yet peace exists—and world peace is thinkable even if it seems very remote.

In short, you would never feel thirsty if there were no such thing as water. Our very desire for a meaning to life strongly suggests that there is such a meaning.

Some may say that the idea that life has a meaning is erroneous because it assumes that life is a signifier like a noun or a verb. Life is no such thing, they would say; it is not a word; therefore it is nonsensical to ask about the meaning of life. But I have used the expression *meaning of life* because it is ubiquitous. That in itself suggests that the question is valid. If it really were nonsensical, no one would have asked it for long, just as nobody asks, "Why is green?" The question of life's meaning, however, *is* asked, continually and relentlessly, and there is something in the human mind that will not let go of it. If I were to replace the phrase with something similar, such as the *purpose of life,* it would come to the same thing, because *purpose* too points to something beyond itself.

We are then driven to conclude that life must have a meaning beyond itself, beyond what Christianity calls "the world."

A Course in Miracles begins its Workbook lessons with meaninglessness: "I am upset because I see a meaningless world. . . . A meaningless world engenders fear" (W, 19, 21). This "meaningless world" is described as "the world I see": "The world I see holds nothing I want" (W, 233).

If we were left at this step, the only result could be nihilism and despair. But, the Course continues, "you cannot stop with the idea that the world is worthless, for unless you see that there is something else to hope for, you will only be depressed" (W, 235). Thus the next lesson says, "Beyond this world there is a world I want" (W, 235).

But the Course's stance differs from the gloomy and pessimistic world denial that theologians criticize (usually in someone else's theology).

> The world is nothing in itself. Your mind must give it meaning. And what you behold upon it are your wishes, acted out so that you can look at them and think they are real. Perhaps you think that you did not make the world, but came unwillingly to what was made already. . . . Yet in truth you found exactly what you looked for when you came.
>
> There is no world apart from what you wish, and herein lies your ultimate release.
>
> Change but your mind on what you want to see, and all the world must change accordingly. Ideas leave not their source. (W, 242)

The ego has arisen from the "tiny, mad idea" that the Son of God could exist apart from his Father, or could create a reality that is not in accordance with his Father's, or indeed his own, wishes. This idea gives rise to fear; in essence, the ego *is* fear. It is frightened by its imagined revolt against God and retreats further into fear. It cannot accept itself as the source of the fear, because that would call its own existence into question. So it projects its fear onto an imagined outside world, "the world I see" (W, 34), the result of "attack thoughts" (W, 40).

The ego sees this revolt as killing God. The killing of the god is a common if not universal theme in many religions. One example is a myth found in the Karadjeri tribe of Australian aborigines. It tells of a pair of brothers, the Bagadjimbiri, who in the Dreamtime came out of the ground in the form first of dingoes and then of giants. They taught many valuable skills to the Karadjeri, including the rites of initiation. But at some point a man killed them with a lance. Resuscitated by their mother's milk, they were transformed into water serpents. Their spirits ascended to the sky, where they took form of the Magellanic Clouds. The Karadjeri meticulously imitate their actions, especially the initiatory rites.[2]

This myth rests upon a profound ambivalence: worship and imitation of the divine brothers, along with an implied guilt because they were killed by the tribe. We can see this as a reflection of the process of which the Course speaks. The ego "revolts" against God, and, in its guilt, imagines that it has killed him. But it is able neither to destroy him nor forget him.

Christianity plays out this dynamic by portraying the murdered god in the form of Jesus. There is much guilt surrounding this act, and it is manifested in a split fashion. On the one hand, Jesus died for the sins of all of us, so in this sense all of us have killed him, and we cling to the consequent guilt. On the other hand, there is an equally powerful urge to get rid of this guilt by projecting it onto the putative culprits—usually the Jews. I do not think it is possible to fully understand anti-Semitism without acknowledging this fact.

This imagined murder of God may illuminate other psychological facts as well. In *Totem and Taboo,* one of Freud's strangest but most evocative books, he proposes that the Oedipus complex and its associated guilt goes back to an incident that took place in the "primal horde" of humans (a concept postulated by Darwin). This was a tribe that was led by the father, who dominated the clan and kept all the women for himself. Jealous of his sons, he expelled them from the tribe. "The expelled sons joined forces, slew and ate the father, and thus put an end to the father horde."[3] Their guilt, echoed down through the generations, manifests in the incest taboo and the Oedipus complex.

It is not clear how seriously Freud took his own theory. One early critic mocked it as a "just-so story," and Freud was amused; as a joke, he said, it was "really not bad."[4] In any case, I am suggesting that the just-so story in *Totem and Taboo* is functionally similar to the Karadjeri myth and countless others, and that the Course casts some light upon it. The ego revolts against God the Father. Again, it interprets this revolt as "killing" God, leaving a guilt that is both profound and deeply hidden. Of course the ego cannot kill God. God cannot be killed, and the ego does not really exist. But it imagines it has committed this crime, and cannot let go of this belief. The fear is played out symbolically through repetition in the initiation ritual of Karadjeris (which must carried out exactly as the brothers did it), and in similar rites in other religions, such as the Christian Eucharist. These considerations may explain the highly obsessive-compulsive nature of ritual as a whole.

This is the world we inhabit. We project our fears onto an imagined world and feel guilt that, having revolted against God, we will be punished by him. Like Cain skulking away from the sight of the Lord, we take refuge in this world, while populating it with innumerable threats—germs, disease, natural disaster, other people.

We are like the man in the box of mirrors. If he acknowledged his own madness, he would grow still more fearful, because he would realize that he is his own worst, indeed only, enemy. So he must protect himself from this fact by projecting his fear outward, onto all the grimacing faces that he sees in the mirrors. He believes that they are other people, some of them friendly, others menacing.

But, you may reply, we do not live in a box of mirrors. We live in a cold, hard, all-too-factual world, where threats are real and real damage can be done. So it would appear. But all this damage, all these threats, can only affect one thing—the body. For the Course, the body is the concretization of the ego's fears—the "'hero' of the dream" of separation (T, 585). "The body is the ego's home by its own election. It is the only identification with which the ego feels safe, since the body's vulnerability is its own best argument that you cannot be of God" (T, 66).

According to the Course, the body, like all things, is produced by thought. Thought is the cause; physical reality is the effect. "Thoughts can represent the lower or bodily level of experience, or the higher or spiritual level of experience. One makes the physical, and the other creates the spiritual" (T, 3).

The physical body, says the Course, cannot be the creation of an all-good God. If it were, it would not be a source of suffering, pain, and treacherous pleasures. Here the Course differs from conventional Christian theology. But in so doing, it evades many of the difficulties that ensue from believing that the body, which for all of its intricacy is far from perfect, is the creation of the perfect God. Instead, the Course says, the body was made by the ego. In terms of the first half of this book, the Fall takes place with the construction of a five-dimensional reality, whose outermost shell is the organs of the body.

But this does not mean that the body should be hated or punished. Instead it is to be regarded as a completely neutral thing (W, 445). "The body, valueless and hardly worth the least defense, need merely be perceived as quite apart from you, and it becomes a healthy, serviceable instrument through which the mind can operate until its [i.e., the body's] usefulness is over" (W, 253). There is no need for austerities or abstinences. The body's sole value is to communicate the Holy Spirit's message of love.

If the body is the work of the ego, what is the ego? The Course uses the term the *ego* in a radically unusual manner.* Usually the term refers to the conscious, street-level self that is ostensibly in control of an individual's mind during the waking state. This is *not* the way the Course uses the word. The ego, in the Course's system, is *not* the street-level self. It is a primordial disassociation, one that is prior to waking existence and indeed to the physical world. The ego gave rise to the cloud of oblivion, out of which in turn our sense of five-dimensional reality arises. The ego, then, is not ordinary consciousness but a loss of consciousness at a level so deep that we do not recognize it has happened.

The Course is designed to strike at this cloud of unknowing. (For an exercise from the Workbook illustrating this point, see page 152.) From its point of view, the clouds are your grievances—the things you hold against other people, against the world, against yourself. These grievances, the products of the ego, serve as cognitive blocks to your perception of what the Course calls the *real world*.

It follows, then, that the way past this cloud of oblivion is letting go of your grievances—in a word, forgiveness. The Course posits forgiveness as the sole possibility of escape for us, the sole hope of escaping from the meaningless "world I see": "Forgiveness is the key to happiness. . . . Forgiveness offers everything I want " (W, 214, 217).

But this is not forgiveness of the conventional kind, which a supplement to the Course calls "forgiveness-to-destroy," contending, "No gift of Heaven has been more misunderstood than has forgiveness. It has, in fact, become a scourge; a curse where it was meant to bless, a cruel mockery of grace, a parody upon the holy peace of God."[5]

"Forgiveness-to-destroy" includes nearly all of what passes for forgiveness in this world.[6] Often it involves a lordly disdain, "in which a 'better' person deigns to stoop to save a 'baser' one from what he truly is." In another form, ostensibly more humble, "the one who would forgive the other does not claim to be better. Now he says instead that

---

*This usage of the term *ego* differs also from its meanings in the passages quoted from Papus (page 16) and Stephan Hoeller (page 53).

here is one whose sinfulness he shares, since both have been unworthy and deserve the retribution of the wrath of God. This can appear to be a humble thought, and may indeed induce a rivalry in sinfulness and guilt."

Still another version of forgiveness-to-destroy takes the form of bargaining: "'I will forgive you if you meet my needs, for in your slavery is your release.' Say this to anyone and you are slave."

Much of what the world calls forgiveness falls into these categories.

True forgiveness, or "forgiveness-for-salvation," is the opposite. It follows rigorously from the premises that the Course sets out. If this world is a fiction concocted by a mad belief in separation, then only one sane response is possible: to recognize that, whatever form sin appears to take, it is part of the "meaningless world" and therefore simply does not exist—in anyone, ourselves as well as everyone else. "Forgiveness . . . is an illusion, but because of its purpose, which is the Holy Spirit's, it has one difference. Unlike all other illusions it leads away from error and not towards it. Forgiveness might be called a happy fiction; a way in which the unknowing can bridge the gap between their perceptions and the truth" (M, 83).

Forgiveness, then, is the principal means of Atonement.

To a mind oriented toward the world we know, this sounds ridiculous—sweet, maybe, noble, maybe, but quite naive. But it may be otherwise. In my book *The Deal: A Guide to Radical and Complete Forgiveness,* I have argued how, even from a conventional point of view, forgiveness is not only more powerful but more advantageous than many believe. Grievances are enormous obstacles to happiness and success. Even apart from any spiritual element, forgiving grievances can provide an enormous boost for anyone who attempts it sincerely. It also follows naturally from the premises that the Course sets out.

The Matrix shows a dystopian future in which humans are kept submerged in a trance while their energy is siphoned off to power a race of automatons. To keep the humans in their stupor, the automatons have created a virtual reality—the Matrix—in which the humans appear to have ordinary existences. (Significantly, the automatons first attempted to create a paradisal Matrix, but the humans would not accept it and obnoxiously kept waking up, so a second version, replicating the relatively sustainable misery of late twentieth-century America, was fabricated.) Nearly everyone submerged in this fictitious reality accepts it as the truth. Only the tiniest remnant are capable of awakening from it.

Everyone in this Matrix accepts it as reality. There are friendships, quarrels, rivalries, just as in the world we know. But all of it is fictitious. What could you say about "injustices" and "crimes" here? They are all equally illusory. Should you hold a grievance against someone who harmed you in this nonexistent world? At the very least it will not improve your chances of waking up.

The world we live in is equally fictitious. There is no point in holding grievances against people for what they are doing here, any more than you ought to be angry at someone who has hurt you in a dream. Holding grievances will only "make error real" (T, 215) and hinder you from awakening.

That is what the Course is trying to say. "The full awareness of the Atonement, then, is the recognition that *the separation never occurred*. The ego cannot prevail against this because it is an explicit statement that the ego never occurred" (T, 98; emphasis in the original).

NINE

From the Unreal
to the Real

Philip K. Dick's 1969 novel *Ubik* posits a weird dimension called "half-life": an after-death state in which individuals keep some of their consciousness and some memory of their lifetime experience, but in a distorted and entropic fashion. Like the half-life of radioactive substances, reality in this dimension dwindles and mutates in a fashion reminiscent of the bardo afterlife states outlined in *The Tibetan Book of the Dead* (to which *Ubik* repeatedly alludes). Eventually this existence diminishes to a vanishing point, and the individual moves on to the next incarnation.

Many of the characters in *Ubik* find themselves in half-life and do not realize it. All they can see is that reality shifts and mutates in ways that are impossible in the earthly world. They themselves dwindle and fade. The only remedy for this is an antientropic substance called Ubik. In mock mid-twentieth-century fashion, it is promoted in brief adlike blurbs that begin each chapter ("It takes more than a bag to seal in food flavor; it takes Ubik plastic wrap—actually four layers in one. Keeps freshness in, air and moisture out.")[1] In one form, Ubik appears as an aerosol product that retards deterioration.

The final chapter has no ad blurb at the beginning. Instead there is the statement: "I am Ubik. Before this universe was, I am. I made the suns. I made the worlds. . . . I am the word and my name is never spoken, the name which no one knows. I am called Ubik, but that is not my name. I am. I shall always be."[2] As the novel tells us, the word *Ubik* is derived from the Latin *ubique,* "everywhere."

Ubik is an allegory about our ordinary reality. Dick wondered if this reality is not in some way fake or delusional. He did not invent the idea. In the West it can be traced back to the earliest Greek philosophers, including Heraclitus, who wrote, "Death is what we see when we are awake; what we see when we sleep is waking life."[3] But in Dick's novel, Ubik, which represents the Holy Spirit, symbolizes the force from outside time that stirs us to awakening. In Dick's exegesis of his novel, he writes: "The Holy Spirit *stands at the right or far or completed end of time,* toward which the field-flow moves (the time flow). . . . The H.S. *is* in time, and is moving retrograde."[4]

Compare this to the following statement from *A Course in Miracles*: "The Atonement as a completed plan has a unique relationship to time. Until the Atonement is complete, its various phases will proceed in time, but *the whole Atonement stands at time's end.* At that point the bridge of return is built" (T, 20; emphasis added). And in the Course the means of the Atonement is the Holy Spirit.

Although Dick could have read the Course—it was published in 1975, and he lived till 1982—I can find no evidence that he did read it or know of it. Thus it is especially amazing that their ideas so closely resemble each other. Dick believes that we may be living in an artificial and ultimately unreal existence, and that the only means of escaping it is through a force sent from beyond this world—symbolized by the spray-can product Ubik, and, in a later novel, as VALIS, an acronym for "Vast Active Living Intelligence System," which is invading this defective universe in order to liberate us. Dick alludes to this process in the title of his novel *The Divine Invasion.*

Although Dick had treated the idea of alternate and fake realities much earlier, the theme came to the center of his life and work as the result of a mystical experience he had in 1974, in which a "beam of pink light" was fired at him from a girl's pendant depicting the ancient fish symbol of the early Christians. Like Paul on the road to Damascus, Dick was temporarily blinded. He described this experience as an "invasion of my mind by a transcendentally rational mind, as if I had been insane all my life and suddenly had become sane."[5]

Many, including Dick himself, have seen a parallel to these ideas in the teachings of the Gnostics. In the Gnostic fable "The Hymn of the Pearl," a young man of royal blood descends to Egypt—long a symbol for the fallen material world, particularly in Jewish mysticism—to retrieve a pearl, but while he is there, he eats of the Egyptians' food and forgets his identity. His parents send an eagle to remind him who he is so he can remember to return home with the pearl.[6] Here the eagle would be the equivalent of the Holy Spirit or the divinely invading VALIS—or Dick's pink beam.

It is wise to be cautious about what the ancient Gnostics were really saying. Their cryptic texts do not explain themselves, and the only surviving explications from antiquity appear in vitriolic attacks by Catholic church fathers. But the same insight may have inspired the Gnostics' works.

Dick was one of those unfortunate geniuses who struggle for recognition during their lives only to attain it right after their deaths. His work first came to mass consciousness when his novel *Do Androids Dream of Electric Sheep?* served as the basis for Ridley Scott's film *Blade Runner,* which came out in 1982, the year Dick died. At just about the same time, the affinities between Dick's ideas and those of Gnosticism began to be publicized. Indeed they were at the centerpiece of the first issue of *Gnosis: A Journal of the Western Inner Traditions,* published in 1985, in an article written by the magazine's founder, Jay Kinney. Kinney was also an early editor of Dick's collection of unpublished papers, known as *The Exegesis.*[7]

This theme of ordinary reality as somehow defective or corrupt began to penetrate mass culture in the 1990s. Echoes of it can be found in the TV series *The X-Files,* and in the last few years of the century, it formed the theme of movies as diverse and powerful as *Dark City, The Truman Show, The Sixth Sense, ExistenZ,* and most importantly, *The Matrix.* In the twenty-first century it is echoed in such works such as *Inception* and *The OA,* as well as in film and television adaptations of Dick's own fiction—*Minority Report, The Adjustment Bureau,* and the television series *The Man in the High Castle.* This series is based on a novel of his, published in 1962, which posits an alternate reality in which the Axis powers won World War II. The end of the novel suggests that this other reality is false, and that, as we all believe, the Allies really won the war. Today the unreliable universe (along the lines of the unreliable narrator of fiction) has become a stock theme.

I cannot point to *A Course in Miracles* as the direct inspiration for these themes in mass culture; Dick's influence is far more evident. But I do find it striking that this motif of a false reality has grown more common and more alluring. To some extent it reflects the artificiality of postindustrial life—such as the barrages of video games and virtual realities—but it may also mirror an impulse toward collective awakening from a fictitious reality, which is something that has never come in all of history. The Course is right when it says, "The world has not yet experienced any comprehensive awakening or rebirth" (T, 18; T 2.I.3.7). But the coming of the Course, along with the surfacing of these ideas in Dick and other visionary writers, suggests that at least there may finally be a collective *thirst* for such awakening.

The Course talks about the real world:

Sit quietly and look upon the world you see, and tell yourself, "The real world is not like this. It has no buildings, and there are no streets where people walk alone and separately. There are no stores where people buy an endless list of things they do not need. It is not lit with artificial light, and night comes not upon it. There is no day that brightens and grows dim. There is no loss. Nothing is there but shines, and shines forever.

The world you see must be denied, for sight of it is costing you a different kind of vision. *You cannot see both worlds,* for each of them involves a different kind of seeing, and depends on what you cherish. The sight of one is possible because you have denied the other. Both are not true, yet either one will seem as real to you as the amount to which you hold it dear. And yet their power is not the same, because their real attraction to you is unequal.

You do not really want the world you see, for it has disappointed you since time began. The homes you built have never sheltered you. The roads you made have led you nowhere, and no city that you built has withstood the crumbling assault of time. Nothing you made but has the mark of death upon it. Hold it not dear, for it is old and tired, and ready to return to dust even as you made it. This aching world has not the power to touch the living world at all. (T, 254; emphasis in the original)

There is a semantic trap in the phrase *real world*. The word *real* connotes tangible, physical substance—as in *real estate*. It is derived from the Latin *res,* "thing," so etymologically it is tightly bound up with the world we see with the body's eyes. Maybe the Course should have used a different term, but it did not. At any rate, the Course acknowledges the reality of the physical world *on its own level*. One important passage says, "The body is merely part of your experience in the physical world. Its abilities can be and frequently are overevaluated. However, it is almost impossible to deny its existence in this world" (T, 23).

In short, the physical world exists on its own level and on its own terms. From the point of view of another level, it does not exist. Certainly it does not have the solid, impenetrable reality that it is supposed to have.

To all appearances the Course is contradicting what science says—because does science not, after all, presuppose the existence of the material world?

The matter is not quite as clear-cut as is often assumed. Indeed it presents a contradiction on which science itself falters, because science presupposes not only the actual existence of the world out there, but its existence *as we experience it.** In the 1980s mathematician John L. Casti surveyed the members of a small university physics department. According to Casti, ten out of eleven of them "claimed that what they were describing with their symbols and equations was objective reality. As one of them remarked, 'Otherwise, what's the point?'"[8] Physicist Nick Herbert has written, "Physicists cannot deny the evidence of their senses. The indubitable reality of measurement results is a solid rock on which to found an empirical science."[9] And yet science itself proves, or appears to have proved, that this claim is completely wrong.

Consider this. Investigations into human cognition show that our experience of the physical world is determined by the limits of our senses. Bees see a different section of the color spectrum than we do. Dogs hear sounds that we cannot. Our own brains and senses thus condition our view of the world; we are frozen into it like Urizen.

Notice a contradiction here. You cannot, on the one hand, say that our human cognition is completely conditioned and limited by our own central nervous systems and then, on the other hand, turn around and claim that this cognition gives a complete and accurate picture of reality—even when enhanced by elaborate scientific apparatus.

Science—or the ideology that has been assembled around science— makes precisely these two contradictory claims. Its epistemological grounds are therefore, on its own terms and by its own reasoning, shaky and in fact fallacious.

It is peculiar that these contradictions have not been criticized much more than they have. I suspect that this is largely because much of the intellectual West today believes that it has two and only two choices: (1) to accept scientism, including its naive materialism, as a pseudoreligion; or (2) to revert to the old teachings of biblical literalism.

---

*The most insightful discussion of this issue that I know of is in Owen Barfield's *Saving the Appearances: A Study in Idolatry.* The "idolatry" mentioned in the subtitle is precisely this mistaking of representations for the actuality.

In other words, if we do not clutch at the flotsam of materialistic belief, we will supposedly sink back into superstition and bigotry. These considerations tell us a great deal about the state of cultural debate today.

In any event, scientific findings have challenged naive materialism in other ways as well. Quantum theory, with its nonlocality and its particles that only seem to appear when observed, suggests that what is "really" going on in the world has very little resemblance to our cognitive experience of it.

Usually materialistic thinkers extract themselves from this difficulty by saying that quantum effects are only manifested at the submolecular level, and that the familiar Newtonian universe still applies for us in everyday life. So it may be in practice; the five familiar senses do enable us to function in this world. Nevertheless, we are now very far from being able to claim that the external world is in any fundamental sense like the way it seems to us from moment to moment.

Therefore the world we see is not the world that is out there that—if you like—God created. Even if we know nothing else, this fact seems to be sure. A hundred years ago, Evelyn Underhill wrote in her famous study of mysticism: "Not merely faith, but gross credulity, is needed by the mind which would accept the apparent as the real."[10] So the Course's claims about the illusory nature of "the world I see" are not so outlandish after all.

If there is a real world beyond "the world I see," we have reason to demand evidence of it. In fact you do not have to page through many mystical texts to find descriptions of this real world. Here is an account from the nineteenth-century author John Trevor, quoted by William James:

These highest experiences that I have had of God have been rare and brief—flashes of consciousness which have compelled me to exclaim with surprise—God is *here!*—or conditions of exaltation and insight, less intense, and only gradually passing away. . . . I find that, after every questioning and test, they stand out to-day as the most real experiences of my life, and experiences which have explained and justified and unified all past experiences and all past growth. . . . It was in the most real seasons that the Real Presence came, and I was aware that I was immersed in the infinite ocean of God.[11]

Note that the word *real* occurs three times in this paragraph. Other accounts of such experiences can be found in James's *Varieties of Religious Experience* (from which this passage is taken), Evelyn Underhill's *Mysticism*, Richard M. Bucke's *Cosmic Consciousness,* and Aldous Huxley's *Perennial Philosophy.*

James also argued that one central feature of mystical experience was its "noetic" quality: "Although so similar to states of feeling, mystical states seem to those who experience them to be also states of knowledge. They are states of insight into depths of truth unplumbed by the discursive intellect. They are illuminations, revelations, full of significance and importance, all inarticulate though they remain; and as a rule they carry with them a curious sense of authority for after-time."[12] That is, these states are not delusory or dreamlike. Quite the contrary: they have, as it were, *more* reality about them. They make ordinary cognition seem dull and false, as we have seen with Jung's near-death experience on pages 24–25.

As a matter of fact, conventional materialism does have to acknowledge the gap between the world as it is and the world as we apprehend it. The mathematician Morris Kline writes: "We have five senses— sight, hearing, touch, taste, smell—and each of these constantly receives messages from the external world. *Whether or not these sensations are reliable,* we do receive them from some external source."[13] Even here there is some admission of a gap between our cognition and what may be "really out there." The difference between scientistic materialism and mystical teachings like the Course is this: Materialism acknowledges that there is a gap between our cognition and reality as it exists apart from that cognition, but it assumes that this gap is either small and unimportant or so impossible to bridge that we may as well not bother about it. Mystical teachings also speak of this gap, but they say it is much larger than we believe. They also say, however, that it can be bridged, that in fact we can and do have access to the real world. The Course says, "No one in this distracted world but has seen some glimpses of the other world about him. Yet while he still lays value on his own [world], he will deny the vision of the other" (T, 255).

Which world, then, do we want?

TEN

CREATING, MAKING, AND THE QUALIA

The first part of this book dealt with the Kabbalah. The second part has focused on *A Course in Miracles*. So it is reasonable to ask if these two theologies fit together.

In fact, they fit together remarkably well. To understand why, we can begin by looking at one of the basic concepts of the Kabbalah: the Four Worlds.[1]

World, in this context, does not mean the familiar realm of life on planet earth. Nor does it refer to anything in the physical universe. The Hebrew word is *'olam,* which means something like "world order." There is no exact equivalent in English, although the ancient Greek *aiōn* comes close, as does the Latin *saeculum.* (These words are usually translated, not entirely correctly, as *age.*) The easiest way to understand this concept is to return again to the five-dimensional schema. This sets out the basic coordinates of reality as we conceive of it; this is the world order that these terms refer to. All that takes place in the world we know takes place within its confines, as Jung sensed in his near-death experience. The rules of another world may be quite different.

In the Kabbalah, the physical universe is only one, and the lowest one, of the Four Worlds. It is called Assiah, the world of "making."

The word is derived from the Hebrew root (עשה), 'asah, "make."

Above Assiah, and interpenetrating it, is the world of Yetzirah, the world of "formation," derived from the root yatzar (יצר), "form." It is the world of images, thoughts, memories, dreams. It too is reasonably familiar to us, as the realm of our own subjectivity.

The relation of these two realms is instructive. Assiah is physical, ostensibly objective experience. Yetzirah is psychological, subjective reality. These two realms interpenetrate and overlap, but they are not the same, and one cannot be reduced to the other.

One of the most famous philosophical essays of the past fifty years is Thomas Nagel's "What's It Like to Be a Bat?" Nagel points out that, in addition to their ordinary vision, which is weak, bats have a sensory apparatus whereby they perceive by means of sonar. They bounce a sonar beam off an object, and the beam, bounced back, tells the bat where and how far away the object is.

Humans can understand all of this—but from the physical point of view only. We know how sonar works and use it ourselves for things such as sounding the depths of the oceans. But, Nagel argues, we do not and cannot have any comprehension of what it is like to have sonar as one of our senses. We cannot know how a bat experiences the world through it, because we do not have this sense and never will. He writes, "Bat sonar, though clearly a form of perception, is not similar in its operation to any sense that we possess, and there is no reason to suppose that it is subjectively like anything that we can experience or imagine."[2]

Nagel's argument has led to a long philosophical debate about *qualia* (from the Latin *qualis*, "what kind," or "of what sort"). As the *Stanford Encyclopedia of Philosophy* puts it, "Philosophers often use the term 'qualia' (singular 'quale') to refer to the introspectively accessible, phenomenal aspects of our mental lives." It goes on to say:

> It is difficult to deny that there are qualia. Disagreement typically centers on which mental states have qualia, whether qualia are intrinsic qualities of their bearers, and how qualia relate to the phys-

ical world both inside and outside the head. The status of qualia is hotly debated in philosophy largely because it is central to a proper understanding of the nature of consciousness. Qualia are at the very heart of the mind-body problem.[3]

In the language of the Kabbalah, the purely physical functioning of sonar belongs to the realm of Assiah. As such it is accessible to and even employable by us. But the Yetziratic aspect of sonar—the qualia, the interiority of sensing, as must occur in the bat—is inaccessible. Thus, from the Kabbalistic point of view, they are different worlds. This second, interior world is Yetzirah.

These ideas cast a great deal of light on the mind-body problem in philosophy, which is essentially an attempt to answer the question "Is the mind the same as the mere physical functioning of the brain?" Or, to quote *The Stanford Encyclopedia of Philosophy* again, "What is the relationship between mental properties and physical properties?"[4] Recent cognitive science has mapped many subjective states onto neural states, and researchers in this field imply or state that the former can be entirely reduced to a function of the latter. But despite its promissory materialism ("we will prove this any day now"), cognitive science has come no closer than it ever has to making such a reduction, or to explaining how subjective experience is possible at all.

To return to the Kabbalah: there are two lower, more or less familiar and accessible worlds, Yetzirah, the realm of the qualia, and Assiah, physical manifestation. Above these is the world of Briah, "creation," from the Hebrew *bara'* (ברא), "create." This is the realm of the spirit, of the archetypes.

The topmost is Atziluth, the divine realm, its name being derived from the Hebrew *'atzal* (אצל), "to be near," this realm being the nearest level to God, who is beyond manifestation per se.

Experience of these two higher realms is very rare. It could be correlated with states of enlightenment or cosmic consciousness. Although everyone probably has some contact with these realms at one point or another, these encounters are usually fleeting and easily obscured or forgotten.

This schema of the Four Worlds is mentioned in Isaiah 43:7, which speaks of "every one that is *called by my name*: for I have *created* him for my glory, I have *formed* him; yea, I have *made* him" (emphasis added). Atziluth is the realm of the divine *names,* which, says the Kabbalah, are the immanent manifestation of God. Briah is the realm of *creation,* of the spirit; Yetzirah, the realm of *forms,* of the psyche; Assiah, the physical realm, of *making.* Here is the sequence, going from top to bottom:

Atziluth	Divine	God
Briah	Creation	Spirit
Yetzirah	Formation	Psyche
Assiah	Making	Body

The accompanying images in figure 10.1 show the worlds in diagrammatic form.

The concept of Four Worlds illuminates many obscurities in the Bible. For example, scholars have been vexed by the dual accounts of creation in Genesis, one in the first chapter, the other starting at Genesis 2:4. Because these accounts use different names for God in Hebrew (Elohim and Yahweh), this duality is typically explained with the documentary hypothesis: the first chapter comes from the Priestly source, the second from the Yahwist.[5] That may be, but it does not tell us why the redactor should have included both.

Here is the Kabbalistic answer: The first chapter emphasizes the verb *bara',* "create," as in "God created [*bara'*] man in his own image, in the image of God created he him" (Genesis 1:27). The second emphasizes the verb *yatzar,* "form," as in "the Lord God formed [*wayiytzer*] man out of dust in the ground" (Genesis 2:7).

The dual accounts in Genesis refer to different levels of manifestation. The first chapter, usually attributed to the Priestly source, describes creation in Briah. The second, usually ascribed to the Yahwist, describes

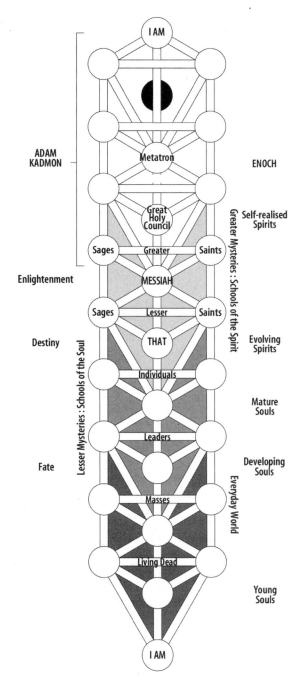

Figure 10.1. The Four Worlds interlocking with each other. In short, the Tiferet ("Beauty," or essence) of one world is the Keter ("Crown," or beginning) of the one below it. Image courtesy of the Kabbalah Society, London.

formation in Yetzirah. Hence these accounts are neither redundant nor contradictory. They discuss two different metaphysical levels. That was likely why both were included in the final redaction of Genesis.

Assiah, from the verb "make" (*'asah,* עשׂה) denotes another level still: the physical world per se. So creation has to do with the level of the spirit, while making has to do with the world of materiality. This terminology exactly parallels that of the Course, as we see on its opening page: "Miracles are thoughts. Thoughts can represent the lower or bodily level of experience, or the higher or spiritual level of experience. One *makes* the *physical,* and the other *creates* the *spiritual*" (T, 3; emphasis added).

In both systems, creating is to the spiritual as making is to the physical.

The Kabbalah says that in between the spiritual and the physical is the world of Yetzirah, of forms, of the psyche. In the Course's terms, this intermediate space is occupied by the *mind.* The mind is the locus of choice and will. It can be turned toward the spirit, or it can be turned toward the ego. "Spirit is the part [of the mind] that is still in contact with God through the Holy Spirit. . . . The other part of the mind is entirely illusory and makes only illusions" (M, 79)—which, as we have seen, include the physical realm.

Here, then, is the Course's system:

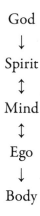

God
↓
Spirit
↕
Mind
↕
Ego
↓
Body

Table 10.1 correlates the two systems.

TABLE 10.1. CORRELATION OF BASIC TERMS IN THE KABBALAH AND *A COURSE IN MIRACLES*.

Kabbalah			A Course in Miracles
Atziluth	Divine	God	God
Beriah	Creation	Spirit	Spirit
Yetzirah	Formation	Psyche	Mind
			Ego
Assiah	Making	Body	Body

Again, the locus of choice—of free will—lies in the realm of the mind, the psyche, which is Yetzirah. Genesis also places the Fall in Yetzirah: "And the Lord God planted a garden eastward in Eden; and there he put the man he had *formed* (*yatzar*, צר, Genesis 2:8; emphasis added). Eden is, in fact, a symbolic name for Yetzirah.

Where in Genesis does the physical level of Assiah, making, come in? At the very end, after the Fall: "Unto Adam also and to his wife did the Lord God *make* [*wayya'as*] coats of skin, and clothed them" (Genesis 3:21). The "coats of skin"—the physical body—are a side effect of the Fall, just as in the Course.

These systems do not agree at all points. Genesis says that God made the body, whereas the Course says he did not. Nevertheless, the parallels between these systems are remarkable.

We can insert another piece into this puzzle. Remember that the five-dimensional framework is described in the *Sefer Yetzirah*. The title of this book is usually translated as "The Book of Formation," and this is accurate as far as it goes, but really it means "The Book of Yetzirah." The *Sefer Yetzirah* may not be talking about all four of the Kabbalistic worlds. It may only be talking about one, the next to lowest one.

Yetzirah is the locus of the Fall. Yetzirah is also the locus of the five dimensions. We are led again to a point made earlier: the five dimensions as we apprehend them are part of the world of the Fall, or, if you prefer, the separation. They are the consequence of the separation and structure the world of separation. In the second century, Clement of Alexandria describes spiritual liberation as freeing oneself from dimensionality:

> We shall understand the mode of purification by confession, and that of contemplation by analysis, advancing by analysis to the first notion, beginning with the properties underlying it; *abstracting from the body its physical properties, taking away the dimension of depth, then that of breadth, and then that of length.* For the point which remains is a unit, so to speak, having position; from which if we abstract position, there is the conception of unity.
>
> If, then, abstracting all that belongs to bodies and things called incorporeal, we cast ourselves into the greatness of Christ, and thence advance by immensity into holiness, we may reach somehow to the conception of the Almighty, knowing not what He is, but what He is not.[6]

Because we cognize the world almost entirely through these five dimensions, our cognition is incomplete and illusory—including our cognition of the physical world. Hence the Course's lessons assert: "I do not understand anything I see" (W, 5), and "I am upset because I see something that is not there" (W, 10).

Furthermore, because this distorted cognition arises from the delusions of the ego, with its fear and hatred, another lesson in the Course says, "What I see is a form of vengeance" (W, 33). Assiah reflects Yetzirah, even when Yetzirah's structure is delusional. This is why the Course also says, "My meaningless thoughts are showing me a meaningless world" (W, 18).

The cloud of oblivion, then, is located in Yetzirah. (In the Kabbalah the cloud is paradoxically called Da'ath or "Knowledge," sometimes known as the Abyss.) But this level of the mind is prior to any conscious awareness, and it is in fact heavily defended against assaults by the conscious awareness. Occult literature sometimes refers to this barrier as the Dweller on the Threshold.[7] The Dweller on the Threshold is the angel with the flaming sword who keeps Adam out of Eden. For us personally, it is the doorway that lies not only behind consciousness, but, strange though it may sound, behind *unconsciousness* as well. If you even touch upon it, you will be hit with a fear so profound and intense that you will wonder if *this fear is you*. You will feel a terror that, if you go past this point, you will be annihilated.

In fact this is not the case: the fear is not you, but the ego, and it is only the ego that is being threatened. But it would be foolish to deny the strength and intensity of this sense of threat (the ego is, after all, powerful enough to have made a world, or a semblance of one), and very few will even want to go near it. Some do inadvertently, as the result of trauma or perhaps of psychedelic experience, but they often end up with permanent damage to their sanity. That is why much mystical literature—particularly that of the Kabbalah—insists that you be firmly grounded in ordinary reality before you make the ascent through the levels. There will come a time when you will see that the world of appearances is illusory, but it is best if this recognition dawns slowly and, as much as possible, in manageable stages.

ELEVEN

The Scandal of Particularity

Most theologians would argue that Christian theology is necessarily Christocentric: that is what makes it Christian. So it is necessary to look into the role of Christ the man in relation to the ideas sketched out above.

It is clear that the epic quest of the historical Jesus, as grand and brave as it was, has not reached its goal and, in the absence of new evidence, is not about to. I have set out my reasons for believing this in *How God Became God,* but here let me restate one of the most important ones in someone else's words. Literary critic Gabriel Josipovici writes:

> My feeling is that we will never be able to know, of Paul any more than of Jesus, just what they said and what was added later, and that such attempts are doomed to circularity: you dismiss as inauthentic what does not fit with your notion of the man, and then use what is left to confirm your vision.[1]

Josipovici makes a similar remark about the circular arguments "common to biblical scholarship, which is so often both meticulous and fantastical in about equal proportions."[2]

For these reasons, I believe it is wise to be conservative when treating the primary sources about Jesus's life. These are principally the canonical Gospels, although I believe that the apocryphal Gospel of Thomas could also date to the first century and may even be older than the New Testament texts.

As has been said often, it is not possible to sift out the genuine acts and utterances of Jesus from those that were fathered upon him later, but it seems sensible to take the core narrative at face value, particularly since, for all their differences, the four Gospels agree about it. This narrative says that there was a man named Jesus, who came from Nazareth in Galilee, was baptized by John the Baptist, and thereupon started on a career as a wandering preacher and healer. He denounced the hypocrisy and corruption of the religious authorities of his day. At one point he defied the priests in their own sanctum—the Jerusalem Temple—and they contrived to destroy him. They persuaded the Roman governor, Pontius Pilate, to have him crucified.* After his death, some of his disciples had visions of him risen from the dead. From this impulse Christianity was born.

The debate about the nature of Jesus Christ, as expressed in the early centuries of the Christian era, has filled many volumes. The positions taken over this period ring practically all the possible changes on such questions as the human versus the divine nature of Christ. These positions are deftly summarized by Ioan P. Couliano in the introduction

---

*One point to note in passing: there is some evidence that the Romans, jealous of the power of administering capital punishment, took this power from the Jewish Sanhedrin around AD 30. If this is true, it could provide the historical context for the crucifixion. The Sanhedrin condemned Jesus as a blasphemer, but no longer had the power to have him stoned to death. They brought him to Pilate, presenting him with a dilemma: Jesus was ostensibly guilty by the Jewish Law but not by Roman law. This fact would explain Pilate's hesitation to condemn Jesus, because, by Roman standards, he was innocent. The stoning of Stephen a year or two later (Acts 6:5–7:60) would suggest that by then the power to condemn a man to death for blasphemy had been restored to the Jewish authorities. For a discussion, see Brown, *The Anchor Bible: The Gospel according to John* 1:337 and 2:849–50. Brown cites the Jerusalem Talmud, Sanhedrin, I 18a, 34; VII 24b, 41.

to his 1992 book *The Tree of Gnosis*. Couliano helpfully sets out the dichotomies of these possibilities (Jesus: divine or human? One nature or two?), and their possible permutations, in a table.[3]

The history of this debate is an unpleasant subject to investigate, because, as Couliano says, "whoever has the slightest knowledge of early Christianity knows how terrible theological debates could be, . . . and how inconceivably obnoxious were many of those whom the Church has canonized."[4] Fortunately for me, this ground has been well covered over the course of theological history, so I don't have to do so here.

The ferocity of the debate over the nature of Christ seems to point to something beyond itself. Why, after all, would the church fathers—who were, for all their nastiness, among the best minds of their time—squabble so bitterly about the degree to which Jesus was divine or human, or about whether he had one nature or two? Although they did not know it themselves, I suspect that, falling into a kind of psychological displacement, they may have been unconsciously fighting about the nature, not of Christ, but of man himself. Is man divine, or merely human? Does he have one nature, or two? Put this way, we can see how the issue would be much more important, indeed crucial, to the goal of human self-understanding. Nevertheless, man's psychological defenses against seeing himself as divine made the question impossible to address directly, so it was projected upon Jesus. This is still the case, more or less.

Maybe this intuition suggests a way out. Maybe the real messianic secret was that Jesus was speaking not only of his own nature but that of all humans.

All this said, most Christian teaching holds that the coming of Jesus Christ was the central moment in history—what Karl Barth called "the Krisis"—the juncture at which God meets humanity.[5] Conventional Christian theology propounds what has been called *the scandal of particularity*—the idea that God would incarnate in human form once and once only. (*Scandal* is used here in its etymological sense: one meaning of the Greek *skándalon* is "stumbling block," as in 1 Corinthians 1:23: "But we preach Christ crucified, unto the Jews a stumbling block, and unto the Greeks foolishness.")

The scandal of particularity, although always a problem for Christian apologetics, was less of one in the early days of Christianity, partly because the conceptual time scale of the era was so small. The Greco-Roman world did not have a well-defined sense of the remote past. The Trojan War (which was more or less accurately dated to around 1200 BC) was always taken as a kind of starting point, before which history was indistinguishable from myth.[6] Although some thinkers, such as Plato in his *Timaeus,* show a wider sense of time, these views do not seem to have penetrated into the culture as a whole.

Thus when Christianity came on the scene and insisted that the Old Testament—and the Old Testament only—gave the correct view of ancient history, the claim seemed at least plausible. And in the context of the four thousand years that had supposedly taken place since creation, it was conceivable that God could come down to earth once and once only.

Today it is different. Current science says the universe came into existence around 13.8 billion years ago, meaning that we humans are late arrivals on the scene. The human race itself (depending on how it is defined) goes back 200,000 or 300,000 years. This scale too makes the scandal of particularity hard to swallow. God came down to earth only *once* in all this time?

Furthermore, some world religions—Hinduism, for example— have a much broader time scale than Judaism and Christianity. Hinduism posits the coming of not one divine being, but of many, known as *avatars,* to the earth over the course of the ages. In this context, it would make sense to do as some Hindus do, and regard Jesus Christ as one, but only one, of many such divine incarnations. But this would topple Christianity's claims to the sole and exclusive franchise on access to the divine.

A Course in Miracles is also Christocentric, but in a different way from orthodox theology. According to the Course, the historical Jesus was not qualitatively different from the rest of humanity, who are all part of the Sonship. Jesus was simply the first human being to fully accept the Atonement for himself. "The name of *Jesus* is the name of one who was a man but saw the face of Christ in all his brothers and remembered. So he became identified with *Christ,* a man no longer, but at one with God" (M, 87; emphasis in the original). That was his distinction. Speaking in the first person, Jesus says, "I am in charge of the process of Atonement, which I undertook to begin." Indeed, he continues, "I am the Atonement" (T, 8, 9).

The Course does not occupy itself with the mystery of the incarnation of Jesus. There was no incarnation, because the physical body, made by the ego as a means of hiding from God, does not ultimately exist. Nor is Jesus different from the rest of us. He is in charge of the Atonement simply because he was the first human being to fully accept it.

Again, the Course uses Christian terms in ways that are radically different from convention. In the Course, the Atonement is simply the process by which God's answer to the "tiny, mad idea" of the ego is worked out in time. But the usual connotation of the word *atonement* has to do with sacrifice: you atone for your sins by repenting and renouncing your old ways and, very likely, accepting some punishment. According to the orthodox doctrine of the vicarious atonement, Jesus, for reasons that are never completely clear, has to offer himself up as an acceptable sacrifice to his Father, thereby appeasing his wrath.

This doctrine was developed only over the course of centuries, culminating with Anselm of Canterbury in the eleventh century, but its roots are not hard to find.* They lie in the New Testament. Ephesians 5:2

---

*The history of this doctrine is more intricate than I am portraying it here. It was, for example, preceded by Origen's theory, accepted by both the church fathers and Augustine, that Jesus's death was kind of a ransom paid to Satan. But Anselm's view, developed in his essay *Cur Deus Homo,* has prevailed in the Western church over the last thousand years. For a concise history of this doctrine, see the article "Atonement," in Cross and Livingstone, *The Oxford Dictionary of the Christian Church,* 122–24.

says, "Christ . . . hath given himself for us an offering and a sacrifice to God for a sweetsmelling savour." Hebrews develops the concept further, making Jesus both priest and sacrifice: "And every priest standeth daily ministering and offering oftentimes the same sacrifices, which can never take away sins: But this man, after he had offered one sacrifice for sins for ever, sat down on the right side of God," thereby becoming "an high priest over the house of God" (Hebrews 10:11–12, 21).

This idea is understandable in its context. The religions of antiquity, Jewish and pagan, were centered around animal sacrifice; it would be only a small exaggeration to say that ancient religion *was* animal sacrifice. Consider the Jerusalem Temple. Certainly it was splendid: Josephus, who provides one of the few surviving firsthand descriptions, says that "it radiated so fiery a flash that people had to avert their eyes as if they were looking directly at the sun."[7] But the Temple had another feature that impressed someone else who saw it firsthand: the author of the pseudonymous *Letter of Aristeas,* usually dated to the second century BC. He writes, "There are many openings for water at the base of the altar which are invisible to all except those who are involved in the ministration, so that all the blood of the sacrifices which is collected in great quantities is washed away in the twinkling of an eye."[8] The Temple had to have an elaborate plumbing system to drain all the blood off.

Why was sacrifice performed? The familiar picture of ancient animal sacrifice is not entirely correct. Many assume that the animal was killed and burned whole on the altar as an offering to the gods. Frequently it was not. As a rule, the bones and entrails were burned. The meat was cut up and served at the sacrificial feast; the surplus was sold commercially. That was why Paul's students had concerns about eating meat offered to idols: it was sold at the butchers' stalls—what the King James Version calls "the shambles" (1 Corinthians 10:25). The animal's blood was carefully collected and sprinkled around the altar.[9]

Originally, then, it was not the meat that the gods desired; it was the blood. As Mephistopheles told Faust, "blood is a very special fluid."[10] It was and is believed to be the vehicle of the life force, known variously by such names as *chi* or *prana*, or in the Hebrew of the Bible, the *nefesh*. Leviticus 17:11 states: "The life [*nefesh*] of the flesh is in the blood." The *Odyssey* illustrates this belief gruesomely: When Odysseus makes sacrifices in preparation for his descent to Hades, he says,

> *I cut the sheep's throats over the pit,*
> *and the dark-clouding blood ran.*
> *And from Erebus gathered the souls of the dead:*
> *Girls and youths and long-suffering elders;*
> *skipping virgins with hearts new to sorrow;*
> *men stabbed with brazen swords,*
> *killed in war, with bloody armor.*
> *The crowd of them flitted around the pit with*
> *   eerie shrieks,*
> *and green fear took hold of me.*[11]

The dead, having no vitality, no nefesh, of their own, try to suck it from the freshly spilled blood. (Vampire myths must have something to do with this belief.) The gods too feed on this life force.

In this context, the early Christians were bound to see the death of Jesus as a sacrifice, however different qualitatively from offerings of lambs and bullocks. The Epistle to the Hebrews illustrates this shift with its ambivalence toward sacrifice. Blood offerings are required for purification: "Without the shedding of blood there is no remission" (Hebrews 9:22). But they do not purify for good, because if they did, "would they not have ceased to be offered?" (Hebrews 10:2). Besides, they only purify earthly things: "It was therefore necessary that the patterns of things in the heavens should be purified with these; but the heavenly things themselves with better sacrifices than these" (Hebrews 9:23). In fact, these sacrifices do not really purify: "It is not possible that the blood of bulls and of goats should take away sins" (Hebrews 10:4). Therefore a better sacrifice was needed: "the offering of the body of Jesus Christ once for all" (Hebrews 10:10).* But the author does not face a deeper question: why blood should purify at all. He simply takes it for granted, on the authority of the Old Testament.

The doctrine of vicarious atonement, developed over the next thousand years, is still defended by learned arguments and celebrated in elaborate rituals. Belief in it is touted as a sine qua non for salvation. But today, when nobody (at least in Western culture) believes that God could be appeased by spilled blood of any kind, it is incomprehensible.

Think of it this way: God is infinite love, but he got mad at the human race because a couple of people ate a piece of fruit in Armenia six thousand years ago. He got so mad, in fact, that he damned everybody for eternity. The only way he could make up for it was to send a part of himself down to earth and have it tortured to death, which somehow made everything all right. Except not really, because unless you believe this story, you will be damned anyway.

Many people accept this doctrine, not because it makes sense to them, but because they have been bullied into it: believe it or face the unquenchable flames.

A few years ago, we had next-door neighbors who were fundamentalist Christians. Despite our religious differences, our relations were amiable, and our sons played with their children. One hot summer day the neighbors put up their aboveground pool. My sons ran over, but one of the neighbors' children said, "You can't come in unless you believe in Jesus!" "I believe in Jesus! I believe in Jesus!" cried my son William, who was thereupon admitted to the glories of the pool.

A cute story about small children, but it is not very different from the situation of the conventional Christian. She has to believe in something

---

*The dating of the Epistle to the Hebrews is as disputed as its authorship. I personally find it difficult to believe that it was written after the sack of the Temple in 70, in the first place because the author does not seem to know of it, and in the second place because the Temple's destruction and the cessation of its sacrifices would have been extraordinarily useful for him polemically. For a summary of the positions, see Brown, *Introduction to the New Testament*, 696–97.

that may not, probably does not, make the slightest bit of sense to her, because she fears that if she does not believe it, she will bring upon herself a far graver penalty than exclusion from a swimming pool. Although Catholicism and liberal Protestantism have backed away from this doctrine in its starkest form, even there it still lies in the background.

For the Course, the redemptive action of Christ on the cross is quite different. It is a kind of object lesson. Speaking in the first person, Jesus says, "I elected, for your sake and mine, to demonstrate that the most outrageous assault, as judged by the ego, does not matter. As the world judges things but not as God knows them, I was betrayed, abandoned, beaten, torn, and finally killed" (T, 93). But in the end it did nothing, because nothing in this world is real, including the body. Jesus does not want anyone else to follow his example: "I will with God that none of His Sons should suffer" (T, 94). Indeed more than once the Course calls the crucifixion the "last useless journey" and warns, "Do not make the pathetic error of clinging to the 'old rugged cross.' The only message of the crucifixion is that you can overcome the cross" (T, 52). Elsewhere it says:

> The crucifixion did not establish the Atonement; the resurrection did. Many sincere Christians have misunderstood this. . . . If the crucifixion is seen from an upside-down point of view, it does appear as if God permitted and even encouraged one of His Sons to suffer because he was good. This particularly unfortunate interpretation . . . has led many people to be bitterly afraid of God. Such anti-religious concepts have crept into many religions. Yet the real Christian should pause and ask, "How could this be?" Is it likely that God Himself would be capable of the kind of thinking which His Own words have stated is clearly unworthy of His Son? (T, 36)

As this passage shows, the Course also accepts the resurrection as a fact, and indeed emphasizes it far more than the crucifixion. The resurrection proved that the body is ultimately inconsequential, and can be destroyed without affecting the Self.

Thus the Christology of *A Course in Miracles* does not posit a Jesus who differs ontologically from the rest of the human race, because the race as a whole constitutes the Sonship. Jesus is merely *primus inter pares*—the first human who has fully accepted the Atonement, and who is therefore put "in charge" of it (T, 8). The passion, death, and resurrection of Jesus is best understood not as a human sacrifice that somehow expiated the sins of humanity, but as an object lesson.

To explain what I mean, let me turn to the ancient mystery religions, such as those of Delphi, Eleusis, and Samothrace. We only have a dim idea of what went on in their initiations, because the initiates were sworn to secrecy, and they kept their word. One clue lies in a remark of Cicero's about the mysteries, "by which we are led from a crude and rustic life to humanity, and are made gentler, so that we have acknowledged these initiations, as they are called, as the true principles of life, and have received a method not only of living with happiness, but of *dying with a better hope*."[12]

The ancient mysteries had to do with death and rebirth. Reductionistic thinkers say they merely commemorated the vegetative cycles of nature, but as far back as the first century AD Plutarch criticized the "dull crowd" that held to this view.[13]

On the passion and resurrection of Christ in relation to the mysteries, P. D. Ouspensky writes:

There is a remarkable analogy between the content of the Mysteries and the earthly life of Christ. The life of Christ, taken as we know it from the Gospels, represents the same Mystery as those which were performed in Egypt on the island of Philae, in Greece at Eleusis, and in other places. The idea was the same, namely the death of the god and his resurrection. The only difference between the Mysteries as they were performed in Egypt and Greece and the Mystery which was played in Palestine lies in the fact that the latter was played in real life, not on the stage but amidst real nature, in the streets and public places of real towns, in real country, with the sky, mountains, lakes and trees for scenery, with a real crowd, with real emotions of love and malice and hatred, with real nails, with real sufferings.[14]

What is the meaning of this sacred drama? That what is true of this god is true for all of us: the death of the body is not the death of the Self, indeed it is ultimately irrelevant to the Self. "Assault can ultimately be made only on the body. There is little doubt that that one body can assault another, and can even destroy it. Yet if destruction itself is impossible, anything that is destructible cannot be real" (T, 92).

This could have been the lesson imparted to initiates by the mysteries, and demonstrated in the passion and resurrection of Christ.

We do not need to imitate this martyrdom. We are merely to learn the lesson that the crucifixion teaches. "You have probably reacted for years as if you were being crucified," says the Course. But "if you react as if you are being persecuted, you are teaching persecution. This is not a lesson a Son of God should want to teach if he is to realize his own salvation. . . . You are not asked to be crucified, which was part of my own teaching contribution. You are merely asked to follow my example in the face of much less extreme temptations to misperceive, and not to accept them as false justifications for anger" (T, 92–93). Hence the final answer is, again, forgiveness.

In any event, let us look at how the resurrection appeared at the time and what it may have meant. The Gospels give only vague clues. The risen Jesus seems at times a phantom, appearing and vanishing at will, at times a palpable being, eating fish and honey. In these instances, we are not dealing with firsthand accounts, except for Paul's description of his encounter with the risen Christ in 1 Corinthians 15:8—but Paul gives us no specifics. All we know, really, is that his experience was enough like that of Jesus's disciples to permit them to accept Paul as one of them.

Paul does not believe in a physical resurrection, which he explicitly denies. The resurrection is of a "spiritual body" or a "glorified body": "It is sown a natural body [*sôma psukhikón*]; it is raised a spiritual body [*sôma pneumatikón*]. . . . Flesh and blood cannot inherit the kingdom of God;

neither doth corruption inherit incorruption" (1 Corinthians 15:44, 50). But he does not say how he conceives of this spiritual body.

For some light on this matter, I will turn to some of the material that emerged alongside of *A Course in Miracles,* by which I mean passages that were dictated by the Voice to Helen Schucman but did not appear in the final, edited version of the Course. In 1976 Schucman and Bill Thetford asked the Voice about the nature of the resurrection. Speaking in the first person as Jesus, it replied:

My body disappeared because I had no illusion about it. The last one had gone. It was laid in the tomb, but there was nothing left to bury. It did not disintegrate because the unreal cannot die. It merely became what it always was. And that is what "rolling away the stone" means. The body disappears, and no longer hides what lies beyond. It merely ceases to interfere with vision. To roll away the stone is to see beyond the tomb, beyond death, and to understand the body's nothingness. What is understood as nothing *must* disappear.[15]

As I have stressed, the Course is self-consistent. If the body is not real, then it does not exist. Under certain circumstances, then, it can simply vanish.

But Jesus did appear to his disciples. What sort of body was that? The Voice continues:

I did assume a human form with human attributes afterwards, to speak to those who were to prove the body's worthlessness for the world. This has been much misunderstood. I came to tell them that death is illusion, and the mind that made the body can make another since form itself is an illusion. They did not understand. But now I talk to you and give you the same message. The death of an illusion means nothing. It disappears when you decide to awaken and dream no more. And you still do have the power to make this decision as I did.[16]

There is not much in the Western traditions that can explain this idea, although it is reminiscent of the concept of the *tulku* in Tibetan Buddhism. The Dalai Lama explains that a fully enlightened being achieves "the empty nature of . . . all-knowing enlightened mind." But such a being can only manifest in its pure form to those who are equally enlightened. For ordinary mortals, such beings manifest as "gods or humans." As such they are "accessible even to ordinary beings." This "emanation body" is known as *nirmanakaya* or, in Tibetan, *tulku*.[17] Descriptions of the tulku bear some resemblance to the form in which the risen Jesus is said to have manifested himself.

These manifestations are supernatural. They are impossible according to the current laws of physics and biology, no matter how creatively interpreted. This may cause some discomfort, because many forms of Christianity today deny or avoid any concept of the supernatural in their theologies. But if you are going to deny any possibility of supernatural manifestations, you may as well drop your religious pretenses and admit that you are a secular humanist.

I also think it best to be cautiously open-minded about the resurrection of Christ. It seems likely that the disciples did have some experience of the risen Christ. But because we have no firsthand accounts of such experiences, we are left with many questions about what that experience was and what it meant. The answers set out above are possibilities and possibilities only. So, for that matter, are all other answers.

If the early followers of Christ believed that the resurrection of the faithful would be a spiritual event rather than a resuscitation of corpses, and the later church believed the exact opposite, we could wonder how this doctrine could have transformed itself so radically. Robert Perry, editor of a recent and comprehensive edition of the Course, theorizes cogently about how the early Christian concept of the resurrection of the body developed.[18] Those who encountered the risen Christ, by all accounts, encountered one with a body that was different from the one he had before. The first step was to conceive of him in a "spiritual body" or "glorious body," as Paul did, for example in

Philippians 3:20–21: "We look for the Saviour, the Lord Jesus Christ: who shall change our vile body, that it may be fashioned like unto his glorious body [*sómati tēs dóxēs*]." (See also 1 Corinthians 15:44, quoted above.) But this glorified spiritual body is extremely hard to conceive of, and in later centuries the concept mutated into the idea of a resurrected *physical* body.

Of course this would mean that the Christian church today teaches the exact opposite of what Christ originally taught. But this is so true of so many aspects of Christian thought that it need not surprise us.

In the end, Christocentrism seems to entail the scandal of particularity in some form, even in the irenic form presented by the Course. In making Jesus the first person in the human race to have fully accepted the Atonement, it seems to push aside all the other great religious figures who preceded him. We are led to suspect that Zarathustra and Lao-tzu and Confucius did not quite grasp the whole picture, and that even the enlightenment of the Buddha was not as complete as he claimed. All this could lead to a religious polemic of the most poisonous variety.

Personally, I do not know who Jesus was. I am familiar with the theories and the doctrines, but that is all they are. To my mind, it makes most sense to think of the nature and person of Christ in this way: Occasionally beings appear who are, both cognitively and ethically, far in advance of the usual run of mortals. Christ was among them, but so very likely were other great spiritual presences. These beings are often seen as divine. They may be, or they may not be; there is no way of saying—if we can even say what *divine* is supposed to mean here. In any event, those of us who are more ordinary have to admit that we have no real criterion for evaluating them: they are, in some important ways, above us, and that is all we can say. But rather than pitching ourselves into a cynical agnosticism or a superstitious credulity—or even a seizure of theologizing—I think we can accept the simple possibility, even the likelihood, that such beings exist and that we can have recourse to their help if we ask for it.

TWELVE

BEING TOWARD DEATH

Martin Heidegger argued that man—or rather Dasein, the human being in the human condition—is a being toward death.[1] By this Heidegger appears to mean that not only death, but the awareness of death, is the central fact of human life. He writes:

> The fact that even everyday Da-sein *is* always already *toward* its end, that is, constantly coming to grips with its own death, even though "fleetingly," shows that this end, which concludes and defines being-whole, is not something which Da-sein ultimately arrives at only in its demise. In Da-sein, existing toward its death, its most extreme not-yet which everything else precedes is always already included.[2]

Death, the grotesque familiar portrayed in the old danse macabre, is always with us, and all our actions are in reference to it. But usually we avoid this fact, for example by deferring the question. "One says that death certainly comes, but not right away. With this 'but . . . [*sic*] the they denies that death is certain."[3] The *they, Das man,* the background of conventional thought and opinion against which we live, defers and denies death. It is common to give even the terminally ill the dishonest reassurance that "you'll be better soon." But the only way to live authentically is to face your own death, and to face it for yourself and only for yourself. "Death does not just 'belong' in an undifferentiated way to one's own Da-sein, but it *lays claim* on it as something *individual*."[4]

Death means one thing and one thing only: the death of the body. In this form it is undeniable and inevitable. Even if physical immortality were possible, it would be monstrous, as we see from the ancient myth of the Sibyl at Cumae. Apollo granted her immortality, but she failed to ask him for eternal youth, so she lived an endless life of progressive decay, dwindling down to the size and shape of a cicada. Swift's *Gulliver's Travels* makes the same point in describing the struldbrugs of Luggnagg, beings who possess immortality without youth: "They were the most mortifying sight I ever beheld; and the women more horrible than the men. Besides the usual deformities in extreme old age, they acquired an additional ghastliness, in proportion to their number of years, which is not to be described."[5] Even if gerontology makes good on its boasts of soon being able to reverse the aging process, no doubt the kind of youth that it would bestow would be as hideous as that of a Sibyl or a struldbrug.

The body *is* death; not now, perhaps, not today, or tomorrow, but inevitably. One could dispute the advantages of being struck down suddenly and cruelly, in the fullness of one's powers, versus those of a lingering experience of being, to use Yeats's phrase, "fastened to a dying animal,"[6] but they come to the same thing. So when Heidegger speaks of Dasein as a being toward death, it is the death of the body he means. To the extent that you identify with the body, this is terrifying: it is inexpressibly bleak if you believe that you are the body and nothing else. Today's astonishing rates of mental illness and depression may be connected with the obstinate insistence by contemporary thought that human consciousness is merely a side-effect of the body's physical functioning and nothing more. This belief could also explain the long-scale trend toward the sanitization and denial of death: it is unpleasant to think of in its own right; it is unendurable if you believe there is nothing else.

The usual retort is that "human kind cannot bear very much

reality."[7] The deep-rooted aversion to this idea—that the death of the body is the death of the self—is usually explained as a refusal to face a hard truth: that the physical body is all we are. But what if it is the other way around? What if we so stubbornly refuse to accept it, not because it is a truth, but because it is a lie?

I strongly suspect—I am firmly convinced—that it is a lie. The very question implies that it is a lie. Because if the human being were simply equivalent to the functioning physical body, no one would ever have thought otherwise. Plotinus would not have been ashamed of being in his body, because the alternative would never have occurred to him.[8] Then there is the evidence of those who have had near-death experiences. Often they see their bodies as alien and repellent. A construction worker from Georgia reported, "I recognized *me* lying there . . . [it was] like looking at a dead worm or something. I didn't have any desire to go back to it."[9]

The pseudoscientific insistence that the human being *is* the body casts light on certain cultural conflicts. In the United States the intelligentsia, who worship scientific thought, are baffled by the belligerent resistance of many religious believers to ideas such as evolution and the big bang. We even see full-size replicas of Noah's Ark and theme parks devoted to the claim that the dinosaurs were contemporaries of Lamech and Methuselah.

On its own terms, this resistance to knowledge is incomprehensible. It is less so in view of what I have just said. Fundamentalists' reaction to current scientific theories is, I believe, less about the theories themselves than about the assertion—not scientific but made in the name of science—that material reality is all the reality there is. In this, apologists for science have overstepped their mark. This claim has not been proved, and, we could even argue, has been disproved. Until the misguided friends of science admit this mistake, cultural clashes will only grow more vehement. Still more unfortunately, present-day theology and philosophy live in such terror of appearing unscientific that they are unable to stand up to the materialists.

We have already seen how *A Course in Miracles* responds to the problem of physical death. If the body is ultimately unreal, its demise is of little importance. Christianity over the centuries has repeatedly insisted upon the body's transiency. That, indeed, was the point of the themes of the memento mori, the danse macabre, and other such motifs. I was most struck by it when visiting Bristol Cathedral in England. There were the usual sepulchers of bishops and noblemen, topped by carved effigies of their bodies in their regalia. But there was one unlike all the others. It was of Paul Bush, the first bishop of Bristol in the sixteenth century, and it showed him as a half-rotted corpse.

These thoughts can easily arouse a hatred of the body, which in turn can generate self-mortification and masochism of the most grotesque sort. Catholic art since the Counter-Reformation, with its crucifixes dripping with blood and hearts of Jesus girded with crowns of thorns, provides the grimmest examples.

The Course will have no truck with such imagery. "The grimness of the symbol [of death] is enough to show it cannot exist with God. It holds an image of the Son of God in which he is 'laid to rest' in devastation's arms where worms wait to greet him and to last a little while by his destruction" (M, 66). Furthermore, "the curious belief that there is part of dying things that may go on apart from what will die, does not proclaim a loving God nor re-establish any grounds for trust. Death denies life. But if there is reality in life, death is denied. No compromise in this is possible" (M, 66).

As for the body, the central and often sole concern in life, the Course advocates neither an obsessive preoccupation with it nor a cruel abuse of it:

The body is in need of no defense. This cannot be too often emphasized. It will be strong and healthy if the mind does not abuse it by assigning it to roles it cannot fill, to purposes beyond its scope, and to exalted aims which it cannot accomplish. Such attempts, ridiculous yet deeply cherished, are the sources for the many mad attacks you make upon it. For it seems to fail your hopes, your needs, your values, and your dreams.

The "self" that needs protection is not real. The body, valueless and hardly worth the least defense, need merely be perceived as quite apart from you, and it becomes a healthy, serviceable instrument through which the mind can operate until its usefulness is over. Who would want to keep it when its usefulness is done?

Defend the body and you have attacked the mind. For you have seen in it the faults, the weaknesses, the limits and the lacks from which you think the body must be saved. You will not see the mind as separate from bodily conditions. And you will impose upon the body all the pain that comes from the conception of the mind as limited and fragile, and apart from other minds and separate from its Source. (W, 253)

We can see why the Course does not really speak of an afterlife. It teaches that the Son is immortal, so there is no death. As for heaven, "Heaven is here. There is nowhere else. Heaven is now. There is no other time" (M, 61). As for hell, "The belief in hell is inescapable to those who identify with the ego. . . . The ego teaches that hell is in the future, for this is what all its teaching is directed to" (T, 301). But "the Holy Spirit teaches thus: There is no hell. Hell is only what the ego has made of the present" (T, 302). Therefore "Atonement might be equated with total escape from the past and total lack of interest in the future" (M, 61).

Strangely in light of these ideas, the Course speaks of reincarnation ambiguously. "In the ultimate sense, reincarnation is impossible. There is no past or future, and the idea of birth into a body has no meaning either once or many times" (M, 61). Nevertheless, the Course stops short of dismissing the concept entirely. "For our purposes, it would not be helpful to take any definite stand on reincarnation. A teacher of God should be as helpful to those who believe in it as to those who do not" (M, 60). It goes on to ask, "Does this mean that the teacher of God should not believe in reincarnation himself, or discuss it with those who do? The answer is, certainly not! If he does believe in reincarnation, it would be a mistake for him to renounce the belief unless his internal Teacher so advised. And this is most unlikely" (M, 61). Robert Perry is probably right in explaining: "How can we actually enter into a succession of bodies over time when bodies and time do not really exist? This does not mean that reincarnation cannot happen within the dream. It just means that if reincarnation does happen within the dream, then like the rest of the dream, it is not real."[10]

The Course seems to be saying this: If the body is a learning device and the lesson of the Atonement is not learned in one lifetime, another body may be taken on. When the lesson is learned completely, the body is set aside. This is more comforting than the conventional Christian doctrine of the afterlife, "and if it heartens [individuals], then its value is self-evident. It is certain, however, that the way to salvation can be found by those who believe in reincarnation and those who do not" (M, 60).

It is reasonable to ask about the nature of embodiment in what the Course calls "the real world." The Course does speak cryptically of "the Great Rays." A prayer toward the end of the Workbook reads in part: "Father, it is Your peace that I would give, receiving it of You. I am your Son, forever just as you created me, for the Great Rays remain forever still and undisturbed within me" (W, 484). It seems to be suggesting that the Great Rays are as we were created by God, but there is no description of them. Conceivably they resemble a vision Helen Schucman had before beginning to write the Course, when she was riding on a dirty, crowded New York subway with her husband. Helen's friend Robert Skutch describes it:

A blinding light seemed to blaze up behind her eyes and fill her mind completely. Without opening her eyes, she seemed to see a figure, which she knew to be herself, walking directly into the light. The figure seemed to know exactly what she was doing; she paused and knelt down, touching the ground with her elbows, wrists and forehead in what looked like an Eastern expression of deep reverence. Then the figure got up, walked to the side and knelt again, this time resting her head as if leaning against a giant knee. The outline of a huge arm seemed to reach around her, and then she disappeared. The light grew even brighter, and Helen felt an indescribably intense love streaming from it. It was so powerful a feeling that she literally gasped and opened her eyes.

She saw the light just an instant longer, during which she loved everyone on the train with that same incredible intensity. Then the light faded and the old reality of dirt and ugliness returned to her.

Shaken, she described her experience to her husband, who said, "Don't worry about it. It's a common mystical experience. Don't give it another thought," and went back to reading his paper.[11]

One glimpses similar things in Christianity. The transfiguration described in the synoptic Gospels, in which Jesus's "raiment became shining, exceeding white as snow" (Mark 9:3), may have been a vision of this kind. The sayings of the ancient desert fathers include this anecdote: "Then came to the abbot Joseph the abbot Lot and said to him, 'Father, according to my strength I keep a modest rule of prayer and fasting and meditation and quiet, and according to my strength I purge my imagination: what more must I do?' The old man, rising, held his hands up against the sky, and his fingers became like ten torches of fire, and he said, 'If thou wilt, thou shalt be made wholly a flame.'"[12]

I have seen people this way a few times myself. They looked like great, intensely bright ovals of light. The physical form did not vanish entirely, but looked like a two-dimensional shadow in front of this light.

Such is the Course's teaching about what Christian theology calls the *particular judgment*—the fate of the individual soul after death. But there is also the *general judgment*: the reckoning of all souls at the end of time.

The existence of both general and particular judgments in Christian eschatology is difficult to explain logically (why judge somebody twice for the same lifetime?) but reasonably clear historically. The Hebrews of biblical times had only a vague concept of the afterlife: "The dead praise not the Lord, neither any that go down into silence" (Psalm 115:17). The Hebrew Sheol, less richly imagined than the Greek Hades, was equally dismal. In New Testament times, the Sadducees, "which say that there is no resurrection" (Matthew 22:23), did so not out of innovation but out of conservatism. Even today many educated and devout Jews insist that Judaism has no teaching about life after death.

Apocalyptic eschatology grew up in the last centuries before Christ, notably in Daniel, which posits a general resurrection, for Israel at least (Daniel 12:1–2). At the time of Christ, the Jews had no clear consensus about what happened to the soul between death and the resurrection. The older view was that they slept "in the dust" (Daniel 12:2), but there was an increasingly popular view, imported from Greek mystery religion, that the soul went into an intermediate state of heaven or hell before then. It was held by the Essenes, according to Josephus.[13] This eschatology is reflected in the parable of the rich man and Lazarus (Luke 16:19–31), which, if it authentically goes back to Jesus, would suggest that he believed in this doctrine too (although the Course would deny this). But the Gospels also presuppose a final resurrection, as we see in Martha's statement about Lazarus: "I know that he shall rise again in the resurrection at the last day" (John 11:24).

Is there some truth to this idea of the Last Judgment? It might be best to approach the subject through reference to another tradition. Mahayana Buddhism speaks of the eventual "enlightenment of all sentient beings." Aspirants are told to desire this goal rather than the more selfish aim of mere personal enlightenment. The thirteenth-century Tibetan sage Longchenpa even says that those who wish to help all other beings achieve enlightenment before themselves will, paradoxically, reach enlightenment first.[14]

This seems peculiar. Why desire the enlightenment of all sentient beings before your own? Why not choose enlightenment for yourself? (After all, until you are enlightened, you have no assurance of doing more good than harm.) The most likely explanation is that because all beings are linked, indeed all beings are one, your own enlightenment will be incomplete until all are enlightened. To understand this fact itself brings you that much closer to enlightenment.

The Course presents a similar train of thought. In its terms, the Atonement is a universal process: it is not complete until it is complete universally. This process is not going to happen overnight: "Just as the separation occurred over millions of years, the Last Judgment will extend over a similarly long period, and perhaps an even longer one" (T, 34). Here we are far from biblical apocalyptic, with its claims that the end of time is imminent—marked by Antiochus Epiphanes's setting up "the abomination that maketh desolate" in the Temple (Daniel 11:31; 12:11), or by a Roman invasion of Judea, as hinted in the apocalyptic discourse in the synchronic Gospels (Matthew 24, Mark 13, Luke 21). We are also far from modern updates, with elaborate calculations of the date of Christ's return (usually six months from now) and raptures causing car crashes. The separation was a cosmic event, taking place over an immense time scale, and so is the Atonement.

The eschatology of the Course is nuanced but clear: The Second Coming "is the time in which all minds are given to the hands of Christ. . . . Every one who ever came to die, or yet will come or is present now, is equally released from what he made. In this equality is Christ restored as one Identity, in which the Sons of God acknowledge that they are all one" (W, 449). To return to my metaphor, it is the moment when the man steps out of the box of mirrors.

In other words, the Second Coming refers, not to a physical descent of Jesus from the skies, but the complete acceptance of the Atonement by all minds. It is "the willingness to let forgiveness rest upon all things without exception and without reserve. . . . The Second Coming ends the lessons that the Holy Spirit teaches, making way for the Last

Judgment, in which learning ends in one last summary that will extend beyond itself, and reaches up to God" (W, 449).

Once the unified Sonship accepts the Holy Spirit's message—forgiveness for "all things without exception and without reserve"—the way is cleared for the Son to reach up to God. And God takes the final step: the Last Judgment. "The final judgment on the world contains no condemnation. For it sees the world as totally forgiven, without sin and wholly purposeless. . . . You who believed that God's Last Judgment would condemn the world to hell along with you, accept this holy truth: . . . To fear God's saving grace is but to fear complete release from suffering, return to peace, security and happiness, and union with your own Identity" (W, 255).

At this point the world vanishes. It has served its purpose, or, rather, it has been discovered to be purposeless, and the Son, which is all of us, is reunited with the Father.

Of all the eschatologies I have ever encountered in all the religions in the world, none compares with this one in sublimity and beauty, and this fact, I believe, is evidence in its favor. Some may dismiss it as wishful thinking. But are we wishing for it *because* it is the truth?

I once interviewed Hameed Ali, a teacher of a spiritual system called the Diamond Approach, who writes under the name A. H. Almaas. He said, "The heart really loves to know the truth. Everybody knows that. Even if you just investigate and find out something for yourself, there is a joy, a satisfaction. The heart really likes it! That is inherent in us, in human beings."[15]

I agree. Admittedly you can arouse a synthetic joy in yourself through self-delusion, but it is the direct opposite of the joy that comes from learning the truth.

This hope is far from the typical Christian apocalyptic, with its vials of wrath, bleeding moons, and beasts slithering out of the abyss. As the Course says, "The world will end in joy, because it is a place of sorrow. . . . It will end in laughter, because it is a place of tears" (M, 37).

THIRTEEN

Relationships, Special and Holy

Is it not well done that our language has but one word for all kinds of love, from the holiest to the most lustfully fleshly? All ambiguity is therein resolved: love cannot be but physical, at its furthest stretch of holiness; it cannot be impious, in its utterest fleshliness. It is always itself, as the height of shrewd "geniality" as in the depth of passion; it is organic sympathy, the touching sense-embrace of that which is doomed to decay. In the most raging as in the most reverent passion, there must be caritas. The meaning of the word varies? In God's name, then, let it vary.

THOMAS MANN[1]

Love is the touchiest of subjects, and the stickiest. We smear the word over everything, but we are often baffled about what it really means. Once on a street in Manhattan, I heard a girl say to another, "So I said to him, 'I like you but I don't love you.' Does that mean we should sleep together?" She might not agree with Thomas Mann that it was a good idea to have a word with so many meanings.

In 2008, I published *Conscious Love: Insights from Mystical Christianity.* Attempting to define love, I said that it "unites self and other." But again this union can take many forms and produce many results, from the ecstatic to the excruciating.

In essence I separated love into two categories. One is *transactional* or *conditional love,* which implies giving and taking, rights and obligations. It is the kind of love that we usually encounter in the world, deny it though we may. A man falls in love with a woman and says, "I don't care what happens between us. I just want her to be happy." Six weeks later, they have broken up, and he wishes nothing but evil upon her.

The other form is *unconditional* or *conscious love,* which is the opposite. It does not set terms or make demands. It gives without thinking about payment. It is the type of love that Paul extols in 1 Corinthians 11. Paul, like the rest of the New Testament, uses the word *agape,* a comparatively rare word outside of Christian contexts. Agape is pure and clean, but it is also somewhat remote. The Greek verb from which it is derived (*agapáo*) is even rather chilly, "often implying regard rather than affection," according to Liddell and Scott's standard Greek lexicon. Jesus displays this love in the Gospels, but then he too is often remote—kind but unsentimental. Certainly he does not extol family values. In one episode, when he is told that his mother and his brothers are waiting to see him, he effectively replies, "Let them wait" (Mark 3:32–35).[2]

Although in *Conscious Love* I often referred to *A Course in Miracles,* I did not say that this distinction between the two loves was inspired by the Course. It does not use my terms, but it makes the same point, contrasting the *special relationship* with the *holy relationship.* I correlate the special relationship with transactional love, and the holy relationship with conscious love.

Some readers thought my characterization of transactional love—which includes romantic love, family love, and friendship—was cold and cynical. So it may have been. But compared to the Course's contrast between these two loves, my view was rather mild.

To understand what the Course means by the *special relationship,* let us go back to the ego. In its pure form, the ego is utter isolation, utter alienation, utter hatred. It is, in fact, very much like the way the more sophisticated Christian theologians characterize hell—not as a place filled with devils and fire, but as a state of total and irrevocable separation from God.

But because the ego is also completely false—it does not exist, except in the mind of the deluded Son, the man in the box of mirrors—this isolation cannot be real; even in the world of appearances it cannot be complete or seem complete. But the Sons of God can accept the lies of the ego to a certain degree; all of us do; otherwise we wouldn't be here. Because of this conflict—between the need for union, which is genuine, and the tendency toward separation, which is false—we feel the need for special relationships. The ego, being necessarily incomplete, has to reach outward for such relationships in order to complete itself.

These relationships are selective. You fall in love with one person, who may or may not care at all; another falls in love with you, and you will have none of it. Hence the term *special relationship.* "To limit love to part of the Sonship is to bring guilt into your relationships, and thus make them unreal. If you seek to separate out certain aspects of the totality and look to them to meet your imagined needs, you are attempting to use separation to save you. . . . To believe that *special* relationships, with *special* love, can offer you salvation is the belief that separation is salvation" (T, 312; emphasis in the original).

We can see this process in romantic relationships. They begin with individuals in need—for companionship, for sexual satisfaction, but above all to fill some sense of an inner emptiness. This need arises out of mistaken thinking, because it implies that there is something lacking in the Son of God that can be filled from outside.

Guilt characterizes the special relationship in another way. It involves obligation—to be sexually faithful, to invite people over for dinner after they have invited you, to exchange Christmas cards every year. Obviously the degrees of obligation vary, but it is never far from the special relationship. And obligations are cemented and enforced by guilt, whether externally imposed ("How can you love me and do that to me?") or internal ("What kind of a friend am I being?"). The Course says:

> It is impossible for the ego to enter into any relationship without anger, for the ego believes that anger makes friends. This is not its statement, but it *is* its purpose. For the ego really believes that it can get and keep *by making guilty.* (Text, 317; emphasis in the original)

This characterization is harsh. It is especially so if you understand the Course—as you could easily do—to mean that all relationships in the world are special relationships. Closer scrutiny reveals that this is not entirely the case. At one point the Course says, "You have made very real relationships even in this world" (T, 358), implying that there are relationships in ordinary life that are *not* special. But even here the passage goes on to say, "Yet you do not recognize them because you have raised the substitutes to such predominance that, when truth calls to you, as it does constantly, you answer with a substitute"—*substitute* apparently meaning something like the ego's goal of specialness (T, 358). So this admission that "very real relationships" exist in the world sounds faint.

If we think of unconditional love, a mother's love for a child comes to mind. But the bond between parent and child can and does turn into a special relationship. In the first place, the love for a child is necessarily special: you love your child *because* she is your child, and you make sacrifices for her that you would not make for someone else's. Furthermore, parents place all sorts of demands upon their children that have nothing to do with unconditional love. Often the child must be perfect, a prodigy, the smartest and prettiest and most popular one in the class. If not, she is deluged with guilt. In a sense, the parent-child connection is the special relationship par excellence.

So far we have been speaking of special love relationships. Whether they are between husband and wife, mother and son, best friends, or any other parties, they are ostensibly positive. You have good feelings toward the other as long as this person meets what you regard as your needs. But there is also the special hate relationship.

The Course's concept of the special hate relationship employs an idea from Freudian psychology (which Schucman knew well): *projection.* It is a tool of the ego. The ego, which "wishes no one well" (T, 317), needs to hide the fact that it is set upon your destruction. As soon as you come near this insight, the ego takes the step of projecting what is in itself onto the special hate object. The choices are endless—your mother-in-law, politicians you detest, the obnoxious person three cubicles away from you at work. None of these people possess these traits *in reality,* because in reality, they, like you, are Sons of God. But you can convince yourself that they do.

> What you project you disown, and therefore do not believe is yours. You are excluding yourself by the very judgment that you are different from the one on whom you project. Since you have also judged against what you project, you continue to attack it because you continue to keep it separated. By doing this unconsciously, you try to keep the fact that you attacked yourself out of awareness, and thus imagine that you have made yourself safe.
>
> Yet projection will always hurt you. It reinforces your belief in your own split mind, and its only purpose is to keep the separation going. It is solely a device of the ego to make you feel different from your brothers and separated from them. (T, 96)

Conveniently, the other person is often making similar projections, in which case you have an enemy. You cannot be enemies *in reality,* because you are both united in the Sonship, but it is very easy to obscure this identity, and you can certainly have enemies in the world of illusion.

How do we cope with these situations? Again, through forgiveness. The Workbook stresses forgiveness relentlessly, for reasons already discussed. If all sin and error are unreal, what is there to forgive? If the body is, as the Course says, "nothing," and the body is the only thing that can be harmed, then harm is impossible. Forgiveness is simply an acknowledgment of the truth.

The means of transcending special relationships, according to the Course, is the *holy instant*. To understand it, we can start with the idea that time, in the Course's view, is illusory. If this is case, then time as such does not exist, and there is only the present. "*Now* is the closest approximation of eternity that this world offers. It is in the reality of 'now,' without past or future, that the beginning of the application of eternity lies. For only 'now' is here, and only 'now' presents the opportunities for the holy encounters in which salvation can be found" (T, 247; emphasis in the original).

The holy encounter is found in the holy instant. Course student Allen Watson writes, "The holy instant is an experience of grace and stillness, an instant in which we set aside some or all of our identification with the ego and our belief in the reality of the world it has projected, and allow the reality of our true Identity in God to shine through, an Identity we share with all the Sonship."[3] The Course says the holy instant is "the little breath of eternity that runs through time. . . . You look upon each holy instant as a different point in time. It never changes. All that it ever held or will ever hold is here right now. The past takes nothing from it, and the future will add no more" (T, 435).

The locus classicus of the holy instant, and the holy relationship that arises from it, is found in the story about how the Course began to be written. In the summer of 1965, Bill Thetford went into Schucman's office before a weekly research meeting. Both of them were dreading the meeting because of the inevitable hostility and competitiveness. As Robert Skutch describes it,

> Bill . . . obviously wanted to say something which he evidently found it hard to talk about. At last he took a deep breath, grew slightly red-faced and delivered a speech. He admitted later that the words

sounded trite and sentimental, and he hardly expected a favorable response from Helen. Nevertheless, he said what he felt he had to say. He had been thinking things over and had concluded that their approach was wrong. "There must," he said, "be another way. Our attitudes are so negative that we can't work anything out." He went on to say that he had therefore decided to try to look at things differently.

He proposed, quite specifically, to try out the new approach that day at the research meeting. He was not going to get angry, and he was determined to look for a constructive side in what the people there said and did. . . .

Then he waited in some discomfort for Helen's response. It was not the one he had expected. She jumped up, told Bill with conviction that he was right, and said she would join in the new approach with him.

At some level this joining represented a *real* commitment that was unprecedented in their relationship, and it seemed to be the signal for the beginning of a series of remarkable events that occurred in the summer of 1965.[4]

Those events led up to the writing of *A Course in Miracles*.

To take a story from my own experience: When I was in my mid-thirties I took a job with a company that required me to move to a completely different part of the country. The boss who had hired me initially seemed agreeable enough, but as soon as I was there, we fell into endless conflicts. In any case, working for this company proved not to my taste, and since I did not try to conceal this fact, I was given my freedom after only nine months, causing me great hardship.

Of course I was seething with rage against my former boss. Being a student of the Course, I tried to apply its principles of forgiveness, but it did not seem to be going very well. Then at one point I ran into him on the street. He stopped and said, "Richard, I know it didn't work out well, and I'm sorry about that." He stretched out his hand, and I shook it. We parted in peace, and after that my grievances against him were gone.

Put simply, the Course's goal is to transmute special relationships into holy relationships. It insists upon transmuting them rather than ending them, which would just lead to seeking out another special relationship, starting the process all over again.

> Now the ego counsels thus; substitute for this [relationship] another relationship to which your former goal [specialness] was quite appropriate. You can escape from your distress only by getting rid of your brother.

To which the Course responds: "*Hear not this now!* Abandon Him [the Holy Spirit] not now, nor your brother" (T, 363; emphasis in the original).* If you refuse to leave the relationship now, but give the Holy Spirit the space to transform it, the relationship will be "reborn as holy."

The Course's contrast of the holy versus the special relationship is stark and absolute, just as everything is either of God or of the ego. There is no compromise, because the ego's motives are never good, and will always bring pollution.

Conceptually, I find the Course's rigid contrast between special and holy relationships plausible, but, more than many ideas in the Course, it seems somewhat removed from the complex reality of human relationships. We live in the mixed world, and our motives are necessarily mixed. This means that love can easily turn to hate, but it also means that a kind of unconditional love can creep even into the most calculated and transactional of relationships. A man is captivated by the curve of a woman's breast: his motive for getting to know her is purely carnal. But then he falls in love with her, and their relationship develops into one that is lasting and mature. A boss hires an assistant: his

---

*The Course uses the term *brother* to indicate all individuals with whom one has a relationship, regardless of the nature of the relationship or the person's gender.

motives are purely commercial; it is simply a matter of work for hire. But here too relations develop. The boss grows fond of his assistant, and eventually becomes a mentor to him. The assistant becomes fond of his boss in turn, and, much later in his career, looks back on him with affection and gratitude. This happens over and over again in life. In fact, I believe, it *should* happen.

So, more than most concepts in the Course, the irreducible dichotomy between special and holy relationships, though useful as a teaching device, does not seem to completely reflect the complexity (and, often, confusion) of human emotions. Or is it rather the Holy Spirit is operating unknown to the people involved?

On a practical note: it can be conceptually useful to draw a sharp distinction between transactional and unconditional love, but reality does not fit well into neat categories. There is no point in drawing up a list of your relationships and dividing it into two columns. At the same time, I think there is some wisdom in grasping that our relationships in the world are characterized by conditions and terms and obligations and rights. That is not likely to change anytime soon. Even so, there is also some wisdom is remembering that something higher and purer can appear in all these relationships—often spontaneously and unexpectedly. That may be what the holy instant is all about.

FOURTEEN

CHURCH AND
SACRAMENTS

Is there still a need for the church? The recent convulsive decline of the mainstream Christian denominations in the United States makes this question a pressing one.

The church—by which I mean the Christian church in all its forms and all its denominations—is an aggregate of organizations. Thus it may be best to begin by looking at organizations in general.

Take the simplest unit of the organization: the individual. Say you have a job you need to have done, and you hire somebody to do it. From the minute this person begins, actually doing the job immediately becomes his *second* priority. His first priority is to keep the job. (It may be that he does not care for the job and does not want to keep it, but in that case he will soon quit or be fired.)

Since an organization, however big or small, is a multiplicity of such individuals, the fundamental problem becomes immediately apparent. The organization's first priority rapidly becomes maintaining the organization. Its ostensible goal often slips into second place.

The problem becomes especially acute when the organization becomes its own objective. This is true above all with the Catholic Church, which asserts, "To believe that the Church is 'holy' and 'catholic,' and that she is 'one' and 'apostolic' (as the Nicene Creed adds), is inseparable from belief in God, the Father, the Son, and the Holy Spirit."[1] Furthermore, "'the Church' is the People that God gathers in the whole world. . . . She draws her life from the word and the Body of Christ and so herself becomes Christ's Body."[2] Indeed "the world was created for the sake of the Church."[3]

From these claims it is easy to conclude that whatever is good for the church is good in itself. This makes the church's recent behavior a great deal easier to understand. Much has been said about pedophilia among the Catholic clergy, but people have been as shocked by the church's obstinately blind eye to this abuse as they are by the abuse itself. This sordid fact can only be understood in this light: the church often acts as if it were more important to protect itself, including its reputation, than it is to stop the sin of child molestation. (After all, the crimes were not uncovered by the church, which indeed made every effort to conceal them; they were uncovered by former victims and by the press.) The church's welfare as an organization trumps its own values. An account of this behavior throughout the church's history would come very close to a history of the church itself.

From here it is only a short step to saying that the church is more important than Christ—precisely the point of Dostoevsky's tale of the Grand Inquisitor: "Everything," the Inquisitor tells Jesus, who has returned but is again not welcomed, "has been handed over by you to the pope, therefore everything now belongs to the pope, and you may as well not come at all now, or at least don't interfere with us for the time being."[4]

For all their faults, the Protestant churches have mostly avoided this trap. They have generally acted on the premise that the church, though valuable in itself, is and must remain subordinate to the teachings of Christ that the church was created to spread. These institutions' problems do not stem principally from regarding themselves as their own objective. Their difficulties lie elsewhere: The evangelical denominations are crippled by an inaccurate and literalistic understanding of the Bible. The liberal denominations are well aware of the Bible's limitations, but, having been based on the Reformers' doctrine of *sola Scriptura,* they are confused and uncertain about how to use the Bible in the light of present knowledge, or, if it cannot be used in the former way, about what to put in its place. To the old dogmas they pay an equivocal lip service.

In the previous chapters, I have relied on *A Course in Miracles* to sort out a number of theological issues, but it scarcely addresses churches or organizations at all. The Course is a program for individual practice and instruction. It does not assume any help for the student except that of the Holy Spirit. It would be possible to do the Course completely satisfactorily without even encountering another Course student. There is only one passage that addresses the idea of the church, and it is a brief one. I will quote it in full:

> I am sorry when my brothers do not share my decision to hear only one Voice, because it weakens them as teachers and as learners. Yet I know they cannot really betray themselves or me, and that it is still on them that I must build my church. There is no choice in this, because only you can be the foundation of God's church. A church is where an altar is, and the presence of the altar is what makes the church holy. A church that does not inspire love has a hidden altar that is not serving the purpose for which God intended it. I must found His church on you, because those who accept me as a model are literally my disciples. Disciples are followers, and if the model they follow has chosen to save them pain in all respects, they are unwise not to follow him. (T, 93)

The Course uses the word *church* in only one other instance: "Sin is but error in a special form the ego venerates. It would preserve all errors and make them sins. For here is its own stability, its heavy anchor in the shifting world it made; the rock on which its church is built, and where its worshippers are bound to bodies, believing that the body's freedom is their own" (T, 475).

These passages allude to Matthew 16:18: "Thou art Peter, and upon this rock I will build my church." As is well known, there is wordplay in the Greek on *Peter* (*Pétros*) and rock (*tê pétra*). But the passage in Matthew and the one in the Course have very different imports. In Matthew, the whole point of the story is that Peter recognizes that Jesus is the Messiah, and that as a result, he is the rock upon which the church is to be built. (I often wonder whether Jesus was merely making a joke.) The Course, by contrast, says, "I must found His church on you." It is the student that, like all students, is the foundation of this church.

Note the mention of the altar. The theme of the altar appears in the Course much more frequently than that of the church. Here *altar* refers to the inner altar, the place in the heart that is devoted to what you hold most dear: "The voice for God comes from your own altars to Him. These altars are not things; they are devotions. Yet you have other devotions now. Your divided devotion has given you the two voices, and you must choose at which altar you want to serve" (T, 77). The "two voices" are those of the Holy Spirit (the "voice for God") and the ego; you must choose one or the other. There are no other alternatives.

The Course says, "A church is where an altar is, and the presence of the altar is what makes the church holy. A church that does not inspire love has a hidden altar that is not serving the purpose for which God intended it." A church too has the choice of which voice to hear. If it "does not inspire love," its hidden altar is at the service of the ego.

This is as far the Course takes us. It has almost nothing to say about ecclesiology. But the point is clear: a church can have any form, any type of organization. If it is devoted to love, then it serves God's purpose. If it is not devoted to love, it does not.

Note also that love in the Course rules out specialness: if the church offers love only to members and excludes everyone else, then its hidden altar is dedicated to the ego. "Love is extension. . . . Love offers everything forever" (T, 499), whereas "specialness is the great dictator of the wrong decisions. . . . Specialness is the idea of sin made real"

(T, 500, 502). Indeed the whole of chapter 24 in the Text, entitled "The Goal of Specialness," is devoted to this theme. If a church offers love only to believers, only to those it holds virtuous, it extols specialness, and serves the purposes of the ego.

Thus the church, like all organizations, must serve some purpose beyond its own survival. If it serves this higher purpose, it will survive. If it does not, it will not. History offers countless examples of institutions that stopped filling a purpose, or fulfilled one that was false or obsolete and thereby perished. As the rabbi Gamaliel said about the early Christian community in Jerusalem: "If this counsel or this work be of men, it will come to nought: But if it be of God, ye cannot overthrow it" (Acts 5:38–39).

We can also see the spirituality of the collective from another point of view. Myth conveys truths that cannot be expressed in ordinary language. Here is my version of one of the most ancient and universal myths.[5]

Once there was a cosmic being who lived on a plane of existence on a much grander scale than our own. Something happened: a fall, what the Course calls the separation. This fall cannot be connected with anything on the time line of history, even the history of the universe. That is because time and space—the background against which history takes place—are themselves the result of this event.

This being was a cosmic, androgynous human. The fall caused this being to shatter into billions of tiny fragments, each of which believed it was alone and independent and forgot that it had ever been—and still was—united with a greater whole.

Each of these fragments is one of us. We imagine ourselves to be isolated and autonomous, but actually we remain inseparably connected to this universal human. We even know this truth at some level. H. P. Blavatsky is quoted as saying, "Universal brotherhood rests upon the common soul. It is because there is one soul common to all men, that brotherhood, or even common understanding is possible."[6]

Although the details vary, we can see this myth at the core of the tale of the biblical Fall of Adam, the Hindu descent of Purusha into *avidya* or obliviousness, the dismembering of Gayomart in the Zoroastrian tradition, among many others. Indeed Adam, Purusha, and Gayomart are only a few of the names that have been given to this cosmic human over the course of time. I believe that this idea is also the central message of James Joyce's *Finnegans Wake*. "Bygmester Finnegan"[7] falls from his ladder and is immersed in a dream where he is a series of characters such as H. C. Earwicker, Anna Livia Plurabelle, and the brothers Shem and Shaun. The key to this book may lie in a remark by Stephen Dedalus in Joyce's *Ulysses*: "History is a nightmare from which I am trying to awake."[8]

Even in this cosmic shattering, some fragments did not forget that they were part of this whole, or remembered comparatively soon. They recognized, and recognize, one another, just as two people who are awake in a roomful of sleeping people soon become aware of each other. They also understood that they had to awaken all the sleepers, not merely as a virtuous action, but because this was the only way that the cosmic being could be restored to his pristine state.

There are names for this group of people who are relatively awake. One of the best-known is the *Brotherhood*. (Of course the term is not gender-specific; it includes men and women equally.) The Brotherhood cannot be associated with any specific organization or tradition. It is not an organization. At street level, it is simply the collection of people who recognize their common origin and work to restore their common life. Beings on higher levels, which some identify with masters on the inner planes, are part of the same movement, but in other realms. We do not know much about them.

Some in the street-level Brotherhood are esotericists; many—no doubt most—are not. Their qualifications come not from any initiatory rites (although these may take place) but from their awareness of their purpose and their commitment to fulfilling it. This Brotherhood can be seen as the divine seed that will bear fruit in the ultimate restoration of this cosmic being.

This could well be the central concept behind notions of secret societies and secret brotherhoods. The Brotherhood is invisible because there is no formal organization behind it. There may be certain lines—such as the Rosicrucians (as confusing and multivalent as that term may be) that are consciously dedicated to these goals—but if so, they are merely part of this larger unit and are in no way to be equated with it. The twentieth-century esotericist Paul Foster Case highlighted this fact in the title of his book *The True and Invisible Rosicrucian Order.* He writes:

> It is a society within human society, which by superior wisdom and power . . . shares in the administration of the Kingdom of God on earth. Its members live in every part of the globe. Some are humble, and their attainments extend just a little beyond those of ordinary human beings. Some are great adepts, charged with powers and responsibilities beyond our ability to imagine. . . . All are sympathetic, compassionate, tender. They rule, but the law whereby they rule is the perfect Law of Liberty, the Law of Love.[9]

As for conspiracy theories about the Illuminati and other such touted leagues of evil, none of these, if they exist, has any connection with the Brotherhood.

To turn to the sacraments, Christendom universally acknowledges two: baptism and the Eucharist. All others are secondary. Although both of these sacraments have had a tangle of ecclesiastical superstition woven around them, at their core we can see two principles.

Say that the man in the box of mirrors wakes up for a few seconds. He has a brief glimpse of the truth. He understands his situation, but he also realizes that he will sink back into delusion almost immediately. In his short stretch of clarity, he commits himself to waking up, no matter how hard it is or how long it takes. This is such a dramatic shift that we can call it being reborn. Say too that he wants to impress this recollection of awakening on himself, and makes some small gesture that marks the occasion and may serve to remind him again. We could connect this gesture with baptism.

The man is now, temporarily, awake. He sees the faces in the mirrors and understands that they are all his own. He wishes to remember this truth as well. So he makes another gesture that he hopes will remind him of the common life behind all these faces after he has drifted back into madness. We can connect this gesture with the Eucharist, the sharing in the common life of the body of Christ—who is, remember, the single being that shines through all of us.

There we have the sacraments. Viewed in this way, they are perfectly clear and simple. We do not need to embroider them with theological superstition. We do not need to spin outlandish philosophical tapestries about the Real Presence, or twist Aristotelian ideas of substance and accidents to make ourselves believe that a flavorless wafer is somehow the flesh of Jesus Christ. We can dispense with all of this. We can haul it all off and rid ourselves of it forever.

Do, then, the outward forms of the sacraments remain? If they serve their true purpose, why not? If they promote idolatry—that is, mistaking the external form for the essence—they are best left behind. Kenneth R. Wapnick, who worked with Schucman and Thetford in editing the Course materials, writes, "Participation in the sacraments, or any formal means of worship or ritual, is directly antithetical to the study and practice of the Course—*if one believes that the form of the ritual is salvific*—for by affirming that the spirit can exist in form, one makes real the error of believing in the reality of the world."[10]

The Course materials do allude to the sacraments. In an early draft, the Voice, speaking as Jesus, says:

> The idea of cannibalism in connection with the Sacrament is a reflection of a distorted view of sharing. . . . I do not want to share my body in communion because this is to share nothing. Would I try to share an illusion with the most holy children of a most holy Father? But I do want to share my mind with you. . . . Would I offer

you my body, you whom I love, knowing its littleness? Or would I teach that bodies cannot keep us apart? Mine was of no greater value than yours. . . . Communion comes with peace, and peace transcends the body.[11]

Although the Course never refers to the Catholic Church or to any church in particular, several of its passages seem to be aimed at sanguinary Catholic iconography. Here is one example:

Where does the totally insane belief in gods of vengeance come from? Love has not confused its attributes with those of fear. Yet must the worshippers of fear perceive their own confusion in fear's "enemy": its cruelty now as a part of love. And what becomes more fearful than the Heart of Love itself? The blood appears to be on His Lips; the fire comes from Him. And He is terrible above all else, cruel beyond conception, striking down all who acknowledge Him to be their God. (W, 327)

This passage probably alludes to the Sacred Heart, with its bizarre image of the heart of Jesus aflame, bound by a crown of thorns, and sometimes pierced with a sword as well. The Sacred Heart was allegedly revealed to Margaret Mary Alacoque in a series of visions from 1673 to 1675—right after the Counter-Reformation, when Catholic thought became obsessed with the sufferings of Christ. This may reflect the influence of the *Spiritual Exercises* of Ignatius of Loyola, which underscores the sufferings of the passion: "I will . . . rouse myself to sorrow, suffering, and deep pain, frequently calling to mind the labors, burdens, and sufferings that Christ our Lord bore from the moment of His birth up to the mystery of His Passion."[12]

I prefer the Course's view:

The journey to the cross should be the last "useless journey." Do not dwell upon it, but dismiss it as accomplished. If you can accept it as your own last useless journey, you are also free to join my resurrection. Until you do so your life is indeed wasted. It merely re-enacts the separation, the loss of power, the futile attempts of the ego at reparation, and finally the crucifixion of the body, or death. . . . Do not make the pathetic error of "clinging to the old rugged cross." The only message of the crucifixion is that you can overcome the cross. (T, 52)

FIFTEEN

THE LADDER OF PRAYER

In the introduction, I suggested that spiritual experience should be central to any new theology. Such a theology would not only have some room for experience, but also open a path to it. This leads us to spiritual practice.

Spiritual practice is a relatively new term. It seems to be an assimilation from Buddhism, which tends to speak of meditation, with some attempt at humility, as *practice.* It is as if you cannot claim to be meditating per se; that would be too great an achievement; the most you can say is that you are practicing how to meditate.

Consequently, *spiritual practice,* as the term is used today, usually connotes meditative practice. Certainly meditation does open up the practitioner to spiritual experience. The most common forms today are Transcendental Meditation, a mantra meditation brought to this country by the Maharishi Mahesh Yogi in the 1960s; *vipassana* or insight meditation, often described in mass culture as "mindfulness" meditation, which comes out of Buddhism; and Zen, which also comes out of Buddhism. Dzogchen meditation—whose directions are essentially to rest in pure awareness—has become popular as well, at least in certain circles; it comes from the Nyingma lineage of Tibetan Buddhism.[1] But there are countless others from all of the great world traditions.

Which of these forms is best suited to any individual? There are many variables. But in general, it is safe to say that meditation, of whatever sort, is best taught by an instructor qualified in that tradition, to whom the practitioner has some access later on for any questions or problems that arise. When I say *taught,* I mean *personally* taught, that is, when the teacher and the student are in each other's physical presence. Probably it is ideal to do this one-on-one, but each teacher and each teaching has its own guidelines in such matters, and generally speaking, the final criterion is what the teacher considers proper.

Not all types of meditation will have the same effects, because they are not all meant to. Vipassana tends to heighten mindfulness. I wonder how appropriate this is for many American students, because mindfulness can be disruptive if the mind is tense to start with, and many people's minds today are tense. Traditionally Buddhism has always emphasized both vipassana, mindfulness, and *samatha,* calmness, and I find myself asking whether many Americans would be better off starting with samatha. But I am not a Buddhist, so I pose these as questions only.

Once a student has learned the practice, all that remains is to do it. In almost all cases, this means *daily* practice as a regular part of your schedule. The amount of time to be devoted to it again varies with the specific type of meditation, but, again as a general rule, you should expect to devote a half-hour a day to it, working up to this by starting with smaller lengths of time as needed. If the teacher has other instructions, you should follow those.

The types of meditation I have just mentioned are from traditions far removed from Christianity. Is this a problem? It is less so if you think of meditation as a means of gaining access to the unconditioned level of the mind (as many types are). The unconditioned level of the mind is by definition beyond the conditioned level, and religion as we know it, with its doctrines and forms, exists at the conditioned level. To use terms employed earlier, religion as a formal system exists *beneath* the cloud of oblivion. Meditation is an attempt to pierce the cloud and, ideally, rise above it.

Several types of Christian meditation have surfaced over the past three or four decades, some of them new, some of them harking back to traditional methods. Thomas Keating's Centering Prayer, for example, takes its inspiration from the passage in *The Cloud of Unknowing* that I quoted earlier (see pages 34–35). Certainly this is legitimate, and practitioners have reported good results with these methods. All the same, I sense that Christianity, having long neglected if not condemned contemplative practice, is now desperately rooting around in its attic to satisfy current market demands.

This is all that I believe can be said in general terms. Let me talk a bit about the Course's approach to spiritual practice.

In fact *A Course in Miracles* is a program of spiritual practice. This is the purpose of its Workbook, with its 365 lessons. These lessons are specific, and the directions are clear. The Course itself says about the Workbook lessons: "The training period is one year. The exercises are numbered from 1 to 365. Do not undertake to do more than one set of exercises per day" (W, 1). I understand this to mean that the student is to do one lesson a day and spend no more than a day on it. Not everyone agrees, including Helen Schucman. In a 1977 preface, she writes: "The Workbook includes 365 lessons, one for each day of the year. It is not necessary, however, to do the lessons at that tempo, and one might want to remain with a particularly appealing lesson for more than one day."[2]

I am not sure that this is a good idea. It seems to me that it could divert a student, who may stay with a lesson for more than one day out of a feeling that she has not done it right. This can lead to discouragement. Admittedly it takes tremendous discipline to do the lessons every day, as directed, but this discipline is part of the point, because, as the Text says, "This is a course in mind training" (T, 16).

This mind training is aimed at spiritual experience: "Some of the later steps to this course . . . involve a more direct approach to God Himself" (T, 16). I will not go into these steps, because that would defeat the purpose behind the Workbook, but I can still make a few comments here.

Lesson 69 is entitled "My grievances hide the light of the world in me." The directions are, in part:

> Very quietly now, with your eyes closed, try to let go of all the content that generally occupies your consciousness. Think of your mind as a vast circle, surrounded by a layer of heavy, dark clouds. You can see only the clouds because you seem to be standing outside the circle and quite apart from it.
>
> From where you stand, you can see no reason to believe there is a brilliant light hidden by the clouds. The clouds seem to be the only reality. They seem to be all there is to see. Therefore, you do not attempt to go through them and past them, which would be the only way in which you would be really convinced of their lack of substance. We will make this attempt today.
>
> After you have thought about the importance of what you are trying to do for yourself and the world, try to settle down in perfect stillness, remembering only how much you want to reach the light in you today—now! Determine to go past the clouds. Reach out and touch them with your hands; feel them resting on your cheeks and forehead and eyelids as you go through them. Go on; clouds cannot stop you.
>
> If you are doing the exercises properly, you will begin to feel a sense of being lifted up and carried ahead. Your little effort and small determination call upon the power of the universe to help you, and God himself will raise you from darkness into light. You are in accord with His Will. You cannot fail because your will is His. (W, 117–18)

Note the resemblance of the cloud motif to the main image in *The Cloud of Unknowing*. We return to the cloud of oblivion, with one important difference: the Course identifies the cloud with grievances—the assortment of fears, resentments, and hatreds that occupy the human mind. Beyond the clouds is the light. Another lesson in the Course says,

"Try to think of light, formless and without limit, as you pass by the thoughts of this world" (W, 70).

We return to the schema mentioned at the beginning of chapter 4: the world we see, the cloud of oblivion, and something beyond the cloud, which here is seen as the light of God. The process outlined in the Workbook shows a way out of the cloud.

What does this spiritual light have to do with physical light? There must be some connection: it is too common and too universal for it to be otherwise. Some mystics, such as Jacob Boehme, were even led to transcendental experience by gazing at physical light—in his case, a gleam reflected off a pewter dish. But the two forms of light cannot be identical.

The opening of the *Bahir*, a Kabbalistic text probably dating to the eleventh century, offers some cryptic insights:

One verse (*Job 37:21*) states, "And now they do not see light, it is brilliant (*Bahir*) in the skies . . . [round about God in terrible majesty]."

Another verse, however, (*Psalm 18:12*), states, "He made darkness His hiding place." It is also written (*Psalm 97:2*), "Cloud and gloom surround Him." This is an apparent contradiction.

A third verse comes and reconciles the two. It is written (*Psalm 139:12*), "Even darkness is not dark to You. Night shines like day—light and darkness are the same."[3]

The similarity to the motifs in the Course is remarkable. The *Bahir*, however, views it from the other direction: God is hidden in the clouds, whereas in the Course it is the student who is hidden in them. The utterance "Even the darkness is not dark to you" can mean, in the Course's terms, that the darkness is simply illusory because it is not real to God.

Henri Coton-Alvart, a French alchemist, has some striking ideas about the relation of spiritual light to physical light. He writes, "These regions whose extent is the order of magnitude that we attribute to the atom or the neutron, are . . . *places devoid of light,* in which nothingness, the spirit of negation, rules exclusively. That is the root of matter. . . . I am saying that *matter is nonlight.*"[4]

Thus the light in the box of mirrors is not the light that is on the outside. It is not the light of God.

Such is what it is possible to say here about meditation, which is, after all, concerned with the ineffable. What about prayer? The Russian novelist Ivan Turgenev said that every prayer can be reduced to the same one: "Please, God, let two and two not equal four."[5]

Although Turgenev may have meant something different, we can interpret his remark to mean that we often pray to escape consequences of our actions that, from any rational point of view, are inevitable: "Please, God, let me not be broke, even though I've gone through my inheritance."

In any case, prayer often seems to spring from confused or ambiguous motives. You feel that you should praise God and thank him for his gifts to you; but all the while you are thinking of the things you will ask for as soon as you have buttered up the Almighty. The petitioner reminds the deity of his greatness, usually adding long epithets of praise that incidentally remind him of past favors done, before getting around to the business at hand. This appears to be an almost universal impulse. Many prayers, including those from the Bible and classical antiquity, take this form.

Our prayers are conflicted and confused because *we* are conflicted and confused. I do not believe that there is anyone alive on this planet in whom the Self that is the Son of God is completely occluded. Nor do I believe that there is anyone who is completely free from the ego. This is the spiritual conflict that each of us faces. It is universal. As a result, you can describe this conflict—and it has been described—in terms of innumerable paths besides *A Course in Miracles.*

The most concise summary of the Course's view of prayer appears not in the Course itself but in a small treatise that is said to have been dictated by the same Voice: *The Song of Prayer.* (It is incorporated into the third edition of the Course published by the Foundation for Inner Peace. It appears at the end and is paginated separately. Quotations will be marked "S.")

The Song of Prayer says the lowest level of prayer is "asking-out-of-need." It is asking for God's help to deal with the problems that continually surface in life.

> At these levels prayer is merely wanting, out of a sense of security and lack.
>
> These forms of prayer, or asking-out-of-need, always involve feelings of weakness and inadequacy, and could never be made by a Son of God who knows Who he is. No one, then, who is sure of his Identity could pray in these forms. Yet it is also true that no one who is uncertain of his Identity can avoid praying in this way. And prayer is as continual as life. Everyone prays without ceasing. Ask and you have received, for you have already established what it is you want. (S, 3)

Prayer of this kind arises out of problems. The question of problems is subtle and mysterious. Certainly some seem to be greater than others. As the adage goes, "A man may have many problems. A man who has no bread has only one." Nevertheless, most people have their own mental lists of problems. Say this list is twenty items long, ranging from the pressing (money, relationships, health) to the less pressing (the garage needs to be cleaned out) to ones that are tiny or insignificant: a man may worry about going bald, or a woman frets about some crow's feet around her eyes. Then of course there are world problems: war, poverty, the environment, corruption in high places. All of these occupy our minds so fully that if you look back on the happiest times of your life, you may realize that they were only brief intervals—maybe an afternoon—in which you felt you had no major problems or were able to set them aside.

This list never ends; the items are never fully checked off. You deal with the first, but the next one rises up to take its place. There are people who, to all appearances, have no serious problems: they and their families are in good health, they have plenty of money, they enjoy high social esteem. Of course they are no happier than anyone else and may be less so. The rich often seem to be infuriated by tiny things—a perceived insult, a minor technical failure, the unavailability of some small item. There are people whose enjoyment of a sumptuous meal has been spoiled by a sidelong glance from a waiter.

"The world is the totality of facts, not of things," said Wittgenstein.[6] We could say instead that the world is the totality of problems. The Course appears to agree. The ego's plan is to keep problems appearing to come up so that "no one could solve all the problems all the world appears to hold. . . . All this complexity is but a desperate attempt not to recognize the problem, and therefore not to let it be resolved" (W, 141).

In reality, the Course says, there is only one problem, and that is separation, or imagined separation, from God. But this problem has already been solved. Therefore in reality you have no problems. "One problem, one solution. Salvation is accomplished. . . . Your only problem has been solved!" (W, 143).

Admittedly, this fact is hard to remember in daily life, but there is an intermediate step: "You have been told to ask the Holy Spirit for the answer to any specific problem, and you will receive a specific answer if such is your need. . . . There are decisions to be made here, and they need to be made whether they be illusions or not" (S, 1–2).

All this needs to be spelled out in practical terms. I will discuss it from my own experience. Most problems are in fact solvable, even the largest ones. The chief obstacle to understanding this is the mess of fear, guilt, and resentment that coats our minds. If we could set this aside, we would see the problem, and we would see a solution. It may drop into your lap out of the blue, but this is relatively rare. Usually a certain amount of clear sight will show you how to solve the problem, even if only step-by-step. You will usually discover that, on the mundane level, *you* are the solution to your problems.

Of course this is all based on the premise that you have turned your problem over to God, or the Holy Spirit, and asked for a solution. It is not always wise to ask for a specific solution. Say you need money. You see a job that, you think, suits you perfectly and apply for it. You pray to get this job.

This could be a mistake. Even at the mundane level, your problem is really money rather than failing to have this particular job. In my experience, it is generally wiser to ask for a solution to your financial problems (or, in the Course's language, ask to recognize that your financial problems have been solved) rather than asking for this job, even if it seems to be the perfect or indeed only way out. Otherwise it could happen that your prayer will be granted, but the job will turn out to be a disaster. Or you pray for a love relationship with a particular person, and you get it, but it too turns out to be disastrous. I have made these mistakes myself more than once. As a result, I find that it works better to pray for the answer to the real underlying problem as you see it (lack of money, lack of love) rather than for one outcome, even if you believe it is the only outcome that will work. And, of course, turn over the matter to the Holy Spirit.

As for praying for your enemies, the Course material is again consistent and logical. To pray for your enemy is, on some level, to acknowledge that this person is ultimately not your enemy, but, like you, part of the Son of God. "An enemy is the symbol of an imprisoned Christ. . . . The poisonous thought that he *is* your enemy, your evil counterpart, your nemesis, must be relinquished before *you* can be released from guilt" (S, 4, 5; emphasis in the original). Enmity is of the ego and exists only on the level of the ego. "The earlier forms of prayer, at the bottom of the ladder, will not be free from envy and malice. They call for vengeance, not for love. . . . Only those who are in hell can ask for hell. Those who have been forgiven, and who accepted their forgiveness, could never make a prayer like that" (S, 5).

Prayer on a slightly higher level occurs when "a vague and usually unstable sense of identification [with the Son of God] has generally been reached, but tends to be blurred by a deep-rooted sense of sin" (S, 3). In this case, you pray for things of this world, but you may also pray for honesty or gratitude or forgiveness. This too is only intermediate. At the highest level, prayer is simply communion:

Prayer is the greatest gift with which God blessed His Son at his creation. It was then what it is to become; the single voice Creator and creation shared; the song the Son sings to the Father, Who returns the thanks it offers Him unto the Son. Endless the harmony, and endless, too, the joyous concord of the Love They give forever to Each Other. (S, 1)

The Song of Prayer speaks of the steps above as "the ladder of prayer"(S, 3), reminding me of a famous Christian text on this subject: *The Ladder of Ascent,* by the seventh-century monk John Climacus. (The name *Climacus* is derived from the Greek *klîmax,* "ladder.") Although its theology cannot be assimilated completely with that of the Course, the end is similar:

Ascend, brothers, ascend eagerly, and be resolved in your hearts to ascend and hear him who says: Come and let us go up to the mountain of the Lord, and to the house of our God, who makes our feet like hind's feet, and sets us upon high places, that we might be victors with His song.

Run, I beseech you, with him who said: Let us hasten until we attain the unity of faith and of the knowledge of God, unto a perfect man, to the measure of the stature of the fullness of Christ.[7]

John's ladder is very much like the one of the Voice that spoke to Helen Schucman. In either case, it appears to us to be a difficult path. We are constantly besieged by the needs and demands of the world, and we take them so seriously that it seems impossible that we could ever look beyond them. We may at times envy the monks and anchorites, who, having few earthly needs, are able to live by the verse that counsels: "Better is a dry morsel, and quietness therewith, than an house full of sacrifices with strife" (Proverbs 17:1).

We cannot deny the difficulty. Climbing this ladder requires a complete reversal of the world's way of thinking, and the world will, at the very least, fail to support those who want to reverse its thinking. But then if the world's own solutions worked, they would have worked long before now.

SIXTEEN

DISPENSATIONS

It is one of those things you own without quite knowing where it came from.

It was taped up above my aunt's desk, and when she died, it came into my possession with the rest of her belongings. But it is not really the sort of thing she would have bought. In fact I might have bought it myself when I was eleven or twelve and was immersed in such things.

But it is a fine old engraving, some three feet wide and one foot high. It is carefully printed in full color, and is hand-colored in places. The design probably goes back to the late nineteenth century. After I took it from my aunt's house, I had it framed, and it now hangs in my office. It is entitled "A Chart on the Course of Time from Eternity to Eternity," and it chronicles the past and future history of the world, starting on the left with "Eternity," or more specifically, "The Eternal Father," "The Eternal Son," and "The Eternal Purpose," and ending, at the right with a "New Heaven," "New Earth," and another "Eternity." In the dead center is a large black cross, with a yellow label to the right saying, "The Gift of Eternal Life."

Anyone familiar with theology will have no trouble identifying it. It is a diagram of the dispensationalist view of history expounded by the nineteenth-century English preacher John Nelson Darby,[1] printed by the Loizeaux Brothers of Neptune, New Jersey. An explanation of the chart by A. P. Booth, its creator, links the dispensations to the six days of creation: "Through six dispensations, God works to recover man from the moral ruin in which Adam's fall has brought him."[2] According to this schema, we are now in the fourth dispensation, "The Present Age and Church Period," subdivided into seven stages linked with the seven churches named in Revelation 2–3. This dispensation will end with the Rapture as described in 1 Thessalonians 4:15–17.

Dispensationalism received a boost from C. I. Scofield's *Scofield Reference Bible,* published in 1909. It became very popular, and updates were published in 1917 and 1967. Since then, dispensationalism has inspired bestsellers such as Hal Lindsey's *Late Great Planet Earth* and the Left Behind novels by Tim LaHaye and Jerry B. Jenkins.

Like practically all forms of apocalyptic, the dispensationalist mindset assumes the imminence of the End Times. I myself have difficulty believing in imminent apocalypse; I find it more plausible to accept the Course's view that "just as the separation occurred over millions of years, the Last Judgment will extend over a similarly long period, and perhaps an even longer one" (T, 34). Even so, some elements of the dispensationalist perspective may be useful.

The most influential of all dispensationalist theories was devised by the Sicilian abbot Joachim of Fiore (ca. 1132–1202). Joachim was not a prophet, but, he said, he drew his visions for the future from "a revelation of the fullness of the Apocalypse and of the complete agreement of the Old and New Testaments perceived with clear understanding by the mind's eye."[3] According to him, there were three overlapping *status* ("states") or *tempora* ("times") in history, corresponding to the Father, the Son, and the Holy Spirit: "The first *status* [that of the Father] is reckoned from Adam to Christ, the second [that of the Son] from King Josiah to the present time, the third [that of the Holy Spirit] from Saint Benedict to the consummation of the age."[4]

The Age of the Father was the age of the Old Testament, when the covenant with Israel was in force. The Age of the Son climaxed with the coming of Christ. The Age of the Holy Spirit would be the next and last, when "the mystical consciousness of God found in spiritual insight would be poured out fully and finally upon both Gentiles and converted Jews," as scholar Bernard McGinn describes it.[5]

Although Joachim believed this new age was imminent, he did not set a date for it. After his death, his followers Albert of Stade and Gerardo di Borgo San Donnino pointed toward the year 1260.[6] When 1260 came and went and all things continued as they were, the vogue for Joachim's three ages evaporated. Nevertheless, his impact remains. He laid heavy stress on monasticism: as the quote above shows, he dated the beginning of the Age of the Holy Spirit with Benedict of Nursia, founder of Western monasticism in the sixth century. In his own day, Joachim foresaw the arising of two new monastic orders, one of preachers and one of hermits. It is easy to see foreshadowings of the coming of the Order of Preachers (the Dominicans) and the Franciscans in the thirteenth century. No doubt they were inspired in part by Joachim's predictions.

Today Joachim is chiefly remembered as a curious chapter in the curious history of Western apocalyptic. But the concept of dispensations did not go away. In the eighteenth century, the coming of a new era was heralded by Emanuel Swedenborg. On the basis of his elaborate visions, Swedenborg claimed that the Last Judgment had taken place in 1757. But it obviously did not occur on the physical earth. Instead, he said that it was a kind of housecleaning of the realm of the spirits (in his system, an intermediate space between heaven and hell). For us on earth, it meant that spiritual truths would be unveiled that in the previous era had been stifled under literalism and dogma. Swedenborg related a vision in which he saw a temple over whose entrance was written "*Nunc licet*"—"now it is allowed"—allowed, that is, "to use our intellect to explore the mysteries of faith."[7]

Swedenborg was the first visionary of the New Age, although he did not use this term. It only came into use in 1864, nearly ninety years after his death, when a minister named Warren Felt Evans published a book called *The New Age and Its Messenger*. In it he sketched out Swedenborg's ideas and proclaimed "a New Age of the Church."[8]

In the 150 years since then, a new age has been foreseen by any number of esoteric thinkers, including H. P. Blavatsky, C. G. Jung, and René Guénon. Some, like Blavatsky and Guénon, associated this new age with the end of the Kali Yuga, the age of darkness in Hindu cosmology.[9] Others, like Jung, connected it with the Age of Aquarius—that is, the time when the sun at the vernal equinox rises with the constellation Aquarius rather than Pisces behind it.[10]

Joachim's system resurfaced in a different form in the thought of the Russian esoteric philosopher Boris Mouravieff (1890–1966). Mouravieff, a Russian émigré who settled in Geneva, published a three-volume work entitled *Gnosis: Study and Commentaries on the Esoteric Doctrine of Eastern Orthodoxy* in the early 1960s.[11] Mouravieff's ideas (which are often at variance with Orthodox dogma) are compelling and profound, but they are also intricate. There is only one aspect of his thought that I want to go into here.

Mouravieff does not mention Joachim, but he must have known of him.[12] Like Joachim with his three "times," Mouravieff speaks of three "cycles": of the Father, the Son, and the Holy Spirit. He equates the Cycle of the Father with the Old Testament period, ending with the coming of Christ, and the Cycle of the Son with the period after Christ, and he says that the Cycle of the Holy Spirit is due to arrive in our own time. (Although he does not give specific dates, he no doubt believed this time was the immediate decades after his writing in the 1960s.)

Mouravieff does not portray this coming Cycle of the Holy Spirit as a divinely ordained certainty. He presents it as a possibility only, and he sees it as the collective crossing of a certain spiritual threshold by humanity, which may or may not happen. As Mouravieff puts it, this is the alternative that faces us: "Either to reach the *Accomplishment* or go down in a deluge of fire."[13] The "deluge of fire" alludes to 2 Peter 3:10: "But the day of the Lord will come as a thief in the night; in which the heavens shall pass away with a great noise, and the elements shall melt with a fervent heat, the earth also and the works that are therein shall be burned up."

It is impossible to read Mouravieff's description without thinking of nuclear holocaust, and that must have been what he had in mind: he was, after all, writing at the height of the Cold War, when the world came close at least once to such a fate.

Suppose that humanity does pass this threshold of "Accomplishment" and passes into the era of the Holy Spirit. What then? Mouravieff's descriptions of this new era are elaborate and sometimes fanciful, covering areas from world government to beauty and women's fashions. But the most important characteristic is that "in the new era, the Cycle of the Holy Spirit, all conditions will be arranged so as to help the *exterior* man to come more easily to esoteric work so that he can become the *new man* who is master of himself."[14]

And what is the new man? Mouravieff writes, "Christ's kingdom is opened to man with the second Birth, that of *Individuality*, when he has reached consciousness of his real 'I' and, through that, has come into contact with the Covenant of Love."[15]

Like many esoteric systems, Mouravieff's posits two main psychological centers in the human being. The first is what he calls the "Personality"* and which we can identify with the street-level self. The second, the "real 'I,'" is the true Self. The "new man," the "man with the second Birth, that of *Individuality*," has shifted his center of gravity from the Personality (where it is for the exterior man) to the "real 'I,'" that is, the Self. One who has undergone the second birth has access to the Self, the true I, the Christ within, continually if not continuously. Mouravieff adds that unless humanity is governed by an elite consisting of such new men, the deluge of fire is a likely outcome.

Mouravieff's vision hardly seems outmoded today, even if anxiety about nuclear holocaust has been surpassed by fears about environmental collapse and climate change (perhaps another kind of deluge of

---

*It is important to avoid confusing this Personality with the ego as described by the Course.

fire?). Nevertheless, I want to pick up two aspects of his concept of the Cycle of the Holy Spirit. The first is that this era could begin in our own time; the second, that this passage is not predestined but is in the hands of human determination.

Like Mouravieff, I think that the coming of this age is a possibility rather than a foregone conclusion. As I stressed in *The Essential Nostradamus,* I do not believe in prophecies of any kind, and this must mean that I am no prophet myself. I am about to sketch out possibilities, which may not come true. Most likely the human race will survive and muddle through regardless. Cataclysms may and will happen, but cataclysms have always happened, and humanity, while supplementing these misfortunes with wars and other acts of collective madness, shuffles along nonetheless.

Unfortunately, shuffling along is no longer enough. Obscurely we sense this. It is in many ways the result of the technological revolution. Before then, the human race was at the mercy of nature. Mortality rates were high, disease was rampant, and agricultural production was never so abundant that it could entirely forestall the chance of famine.

Today the relation between humanity and nature has flipped: now, it would appear, nature is at the mercy of humanity. This is such a radical upheaval that we have not absorbed the shock. Indeed we could trace the environmental crisis to this reversal and to the failure of human thinking to adapt to it. (In fairness to human thinking, this change is so great that it would have to take generations to come to terms with it.)

In any event, we have the means to put an end to practically all the great problems of human life. It would be easy enough to clean up the environment and provide a minimally decent living to the entire human race if the will were there. That leads to the crux of the situation. Is the human race able to change its course to the point where the all-too-human attributes of greed, aggression, and ignorance no longer stand in our way?

There is a vague but widespread belief that humanity is awakening and that a new period of enlightenment is about to dawn (if we manage to avoid any number of disasters in the meantime). At this point no one can say whether this is really happening. But I think it is safe to say, if not that the human race is waking up, at least that it is trying to wake up—probably for the first time.

Let me go further into the three ages of Joachim and Mouravieff in relation to the history of religion. To begin with, there is an impassible gulf between human memory as preserved in written form and memories preserved orally. The latter are not necessarily less true—human collective memory over the long term has proved more accurate than many have believed—but, to our minds at least, they are less credible, and they are usually less precise.

The chasm that separates these two phases lies around 3000 BC. This era marks the beginning of the dynastic age in Egypt and the cuneiform texts of Sumer. Before this, the picture is much less clear. Incidentally, traditional views of historical cycles also begin at this time. The Maya, for reasons that are impossible to discover, began the present era in 3114 BC. Hindu civilization tells us that the present age of the Kali Yuga began with the death of Krishna, avatar of Vishnu, in 3012 BC. The traditional Jewish date for the foundation of the world is 3761 BC. These dates do not coincide exactly, but they all point to a widespread view even in traditional cultures that there is a break, a gap, between the period before approximately 3000 BC and the age we are now in.[16]

So the first age about which we can say anything substantial starts around 3000 BC. As I pointed out, the religion of this era was centered on animal sacrifice. But as concepts of God became more universal, it became harder to believe that the divine could take any interest in the blood of lambs and bullocks, and people began to put less trust in animal sacrifice. This started during the Axial Age, famously described by Karl Jaspers as the period between the eighth and the third centuries BC. "In this age," Jaspers writes, "were born the fundamental categories within which we still think today, and the beginnings of the world religions, by which human beings still live, were created."[17]

Jaspers's views have been criticized: present-day academics do not have his generation's taste for panoramic generalizations.[18] But something significant does appear to have happened in that period: humanity's spiritual outlook was exalted and transformed by the Hebrew prophets, the Greek philosophers, the Upanishads, and figures ranging from Pythagoras to the Buddha to Lao-tzu and Confucius.

This era started to turn against animal sacrifice. Hosea, one of the first of the Old Testament prophets, writing in the eighth century BC, tells the Israelites on behalf of Yahweh, "For I desired mercy, and not sacrifice; and the knowledge of God more than burnt offerings" (Hosea 6:6).[19] No doubt the biblical authors meant their criticisms rhetorically: they are not criticizing animal sacrifice per se, but the hypocrisy of offering sacrifices in a state of moral baseness.[20] Nevertheless, their comments mark the beginning of a phase, which begins to see moral integrity as the supreme offering. "The sacrifices of God are a broken spirit: a broken and contrite heart, O God, thou wilt not despise" (Psalm 50:17).

In the pagan world, animal sacrifice remained universal, but even here sentiment began to go against it, first among the philosophers. It is often said that Pythagoras, in the Greece of the sixth century BC, practiced vegetarianism and refrained from animal sacrifice, but the evidence is ambiguous. The historian Diogenes Laertius, writing probably in the second century AD, says that Pythagoras taught his followers not to offer animal sacrifice. But Diogenes goes on to say that Pythagoras sacrificed a hecatomb (of 100 oxen) to celebrate the discovery of his famous theorem. In any case, it is true that Pythagoreans centuries later abstained from both animal sacrifice and eating meat.[21] In India at roughly the same time, the Upanishads extolled mystical insight rather than Vedic sacrifice as the summit of religious observation and human perfection.[22]

In the fourth century BC, Plato's *Laws* makes a point like those of the Hebrew prophets: "The wicked man is unclean of soul, whereas the good man is clean; and from him that is defiled no good man, nor god, can ever rightly receive gifts. Therefore all the great labor that impious men spend upon the gods is in vain."[23] Again, moral integrity trumps sacrifice.

A major turning point came in AD 70, when the Romans sacked the Jerusalem Temple. Up to that time, Jewish religion was centered on the Temple and its endless animal sacrifices, but after the Temple was gone, sacrifice was no longer possible, and rabbinic Judaism, picking up the pieces, refocused the Jewish religion onto Torah study and observance.

Early Christian positions are not easy to tease out. It is likely that the Jerusalem church, led by James, the brother of Jesus, continued to assist at Temple offerings until its destruction. Paul believes that Christians should not assist at pagan sacrifices, but he leaves his Corinthian students free to decide whether they should eat meat sacrificed to idols. (If one reads 1 Corinthians 8 and 10 with some dispassion, it seems clear that his chief concern is to keep people from fighting over this issue.) But he argues against circumcision for Gentile believers: "For in Jesus Christ neither circumcision availeth anything, nor uncircumcision" (Galatians 5:6). He is saying that Gentile Christians do not need to observe the Mosaic Law. It would follow that he did not believe that they should offer sacrifices to the God of Israel either.

After the sack of the Temple, the issue was moot. All Jewish sacrificial worship had been centralized there, and now it was gone. Jews themselves could no longer offer animal sacrifices, and from the Christian point of view, pagan sacrifices were made either to nonexistent gods or to inferior ones. (Paul himself seems to veer back and forth about this point.) So Christians had no reason or opportunity to perform animal sacrifice.

At the same time, as we saw in chapter 11, Christianity was beginning to formulate its theology. It came to see Christ's death as a sacrifice that united God and man unequivocally and for all time, so other sacrifices were no longer needed. This is one of the main points of the Epistle to the Hebrews. Christian sacrifice, in the form of the

Eucharist, took the symbolic form of the offering of bread and wine. After Christianity became the official religion of the Roman Empire at the end of the fourth century, the pagan temples were closed, and their sacrifices ceased.

So far, we are seeing three major phases in the religious development of humanity (with huge overlaps):

1. Prehistory, before 3000 BC, with no written records. Here it is possible to say almost anything or nothing: the mute artifacts serve as Rorschach blots upon which theorists can project whatever they like. For our purposes it is best to say nothing.

2. The first phase of history, from 3000 BC to AD 500, the first epoch about which we can say anything concrete: religion focused on animal sacrifice. Let us correlate this to the Age of the Father, the God worshiped by the Hebrews in the first millennium BC.

3. The age of the great world religions. This period started with the beginning of the Axial Age around 700 BC. Animal sacrifice was supplanted by adherence to ethical precepts and to doctrine expounded in sacred texts. These religions for the most part traced their origins to a single founding figure—the Buddha, Christ, Muhammad—and, with rare exceptions, proclaimed themselves as the sole and exclusive access points to the realm of the divine. (If the founders did not make such claims, their followers did so on their behalf.) In a Western context, we could associate this period with the Age of the Son, because it is the period during which Christ has been worshiped. As Jaspers stressed, it is still with us today.

Today the Age of the Son seems to be fading. In the West, this process began with the Reformation. In one respect it revitalized Christianity, not only by creating new theologies but by forcing the ossified Catholic Church to reinvent itself. But this revitalization was temporary and incomplete. The Reformation led to the horrific wars of religions in the sixteenth and seventeenth centuries, culminating in the Thirty Years' War. By the time it ended in 1648, educated Europe was growing sick of its religions, both Catholic and Protestant. Perhaps the Enlightenment a century later was the result of this exasperation as much as or more than it was of scientific breakthroughs.

Now, in the early twenty-first century, Christianity no longer provides us with certainties. Its cosmogony bear little resemblance to those of science (in which we place much more trust), and the Deity as they picture him is connected with the universe hardly at all. Also, its hypocrisies and moral contradictions, denied for so long, are now shoved in its face.

The bankruptcy of Western religion stems in part from an imperfect universalism. The old age of animal sacrifice was not universalistic: people could barely conceive of the world beyond their localities. The world religions represented an advance: arising from a wider worldview, they asserted their universal validity. But to assert your own universal validity is to deny everyone else's: hence the start of religious warfare. Some religions have tried to subsume their predecessors into a grander integration of faiths: this appears to have been the case with Baha'i, Sikhism, and no doubt early Islam. But in the end they too have had to take their place in the lengthening line of sects.

It has been said that one sign of the passing of an age is that the old gods are mocked.

Certainly this was true in classical antiquity. We can see it in the treatment of the gods in Greek Old Comedy and the satyr plays of the fifth century BC; in the satires of Lucian in the second century AD; and often in between, for example with the satire known as the *Apolocyntosis of Claudius* in the first century AD, attributed to Seneca the Younger. *Apolocyntosis,* meaning "pumpkinification" (as translated by Robert Graves), is a made-up word spoofing *apotheosis*—mocking the Roman Senate's practice of decreeing divine honors for its deceased emperors, which Seneca believed Claudius did not deserve. Seneca aims plenty of jabs at the gods themselves: Janus, with his two faces, is described as "a brilliant fellow, with eyes on the back of his head."[24]

We see the same thing in the present. We can trace modern sarcasm toward religion at least as far back as Voltaire, but in popular culture it began in the mid-twentieth century, first with pokes at religious hypocrisy by comedian Lenny Bruce ("Did you hear that General Motors is holding a raffle? They're giving away a 1958 Catholic church") and in the TV program *Rowan and Martin's Laugh-In*. The rock opera *Jesus Christ Superstar* came out in 1970; it could hardly have been staged twenty, even ten, years earlier. Since then we have had films such as Monty Python's *Life of Brian* and Kevin Smith's *Dogma,* in which singer Alanis Morrisette plays the Supreme Being. In the 1990s, singer Joan Osborne wondered if God was "just a slob like one of us." In the visual arts, the most famous example is *Piss Christ,* the 1987 image by Andres Serrano, which shows a crucifix submerged in a glass tank containing the artist's urine. A person coming to our era from a century ago would be incredulous to see such things, but we shrug them off, and even laugh ourselves. The old gods are mocked.

This leads us to the third age, the Age of the Holy Spirit. Jaspers obscurely foresaw such a transition: "Perhaps mankind will pass through . . . to a new axial age, still remote, invisible, and inconceivable, an axial age of authentic human upsurge."[25]

SEVENTEEN

THE AGE OF
THE HOLY SPIRIT

In 1909, the Belgian scholar Franz Cumont wrote about the Roman
world of the early fourth century AD:

A hundred different currents were pulling jolted and recalcitrant
minds in all directions; a hundred opposed teachings were appealing to the human conscience. Imagine that, in modern Europe,
we saw the faithful abandon Christian churches to worship Allah
or Brahma, follow the precepts of Confucius or Buddha, or adopt
the maxims of Shinto. Picture a great confusion of all the races of
the world, where Arab mullahs, Chinese scholars, Japanese bonzes,
Tibetan lamas, and Hindu pundits were preaching, all at the same
time, fatalism and predestination; the cult of ancestors; veneration
of the divine sovereign; or pessimism and deliverance through anni-
hilation. In our cities, these priests would erect temples in exotic
architectures to celebrate their various rites. This dream, which will
perhaps become reality in the future, offers us a reasonably accurate
image of the religious chaos in which the ancient world was floun-
dering before Constantine.[1]

Cumont was right to suppose that the same thing might happen in the modern West, because it did. The world of Western religion today is very much the farrago he describes.

When Cumont mentions Constantine, he is talking about the Roman emperor Constantine's Edict of Milan, decreeing toleration of Christianity in 313 and leading to its eventual triumph as the official religion of the Roman Empire.

To the citizens of Constantine's realm, the empire *was* the world; even the learned had only a dim idea of what went on outside the bounds of the imperium. And one man was the ruler of this world. He could decree sweeping reversals of laws and customs, and they would be enforced.

There is (fortunately) no such world ruler today. So, like all analogies, this one cannot be pressed too far. But it does lead us to ask: is the world looking for a new religious vision that will surpass those of the world religions just as the latter surpassed the old religion of animal sacrifice? I believe it is. Very likely Mouravieff and the other visionaries of the New Age were pointing to this possibility.

We might ask what this new synthesis might be like. In the first place, *it may not look like a religion in our sense of the word*. The priests of the Age of the Father, whose job centered on sacrifice, would probably not have recognized their successors as religions: remember that one of the charges the pagan Romans leveled against the Christians was atheism.[2] In the second place, it will almost certainly *not* be a mere synthesis of the current religions, as is sometimes imagined. It will go as far past them as the Age of the Son went past the Age of the Father. (Many of my comments below are couched in terms of present-day religion, but that is only to say that I was born and raised in the context of this religion and can see only the tiniest distance beyond it.) Prefaced by these caveats, these would appear to be some of the chief features of this coming religion:

An internalization of the divine. The Theosophist G. R. S. Mead, writing in 1906, characterized this perspective as "Gnosis": "I doubt that the Gnosis of the new age will be new. Certainly it can be set forth in new forms, for the forms can be infinite. . . . Indeed, if I believe rightly, the very essence of the Gnosis is the faith that man can transcend the limits of the duality that makes him man, and become a consciously divine being. The problem he has to solve is the problem of his day, the transcending of his present limitations."[3] In 1954, Jung, who was influenced by Mead, wrote that in the new age "man will be essentially God and God man."[4]

In one sense, this is nothing new: for two thousand years, Christianity has been proclaiming the coming of the God-man. But here I think it will mean something different. As the Course says, we will discover that each of us is the Son of God: Jesus Christ differed only in discovering that truth first. Thus the Self dwelling within will be recognized, not as God in the transcendent sense, but as the point of contact between the human individual and God. In short, worship of the external God without will be replaced (or complemented) by the knowledge of the presence of the God within.

Many of the things described below, in one way or another, reflect and amplify this central feature.

Inner experience as the center of religion. Up to now, personal observance in Christianity has mostly taken the form of petitionary prayer. But the swell of interest in meditation suggests that the faith of the coming age will have more to do with inner silence and concentration than with verbal utterances—and with opening oneself up to direct experience of the divine.

Scripture used for advice and inspiration, not as a source of dogma. The sacred scriptures of the world offer tremendous resources and insights, but these are obscured once the focus is laid upon the letter of law and upon taking everything in scripture as explicit commands. (Notice how this process took place in regard to the epistles of Paul, who said he was not interested in laying down new sets of rules.)

A transformed clergy. In the introduction, I brought up many of the issues that are most important here. In the first place, the clergy are trained in theology and biblical hermeneutics—but somehow they never end up applying what they have learned, permitting their congregations to hang on to outmoded and simplistic beliefs. This is largely because the clergy have no clear idea of what to replace these with, or, in many cases, of what to tell their congregations at all.

Few of the laity care much about theological intricacies. But laypeople *are* interested in spiritual experience (if only at times of crisis or transition in their lives), and the clergy have not been trained to guide them through such experiences. Consequently, if the clergy are to remain useful, they will both have to give some instruction about people's individual experiences and to show how such spiritual experience can be cultivated. They will have to have this knowledge themselves—or, at the very least, be able to consult those who do. Alan Watts describes the situation in a 1947 letter:

All great religions, although their inner essence is esoteric and inevitably the province of the few, have to make some provision for the world at large. This involves a hardening and conventionalizing process which renders all popular religion . . . superficial—an imperfection which is simply inevitable, but which we must no more resent or deplore that the fact that children of six cannot be taught the calculus. When certain persons insist that this exoteric religion is the whole truth, and that there is no other way of salvation, we have fanaticism, which is almost inevitable.

Little real harm is done by this process, so long as a nucleus of persons maintains the interior religion, which is substantially the same in all places and periods. I see no particular point in changing the external form of the religion of the West. . . . Indeed I think it would do a great deal of harm. My concern is that the inner religion should flourish within official Christianity so that the Church will be able to instruct and guide the increasing, but still relatively small, number of persons who are ready to profit by it. Furthermore, where such a nucleus does not exist, there is a general decline of the religious and social order. But the constructive influence of such a nucleus is out of all proportions to its numbers. I do not think that the interior religion should be given a name or form so as to be externally recognizable, for it will thus be rushed into the position of a sect and involved in argumentation, propaganda, and controversy, the terms and methods of which are radically inapplicable to mystical knowledge.[5]

Two tiers, then: exterior religion, which is for the many and which can provide them with advice and consolation when they need it; and esoteric religion, consisting of those who have enough inner experience to provide some guidance to others—even to ordinary clergy, who may not have much of this experience themselves. As Watts says, if these tiers are institutionalized, they will lead to nothing but more priestcraft.

This is a serious issue that Western civilization has not yet solved (at least in recent times). Watts's verdict about it may be gauged from his life. When he wrote the words above, he was an Episcopal priest: three years later he laid his vocation aside. The overall situation does not appear to have changed significantly in the seventy years since he was writing.

A more flexible use of ritual. It is naive to think that ritual is unnecessary or dispensable. In certain contexts, it may become more important than ever (something we see in the Wiccan and Neopagan movements). But it will be based more on certain fundamental principles that can be used flexibly than on forms that have been followed rigidly and mechanically.

The restoration of beauty to religion. In the Middle Ages and in many traditional cultures today, people have lived in squalor and misery, but they could always go to the church or the temple and submerge themselves in beauty and the life of the spirit at the same time. This is hardly possible today, especially in the United States. American culture is indifferent or hostile to beauty in any but the shallowest and most commercial forms, and religious culture is no exception. The typical American church looks like a veterans' hall with a large cross hanging at the back. Author Edward Robinson observes that today there is "indeed an almost complete separation between the world of religion and the world of the contemporary arts."[6]

This relentless onset of featurelessness, indeed ugliness, has had consequences: it must have something to do with the current plague of mental disorders. A religion—or, if you prefer, a spirituality—that provides this missing element could do much to heal the human soul.

Humanistic ethics. The Deity will not necessarily be viewed as remote and indifferent to human behavior, but people will acknowledge that it is not God that they are hurting when they do wrong, it is themselves and one another. The basic ethical tenets, which are universal—exemplified in the Sermon on the Mount and the Eightfold Noble Path of the Buddha—will remain as they are. Time has proved their value: newer models of morality—like utilitarian philosophy—affirm much the same ethical rules without invoking God. At the same time, moral injunctions that reflect the thinking of earlier ages and are of no present use (even if they are embodied in scripture) will be permitted to fade away. (To take one more or less uncontroversial example, ancient religious precepts often involve rites of physical purification. These are less useful today in the light of modern hygiene and sanitation, even if ritual purification still has value.)

A recognition that the many forms of religious thought and representation are undergirded by certain universal truths. It will be easier to see the same ideas and principles embodied in the gods of all faiths, even if they cannot be simplistically reduced to a single essentialist denominator.

A more rigorous theology. This feature would seem to run counter to many of the ones that I have already set out. But if religious dogmatism continues to weaken, it will be necessary to reformulate theology in an intellectually convincing way. That is what I have tried to do with Christian theology in this book.

Is theology necessary? Some have tried to dispense with it, but this is not so easy. It creates an ideological vacuum that will have to be filled. Some will give up and take refuge in old doctrines and rituals. Others will be—and have been—drawn to the wildest and most dangerous political and social theories. As was once said, "Those who do not believe in God will not believe in nothing. They will believe in anything." An epitaph for the twentieth century.

Resilient worldviews. Take the human body as an analogy. A resilient body is strong, flexible, and able to shake off shocks with ease. An ailing body is rigid and hypersensitive to irritation. Similarly, a resilient worldview can easily adjust and respond to discomfitures such as opposing ideas. It does not seek out disruption, but can handle it easily when it occurs. I think that the coming age will be marked, not so much by a single, overarching worldview (as was the case with Christian civilization), but by a number of worldviews, ranging from the deeply religious to the totally secular, that can live with one another and accept that no single one is likely to give a complete picture of the truth.

A recognition of the limits of science. I do not think that the Age of the Holy Spirit will be subservient to science as the Age of the Son has been in its waning centuries.

In the first place, as I suggested earlier, science is a method, not a doctrine. It is a particular approach to solving particular, and quite limited, questions. Its findings can never be taken as dogma. As Karl Popper said, these findings always remain subject to future falsification: "The game of science is, in principle, without end. He who decides one day that scientific statements do not call for any further test, and that they can be regarded as finally verified, retires from the game."[7]

In the second place, science is facing its own epistemological problems, which are likely to grow more acute. These are not problems with the scientific method as such, but rather with current scientific findings that are dishonestly held up as ultimate truths. Earlier I mentioned what I might call the neurological loop: science has shown that our cognition—at least our ordinary cognition—is heavily circumscribed by our perceptual apparatus. If so, why should we suppose that the data given by this apparatus give us any complete picture of the universe?

Another problem is that science—particularly physics—is producing conclusions that are more and more remote from our daily experience and in many ways contradict it. This may be the sign of a late paradigm (in the terminology of Thomas S. Kuhn) that is about to be overturned, just as the increasing complexity of epicycles in the late versions of the Ptolemaic theory showed the need for the Copernican paradigm. Be that as it may, "science" has often come to refer to a naive materialism that is supposedly vindicated by scientific findings, a view that I call *scientism*. This pseudoreligion insists that there is nothing more than matter and that this is matter as commonly understood. But scientism cannot have it both ways. It cannot *both* place its faith in scientific findings *and* try to pretend that these findings validate the ordinary view of reality.

As a result, it is hard to predict how this nascent faith will jibe with science. But that is not because of a rise of irrationalism (or it need not be), but because science needs to start answering certain crucial questions that it has long been permitted to beg.

Furthermore, it seems that science is beginning to rethink its own premises. In my book *The Dice Game of Shiva: How Consciousness Creates the Universe,* I argued for the primacy of consciousness in reality as we know it. Now, ten years after the book was published, the idea is becoming increasingly reputable. On the Quartz website, writer Olivia Goldhill observes:

Consciousness permeates reality. Rather than being just a unique feature of human subjective experience, it's the foundation of the universe, present in every particle and all physical matter.

This sounds like easily-dismissible bunkum, but as traditional attempts to explain consciousness continue to fail, the "panpsychist" view is increasingly being taken seriously by credible philosophers, neuroscientists, and physicists, including figures such as neuroscientist Christof Koch and physicist Roger Penrose.[8]

We should be cautious, then, in speculating about the future relations between science and religion when both could soon turn out to be quite different from what they are now.

It is an open question too what relation this new faith will have toward the political and social order. As Lao-tzu understood, the presence of laws is evidence of a decay of morals; the presence of morals is evidence of a separation from inner truth.[9]

Of course we need government—what Hobbes called the "Sovereign"—to keep the beasts within us in check. Or do we? The Chinese novelist Yu Hua writes about the mood in the Chinese capital during the Tienanmen uprising:

> Beijing in the spring of 1989 was anarchist heaven. The police suddenly disappeared from the streets, and students and locals took on police duties in their place. It was a Beijing we are unlikely to see again. A common purpose and shared aspirations put a police-free city in perfect order. As you walked down the street you felt a warm, friendly atmosphere all around you. You could take the subway or a bus for free, and everyone was smiling at one another, barriers down. We no longer witnessed arguments in the street. Hard-nosed street vendors were now handing out free refreshments to the protesters. Retirees would withdraw cash from their meager bank savings and make donations to the hunger strikers in the square. Even pickpockets issued a declaration in the name of the Thieves' Association: as a show of support for the students, they were calling a moratorium on all forms of theft. Beijing then was a city where, you could say, "all men are brothers."[10]

The optimist in me sees this as a presage of times to come.

In human life as in Newtonian physics, each reaction produces an equal and opposite reaction. We see this fact embodied in the term *reactionary*. Thus any given trend is unlikely to advance in a steady, unimpeded, linear way. There will be waves and counterwaves, even if the long-term movement is going in a single direction. The most obvious type of religious reaction is fundamentalism. It will probably not vanish any time soon.

As I have said above, I am describing possibilities rather than making predictions. But I think there is some hope that many of these features, which after all are already present, will take root and grow over the next century.

If I am talking about an Age of the Holy Spirit, I have to deal with the biggest piece of evidence on its behalf in present times: Pentecostal and charismatic Christianity, which are inspired by an outpouring of the Holy Spirit. I could hardly ignore it in any case: one frequently cited statistic says that there are 500 million Pentecostals worldwide (a quarter of all Christians), with some 80 million in the United States. The movement is estimated to be increasing at a rate of 13 million people a year, with growth particularly strong in regions as far-flung as Latin America, Africa, and Southeast Asia.[11]

The roots of the American Pentecostal movement go back to Holiness revivals held after the Civil War.[12] But its present-day origin has usually been traced to an "infilling of spirit" that one William J. Seymour claimed to have during a revival at a private home in Los Angeles in 1906. Several days later he had a similar experience, and others joined in. News of the event spread fast. An article in the *Los Angeles Times* from April 18, 1906 (coincidentally, the same day as the great San Francisco earthquake), described the movement in an article headlined "A Weird Babel of Tongues: New Sect of Fanatics Is Breaking Loose." Believers rented an abandoned church on Los Angeles's Azusa Street, forming the first Pentecostal congregation. Donald Miller of the University of Southern California describes how the movement was spread by missionaries who "were able to communicate with people in plain language, and they followed the practice of Jesus' disciples by casting out demons, healing the sick and experientially demonstrating the truth of the Christian gospel."[13]

Miller's comments explain the movement's popularity. Its beliefs are simple and fundamentalist: the divinity of Christ, the vicarious atonement, the immanence of the Second Coming. These doctrines, hard for an intellectual to swallow, appeal to many people because they are set out simply and plainly. As such, they are easy to grasp (provided one does not attempt to sort through their contradictions) and far from the complicated and equivocal theology of mainstream Protestantism. Furthermore, Pentecostal manifestations of the spirit—speaking in tongues, healing, casting out demons—resemble what Christ and his disciples did, according to the New Testament.

Is the Holy Spirit really present in these gatherings? It is hard to draw a line between the ecstasy of a Pentecostal congregation and the enthusiasm of a rock concert or of a stadium full of sports fans, if only because the collective psychology of humanity—particularly of crowds and mobs—is poorly understood. But the astonishing spread of Pentecostal movements in little over a hundred years testifies on behalf of some genuine spiritual outpouring.

American Pentecostalism parallels the New Thought movement. New Thought, which arose in the mid-nineteenth century, said that mind was the primary force in healing: Christian Science is its most famous example. The Course resembles New Thought in insisting that healing is of the mind alone, although the Course also says that the student should not reject standard medical procedure if doing so would cause fear. "Physical medications are forms of 'spells,' but if you are afraid to use your mind to heal, do not do so. The very fact that you are afraid makes you vulnerable to miscreation. . . . Under these conditions, it is safer for you to rely temporarily on physical healing services" (T, 25).

In the twentieth century, New Thought turned more and more toward prosperity. Its chief slogan is summed up in the 1938 best seller by Napoleon Hill—*Think and Grow Rich.*

Pentecostalism too has taken up the prosperity gospel—the belief that God not only wants to save your soul, but wants you to become rich. Much like Weber's Protestant ethic, it regards wealth as a sign of divine favor. Mitch Horowitz, author of *One Simple Idea: How Positive Thinking Reshaped Modern Life,* contends that Oral Roberts was the key figure in this transition. While earlier Pentecostalism promoted healing through spirit, "the Oklahoma-based minister and university founder began emphasizing prosperity over healing. Hence, Pentecostalism traveled the same trajectory as New Thought, shifting its focus from healing to prosperity."[14]

According to the prosperity gospel, wealth—your share of the limitless abundance of the universe—is your birthright. Joe Vitale, a promoter of this approach, says:

> Your job is to declare what you want from the catalogue of the Universe. If cash is one of them, say what you would like to have. "I would like to have twenty-five thousand dollars, unexpected income, in the next thirty days," or whatever it happens to be.[15]

Of course this sounds crass, but then sometimes you do need a certain amount of money in a certain amount of time (taxes, medical bills). In that case you will probably pray for it whether somebody else thinks you should or not.

In any event, some say the Course teaches the prosperity gospel. In their book *Prayer: A History,* Philip and Carol Zaleski lump it in with teachings of this kind, claiming: "Prayer for good things such as health, happiness, prosperity, and love is their stock-in-trade."[16]

But the Course does *not* tout a prosperity gospel. According to the Course, such things are worthless because the world is worthless:

> You really think that you would starve unless you have stacks of green paper strips and piles of metal discs. You really think a small round pellet or some fluid pushed through your veins through a sharpened needle will ward off disease and death. . . . It is insanity that thinks these things. (W, 134)

The Course teaches that the Holy Spirit will provide for your needs, but not because the universe will deliver your order like a fast-food clerk. When it speaks of miracles, it is not talking about Rolls-Royces materializing in your driveway. Those who think the Course teaches the prosperity gospel have not read it carefully.

In any case, the Pentecostal surge ties in to what I said at the start of this book. In the first place, there is a terrible thirst for spiritual experience; it is a fundamental human need and, like all such needs, will find ways of fulfilling itself. In the second place, this experience is usually devoid of theological content. Jesus may appear to a man and tell him to clean up his life, but he will probably not go into detail about what the man should believe.

Pentecostalism has a number of the features I have sketched out for a religion of the coming age. With its outpourings of the Holy Spirit, the movement does point toward an internalization of the divine. It sees inner experience as the center of religion. Ritual too is looser and more ad hoc.

Other features are absent. Pentecostal ethics are rooted in the Bible as narrowly understood. The charismatic clergy are often more domineering than their conventional counterparts. Beauty is no more prized than it is in the rest of the bleak landscape of American mass culture. There is no universalism: Jesus and only Jesus is the way. For many people, this fundamentalism, rigid and exclusive for all its surface warmth, does not inspire but arouses suspicion.

And yet the need for theology remains real and urgent. One way or another it will come. But whose?

I have framed the discussion in the two chapters above in terms of dispensationalism—the belief that there are certain fairly clearly delineated periods in human history, each with its own characteristics. We seem to be witnessing another turning of the age. But I do not believe that this will lead in any immediate way to a millennial utopia, or to the Atonement. As foreseen by *A Course in Miracles,* the Atonement will probably take place over a much longer, indeed colossal, time frame. This next step, however, could take us some distance further.

EIGHTEEN

SUMMA THEOLOGIAE

In the previous chapter, I set out some possible features of a coming religious vision, I have yet to discuss the last and most important: a confrontation with dogmatism.

I say *dogmatism* rather than *dogmas* because the problem is not with any specific dogma, but with the habit of the human mind to take a set of beliefs and turn it into a vicious absolute, a Moloch demanding human sacrifice. I have also written *confrontation* rather than *victory* because it does not seem certain that this habit will be overcome. So far we have simply upgraded dogmas, version 2.0 replacing 1.0 and so on: neo-Darwinism supplants Genesis.

Author and rabbi Rami Shapiro offers one answer to this problem—holy rascality:

> Using humor, play, and fearless joy, holy rascals free people from idolatry and open them to the creative art of meaning making at the heart of human religiosity. In so doing we free brand-name religions from the madness that robs them of creativity and meaning as well.[1]

It is misguided to mock the old gods. The gods are not the issue. What we must do is mock the dogmatic frame of mind that turns gods into idols. Similarly with political, economic, and sociological systems, however beguiling.

Of course the theology I have outlined here could, like its predecessors, turn into another set of manacles for the mind. To a degree, this has already happened, with various groups championing their own interpretations as well as their own favorite versions of the Course. Having been in circulation only for some forty years, the Course is still new, so these disagreements have usually (though not always) been mild and amicable. For future generations, it may not go so well. I find myself paraphrasing Gurdjieff: sooner or later it all ends in people breaking one another's heads.[2] Although the Atonement is ultimately certain, there may well be steps forward and back in the meantime.

I feel the need to make these points before summarizing the Course's theology. As the Course itself says, "A universal theology is impossible, but a universal experience is not only possible but necessary." It also calls itself "a special form of the universal course. There are many thousands of other forms, all with the same outcome" (M, 77). So we are not striving for a new set of creeds, but for a theological approach that is fresh and consistent and frees the mind instead of imprisoning it. It is best approached with an attitude that is both flexible and rigorously logical; otherwise the religious mistakes of the past two thousand years will simply repeat themselves.

Tara Singh, a teacher of the Course, writes: "Religion is a State of Being and remains innocent and silent. It requires understanding why we compromise. Find out whether you really want a religious life that is a State and not a dogma."[3]

With these caveats, let me set out the doctrines of *A Course in Miracles,* using the familiar categories of systematic theology.

THEOLOGY PROPER

The Nature of God

God, the Father, is one. He is the origin and the creator of all things.

Out of his limitless love, the Father created the Son. The Son possesses all the attributes of the Father except one: the Father created the Son; the Son did not create the Father. This aspect of their relationship is not reciprocal. This is the only difference. Otherwise the Son possesses the full power of the Father, and lives with the Father in an endless relationship of reciprocal love.

CREATION

God's creation is wholly good. There is no evil in it. God the Father does not know of evil: if he did, it would exist, and it does not. But because the world as we know it apparently contains evil, it was not created by God. Rather it was made by the ego.

HAMARTIOLOGY

The Nature of Sin

At some point, the Son had a "tiny, mad idea" that he could be separate from the Father. This "idea" is the *ego*. It is an imagined revolt from God. Because God did not will it, it did not happen in reality. But the Son chose to believe the ego's lies, and this precipitated the *separation,* producing an illusion that we experience as the physical world. The body is the result of this fall. Unlike the Son, the body encounters good and evil in a world in which good and evil appear to be possible.

The body feels no guilt; *we* do, when we identify with it. This sense of guilt leads us to expect retaliation from God for our "sin" of separation, and then in turn to a fear of God.

The "sin" of separation is not real, but the ego thinks it is. When we follow it, we feel guilt for having revolted against God, even, in our own mind, for killing him. This is the root cause of the human feeling of guilt and belief in sin. The separation also produced an apparent split in the Son, by which he deludedly believes that he is divided into separate selves in separate bodies, all in conflict with one another.

PNEUMATOLOGY
The Doctrine of the Spirit

Because God did not will the separation, it did not happen. But the Son believes that it has happened. Therefore there was a need for a reconciling principle. This principle is called the Holy Spirit. Like the Son, the Holy Spirit was created by God and has always existed. But after the separation, there was a need for a "Communication Link" between the Father and the apparently fallen Son. The Holy Spirit fulfilled this role. After the coming of Jesus, he was "called down" to earth in the sense that it was now possible to hear his Voice (M, 89–90; C 6.1.3).

THEODICY
Divine Justice

There is, in essence, no problem of divine justice. God wills nothing but good for all his Sons collectively and individually. Evil is the product of the ego. Because the ego is ultimately unreal, evil is unreal as well. It appears to exist on earth because the separated Sons believe in it and act in ways that reinforce their sense of separation. They will not be punished for this now or in the afterlife, because God does not know of punishment, but this mistake causes incalculable suffering in the physical world insofar as the Son continues to accept it.

SOTERIOLOGY
The Doctrine of Salvation

Salvation in the strict sense is unnecessary, because there is nothing real to be saved *from*. But there was a need for healing and correcting the mind of the Son, and this need produced a plan for "an interlocking chain of forgiveness" called the Atonement (T, 4). Its goal is to enable all the Sons of God to remember that they are one, they never sinned, and they have never been separated from God, no matter what they believe.

But the Son has all the power of the Father, so his miscreations—the ego and the separation—can seem to have enormous force. They have fabricated an apparently real but ultimately fictitious realm of time and space. The Atonement is the return from the separation enacted through time. The miracle is a way of shortening time. It consists of removing the blocks to our awareness of love's presence, and it can have apparently supernatural results. But ultimately the miracle is simply a means of shortening the time length of the Atonement. The *end* of the Atonement is certain, but the Sons of God can choose to accelerate it or delay it by accepting or temporarily refusing their roles in God's plan for salvation.

CHRISTOLOGY

Christ is another name for the perfect Son of God. Therefore each of us is one with the Christ. This has never changed, despite our belief in the separation. If we recognize this truth, we will recognize the *face of Christ* in everyone.

The historical Jesus was an individual who saw this face of Christ in everyone. He was a man who is in essence no different from the rest of us ("Is he the Christ? O yes, along with you," M, 87), except that he was the first to fully accept his part in the Atonement. Thus he was put in charge of the process of the Atonement. In this sense, and in this sense only, he is superior to us. But because he is ahead of us, we can request his help. At the same time we are not to mistake him for God or feel awe toward him in a way that is proper only for the Father.

The passion and resurrection of Jesus Christ happened (in the restricted sense that anything happens in this unreal physical world) more or less as the Gospels describe. But Jesus did not die as an offering to God for our sins, because such an offering would be meaningless to God. It was rather a kind of object lesson. Jesus suffered the most incredible tortures, humiliations, and execution, but he did so only to show us that even the grossest physical harm does not affect the truth of the Son of God. The resurrection demonstrated this fact, although the disciples did not understand it.

MORAL THEOLOGY

The belief in sin is illusory. To hold fast to it is to reinforce attachment to a belief in the physical. Therefore the only proper response to apparent sin in all its forms is to recognize that it is unreal. This is forgiveness in the true sense of the word. The proper response of the Sons of God to one another is love in any and all circumstances. Hatred, anger, fear—no matter how horrific—are all calls for love, and thus the correct response to them in all their forms is love and forgiveness. If we ourselves feel such negative emotions, it is best for us simply to acknowledge them and "choose once again" (T, 666).

THE AFTERLIFE

In the strict sense, there is no afterlife because there is no death. The body ultimately does not exist, and its demise does not constitute a loss of anything real. While we appear to have bodies, they are useful as learning devices—and it is only as learning devices that we should ascribe any degree of reality to them (T, 25). When they have fulfilled their purpose, they will be dropped.

Heaven is ever-present, if we can open our awareness to it: "Heaven is here. There is nowhere else. Heaven is now. There is no other time" (M, 61). Hell is simply the belief in separation, and "hell and oblivion are ideas that you made up" (T, 245).

Nevertheless, some people drop their bodies without having fully learned the necessary lessons. Reincarnation is thus a possibility in the dream—as long as we acknowledge that embodiment in itself has no ultimate reality.

ESCHATOLOGY

The Last Judgment will take place, though on a time scale far beyond what we conceive of as the historical time line. *When* exactly it will happen cannot be predicted, because it is determined by the free will of each Son of God. It can be accelerated, however, by individual Sons of God who see all things through the light of forgiveness. The judgment will be visited upon each individual, and for all of them the verdict will be the same:

Holy are you, eternal, free and whole, at peace forever in the Heart of God. Where is the world, and where is sorrow now? (M, 38; emphasis in the original)

ECCLESIOLOGY

The Course does not say much about the church. A church can be helpful as a gathering place for like-minded people who want to strengthen their aspirations for the Atonement. But if these people see themselves as a group of "elect" who are superior to outsiders, it is not useful and is best discarded. "A church that does not inspire love has a hidden altar that is not serving the purpose for which God intended it" (T, 93).

The Course also says nothing about a clergy. It does speak of "teachers of God":

A teacher of God is anyone who chooses to be one. His qualifications consist solely in this; somehow, somewhere he has made a deliberate choice in which he did not see his interests as apart from someone else's. Once he has done that, his road is established, and his direction is sure. . . . He has become a bringer of salvation. He has become a teacher of God.

They come from all over the world. They come from all religions and from no religion. They are the ones who have answered. The Call is universal. (M, 3)

The Course also says that the teacher of God "cannot claim that title until he has gone through the workbook, since we are learning within the framework of our course" (M, 40). I do not think that the term *title* should be taken too seriously here. The Course is simply distinguishing between those who are still working within the framework of the Workbook and those who have finished with it, for whom "individual need becomes the chief consideration" in spiritual practice (M, 40).

Even if you have completed the Workbook as directed, if you are hanging too much importance upon the title *teacher of God*, it is almost certain that the ego is involved.

MISSIOLOGY

Because the Course does not emphasize the idea of the church, it naturally follows that the Course has little to say about the church's mission. The mission of God's teachers is to advance the Atonement, however they understand it and however they are best equipped to do so, as guided by Jesus and the Holy Spirit. The Course says (speaking in the person of Jesus): "As you share my unwillingness to accept error in yourself and others, you must join the great crusade to correct it" (T, 9). But again it would be unwise, I think, to place much stock in the literal sense of the word *crusade*. *Crusade* is simply another way of describing the Atonement.

REVELATION

Revelation does not mean the same thing in the Course as it does in conventional Christianity. The latter generally sees revelation as the process of God revealing himself in history, first to Abraham and his offspring and finally through Christ. This revelation is entirely historical, and it is historically complete (or at least theologians tend to speak of it that way): the age of revelation, like the age of miracles, has passed.

The difficulties here are immediately apparent. If revelation occurred once in historical time and once only, it is frozen. All situations, all questions have to be referred back to this revelation, although it was given in inconceivably different circumstances and to equally different mentalities. Most of the Christian church is still clinging, often pathetically, to revelation in this sense; the rest realize that this is impossible but have found nothing to take its place.

For the Course, revelation is accessible to everyone: "Revelation unites you directly with God. Revelation is intensely personal and cannot be meaningfully translated. That is why any attempt to describe it in words is impossible. . . . Revelation is literally unspeakable because it is an experience of unspeakable love" (T, 7).

The Course regards itself as a kind of preparation for revelation—that is, a direct experience of God. But some preliminaries are required. "Some of the later steps to this course . . . involve a more direct approach to God Himself. It would be unwise to start on these steps without careful preparation, or awe will be confused with fear, and the experience will be more traumatic than beatific" (T, 16).

This is a summary of the Course's views on the major themes of systematic theology. They can be set out so succinctly and coherently because the Course's theology is clear and consistent. Its conclusions follow simply and naturally from its premises.

In 2002 I published *Inner Christianity: A Guide to the Esoteric Tradition*. I had two motives for writing it, one stated, one unstated. The stated motive was that the esoteric tradition of Christianity had not been described recently in clear and contemporary language; I tried to do so. The second, unstated motive was inspired by the *Corpus Hermeticum,* a body of texts, written in Greek, that probably date to the first through third centuries AD. It was long assumed that these books were a mishmash of Greek, Jewish, and Christian ideas thrown together for reasons that are unknown and hard to divine. But I think these works were of quite another nature. They were not a syncretistic mishmash, but an attempt to restate the esoteric tradition of Egypt and express it in the language of the Greeks before that tradition died out utterly. One of these texts, the *Asclepius,* speaks of this heartbreakingly:

> O Egypt, Egypt, of your reverent deeds only stories will survive, and they will be incredible to your children! Only words cut in stone will survive to tell your faithful works, and the Scythian or Indian or some neighbor barbarian will dwell in Egypt. For divinity goes back to heaven, and all the people will die, deserted, as Egypt will be widowed and deserted by god and human. . . . Whoever survives will be recognized as an Egyptian only by his language; in his actions he will seem a foreigner.[4]

In *Inner Christianity* I tried to make a similar formulation. In this sense it was backward-looking. I attempted to summarize the ideas of esoteric Christianity in a form that, if it lasted, would preserve the tradition's essence.

Today much of what has been called Christianity is tottering. But the theology in this book may provide a new life for the faith and free it from the bizarre belief in an all-loving God who is nonetheless remorselessly vindictive.

It would be foolish to expect this theology to transform today's centers of religious learning or the people in charge of them; most of them will probably either ignore this book or dismiss it with a glance. But I am not writing for them. I have in mind a generation or two ahead of now, when the current leadership has gone to its reward and a new set of minds is tackling these issues. They may find something here.

In any case, it is possible to work with the Course without any ties to conventional religion; most of its students do. Indeed the Course probably appeals most to people described as "spiritual but not religious."

Theology cuts against the grain of current times, particularly in the United States. Americans think of themselves as pragmatic: if something has no immediate practical value, whether to a company's bottom line or to personal betterment, it is seen as garbage. And what could be more irrelevant to practical concerns than theology?

We cannot live with this fiction any longer. The twentieth century, disgusted by the crimes and hypocrisies of Christendom, tried to discard it. But the Western mind did not rise up in exuberance. Instead it took refuge in social and political theories—such as fascism and communism—that can be most charitably described as insane.* The Second World War and the collapse of the Soviet Union proved that these ideas were worthless. Over the last several decades, liberal capitalism has been trumpeted as the only way forward, but it is obvious now that liberal capitalism, as a source of absolute values, can be nearly as bad as its old enemies. (Western culture seems to be coming to this conclusion belatedly.)

Theology is not a vestigial organ. It cannot be cut out without causing damage. The void will be filled by something else— materialistic scientism, capitalism viewed as a quasireligion, or various forms of extremism—but it will be filled. It would be good if the human longing for the divine were taken at face value, for what it is, rather than as a neurosis. It would also be good if this longing were expressed by a theology that held humanity to its highest possibilities, not only ethical and experiential but intellectual. I believe that the theology presented here can do this; thus this book is forward-looking. (Nonetheless, this book represents a development rather than a rejection of the ideas in *Inner Christianity*. I had been

---

*Jung saw this over eighty years ago. In a 1937 lecture, he said, "But if [man] declares this 'tremendum' to be dead, then he should find out at once where this considerable energy, which was once invested in an existence as great as God, has disappeared to. It might reappear under another name, it might call itself 'Wotan' or 'State' or something ending with -ism, even atheism, of which people believe, hope, and expect as much as they did of God." Jung, *Psychology and Religion*, 104. "Tremendum" refers to the *mysterium tremendum et fascinans,* the "awesome and beguiling mystery" of Rudolf Otto, referring to the experience of the divine.

studying the Course for twenty years when I wrote *Inner Christianity*.)

This is the only theology I know of that is both coherent and inspiring in the framework of the Christian heritage. What Christianity will make of it only the future can tell. And by *future* I mean not months or years, but decades and centuries.

STUDYING
A COURSE IN MIRACLES

A Course in Miracles has a readership in the tens of millions, many of whose lives have been transformed by it. But the Course is not always easy to approach, so it may be in order to give some advice about beginning to study it.

The Course is in three major parts: the Text, the Workbook, and the Manual for Teachers. The Course itself says, "In some cases, it may be helpful to read the manual first. Others might do better to begin with the workbook. Still others may need to start at the more abstract level of the text" (M, 70). What follows consists purely of my own personal advice.

Although the Text is the first volume, I have found very few people have managed to get very far into the Course by reading it at the outset. Neither could I. When I brought the books home in 1981 (the Course was in three volumes then), I read about twenty pages of the Text but could make nothing of it. It used terms like *revelation, Atonement,* and *miracles* in quite different senses from those familiar to me. So I set it aside.

I did notice, however, that the Workbook was broken down into 365 daily lessons, and that the lessons were very simple and brief. I started to do them. I managed to get through all of the lessons, doing one a day, so that I finished in a year.

About three or four months into doing the Workbook lessons, I began to look into the Text, and by that time I found it much more comprehensible. I went on to read it. At some point, I began reading the Teacher's Manual and found it among the most powerful parts of the Course. About six months into the Workbook, I found a group that was meeting to study the Course, and I joined it.

This process worked for me. I would recommend it for people who are interested in studying the Course: beginning with the Workbook and going later into the Text and Teacher's Manual.

The edition I recommend to begin with is the one published by the Course's original publisher, the Foundation for Inner Peace, the third edition of which I quote in this book. Its first edition was the only one available in 1981, when I started to study the Course.

The Course is (for complicated reasons) not under copyright, and many editions have been published. These tend to differ from one another mostly at the beginning, because the Course's original editors, including Helen Schucman, took out some early personal material that came to her and Bill Thetford. This material (some of which I have quoted in this book) is available, again in a number of versions. The best is the one edited by Robert Perry and published by the Circle of Atonement in 2017 (full publication information is in the bibliography). I find this additional material extremely interesting, but most of it relates personally to the people who wrote down the Course—Schucman and Thetford—and I think a beginning student would find it distracting. Thus I would recommend it only to intermediate and advanced students of the Course (say someone who has gone through the whole Workbook as directed).

All of this is advice only, but it does come from almost forty years of personal experience, along with my observations of many other students. In any event, as the Course says, "The curriculum is highly individualized, and all aspects are under the Holy Spirit's particular care and guidance" (M, 70).

Notes

INTRODUCTION

1. Ricoeur, *The Symbolism of Evil,* 351; emphasis Ricoeur's.
2. Richard Smoley and Jay Kinney, "A *Gnosis* Interview with Huston Smith," *Gnosis* 37 (Fall 1995), 33.
3. Charlesworth, *The Good and Evil Serpent,* 7.
4. "The Stand," *The Economist,* November 4, 2017, 41.
5. See Riley, *One Jesus, Many Christs.*
6. In Ouspensky, *In Search of the Miraculous,* 74.
7. See, for example, Emily Chandler, "Religious and Spiritual Issues in DSM-5: Matters of the Mind and Searching of the Soul," *Issues in Mental Health Nursing* 33, no. 9 (September 2012): 577–82; and W. K. Mohr, "Spiritual Issues in Psychiatric Care," *Perspectives in Psychiatric Care* 42, no. 3 (August 2006): 174–83.
8. I discuss this matter in *How God Became God,* 188–91, and will go into it later in this book.
9. Miguel de la Torre, "The Death of Christianity in the U.S.," Baptist News Global (website), November 13, 2017.
10. See my *How God Became God,* xviii. The word is a translation of Heidegger's *Geworfenheit.*
11. Jacques Derrida, "Structure, Sign, and Play in the Discourse of the Human Sciences," 1970, 6.

1. WHAT IS GOD?

1. In Matt, *The Essential Kabbalah,* 29.
2. *The Zohar* 1:15a, in Matt, *The Zohar,* 1:107–9.
3. Papus, *The Tarot of the Bohemians,* 21.
4. *Tao Te Ching* §§1, 42, in Wei, *The Guiding Light of Lao Tzu,* 129, 181.
5. Blakney, *Meister Eckhart,* 200–201.
6. Guénon, *The Great Triad.*
7. In Barker, Humphreys, and Benjamin, *The Mahatma Letters to A. P. Sinnett,* 52.
8. Henry Fountain, "Two Trillion Galaxies, at the Very Least," *New York Times,* October 17, 2016.

2. THE FIVE-DIMENSIONAL BOX

1. *Sefer Yetzirah* 1.5, in Friedman, *The Book of Creation: Sepher Yetzirah,* 1. Transliteration of Hebrew words vary from author to author (*sefer* vs. *sepher,* etc., *waw* versus *vav*). The word Friedman translates as "alone" is the Hebrew *belimah,* a word of obscure and disputed meaning. It is often taken as deriving from *beli mah,* "without what," and thus is sometimes translated as "nothingness," i.e., "ten *sefirot* of nothingness." It appears to have this meaning in its sole occurrence in the Hebrew Bible, in Job 26:7. See Kaplan, *Sefer Yetzirah,* 25. The *Sefer Yetzirah* exists in a number of editions and translations. I am using three different versions in order to highlight certain points.
2. The whole vision is recounted in Jung, *Memories, Dreams, Reflections,* 289–95.
3. Sudman, *Application of Impossible Things,* 4–6. See also my article "Natalie Sudman: Prophet of Another Reality," *New Dawn* (November–December 2016): 31–36; reprinted in *Quest: Journal of the Theosophical Society in America* (Summer 2017): 14–19.
4. Plato, *Republic* 614a–621d, trans. Paul Shorey, in Hamilton and Cairns, *The Collected Dialogues of Plato,* 838–46.
5. Sudman, *Application of Impossible Things,* 38; emphasis Sudman's.

6. Sudman, *Application of Impossible Things,* 44; emphasis and expurgation Sudman's.

7. Van der Post, *The Lost World of the Kalahari,* 210.

8. Sudman, *Application of Impossible Things,* 27; emphasis Sudman's.

9. For my information about the war hostel, I am relying on Tripadvisor; see the reviews of the Sarajevo War Hostel on that website.

10. Sudman, *Application of Impossible Things,* 43.

11. Plato, *Cratylus* 400c.

12. Plato, *Phaedo* 62b; my translation.

3. THE CLOUD OF OBLIVION

1. For a discussion of the translation of the opening word in Genesis, see Josipovici, *The Book of God: A Response,* 53–59. Josipovici argues, correctly, I believe, that the standard translations of this verse are theologically tendentious and grammatically unconvincing. As for the Greek, technically the ē in both *tē* and *archē* includes an iota subscript, indicating the dative case, but I have omitted them from my transliteration.

2. See Robertson, *Jungian Archetypes: Jung, Gödel, and the History of Archetypes,* 92.

3. Pseudo-Dionysius, *Mystical Theology* 1.1; Gregory of Nyssa, *Life of Moses,* 2.163; and Corbin, *The Man of Light in Iranian Sufism,* 99–120. For these references I am indebted to Matt, *Zohar* 1:107, which provides other examples as well.

4. *The Cloud of Unknowing,* §4; University of Rochester, Middle English Texts Series (website). Emphasis added.

5. Quoted in Corbin, *Man of Light in Iranian Sufism,* 112; emphasis in the original.

6. *Chāndogya Upanishad,* 8.11.1, in Hume, *The Thirteen Principal Upanishads,* 271.

7. Swami Jnaneshvara Bharati, "Yoga Nidra: Yogic Conscious Deep Sleep" (website).

8. *The Cloud of Unknowing,* §7.

4. THE REIGN OF NUMBER

1. Quoted in Jung, *Mysterium Coniunctionis,* 429.
2. Plato, *Timaeus* 17a, trans. Benjamin Jowett, in Hamilton and Cairns, *The Collected Dialogues of Plato,* 1153. Cf. Jung, *Mysterium Coniunctionis,* 212.
3. Jung, *Mysterium Coniunctionis,* 210.
4. Jung, *Mysterium Coniunctionis,* 186.
5. In Kant, *Critique of Pure Reason,* 212.
6. Jung, *Synchronicity: An Acausal Connecting Principle,* §§870–81; see also my *Inner Christianity,* 197–98.
7. Robertson, *Jungian Archetypes,* 269–70.

5. OF MIRRORS AND MADNESS

1. Kevin Loria, "Neil deGrasse Tyson Thinks There's a 'Very High Chance' That the Universe Is Just a Simulation," *Business Insider* (website), December 23, 2016.
2. Plato, *Republic* 515a; my adaptation.
3. I am taking this quote from Campbell, *The Masks of God: Creative Mythology,* 344. Campbell is quoting (and presumably translating) from Schopenhauer, *Sämtliche Werke* (Stuttgart: Cotta'sche Bibliothek, n.d.), 8:220–25.
4. Prabhavananda and Isherwood, *Shankara's Crest-Jewel of Discrimination,* 90–91.
5. Zur and Davies, *Sepher HaBahir,* 167.
6. Zur and Davies, *Sepher HaBahir,* 171. There is some dispute about the exact translation of the Hebrew terms for some of the organs. On this point, see Kaplan, *Sefer Yetzirah,* 212–14.
7. Kaplan, *Sefer Yetzirah,* 8–9.
8. Agrippa, *De occulta philosophia* 1.13, pp. 111–12; my translation.
9. On the authenticity of this maxim, see Bill Cherowitzo, "Let No One Ignorant of Geometry Enter Here," PowerPoint presentation, Department of Mathematics, University of Denver (website).
10. For further discussion of this issue, see my articles "The Fires of Artifice,"

Gnosis 26 (Winter 1993): 14–17, and "From the Editor's Desk," *Quest* 103, no. 1 (Winter 2015): 2.

11. Hoeller, *The Gnostic Jung and the Seven Sermons to the Dead,* 38.

12. Genesis 2:21. Cf. *A Course in Miracles* (T, 18).

6. A SUPPOSITIONAL MOMENT

1. Harman, foreword to Robert Skutch, *Journey without Distance,* i.

2. Quoted in Miller, *The Complete Story of the Course,* 126.

3. See Miller, *Complete Story of the Course;* Skutch, *Journey without Distance;* and Wapnick, *Absence from Felicity.*

4. Quoted in Skutch, *Journey without Distance,* 134–35.

5. Herman Melville, *Moby-Dick,* chapter 36; in Hayford and Parker, 144.

6. [Tomberg,] *Meditations on the Tarot,* 142. This work was originally published anonymously; emphasis in the original.

7. THE LAW ON TWO LEVELS

1. Quoted in Ouspensky, *In Search of the Miraculous,* 84.

2. Besant, *Dharma,* 17.

3. Goethe, *Die Geheimnisse* [The secrets]; my translation. The original reads, "Von der Gewalt, die alle Wesen bindet, / Befreit der Mensch sich, der sich überwindet."

4. The Course materials include some supplements that are not strictly part of the Course itself, but are held to be the work of the same Voice that dictated it. This passage comes from a short treatise of this kind called *Psychotherapy: Purpose, Process, and Practice,* 1. Originally published separately, it is reprinted in the third edition of the Course.

8. MEANING FOR A MEANINGLESS WORLD

1. [FitzGerald], *Rubáiyát,* stanza 27, p. 38.

2. I am taking this account from Eliade, *Myth and Reality,* 101.

3. Freud, *Totem and Taboo,* 122.

4. Gay, *Freud: A Life for Our Time,* 327.

5. *The Song of Prayer: Prayer, Forgiveness, and Healing,* 11. *The Song of Prayer* is another supplementary treatise to the Course, dictated by the same Voice. It too can be found as a supplement to the third Foundation for Inner Peace edition of the Course, but is paginated separately. Subsequent references to this supplement are cited using the method used for other Course Materials, i.e. (S, 11), "S" for *The Song of Prayer* followed by the page number.

6. The discussion of this topic, along with the quotations cited, are from *The Song of Prayer,* 11–12.

9. FROM THE UNREAL TO THE REAL

1. Dick, *Ubik,* 192.

2. Dick, *Ubik,* 226.

3. Heraclitus, fragment 21 (Diels-Kranz). I am accepting Marcovich's emendation of this text in his *Heraclitus: Greek Text with a Short Commentary,* 247.

4. Dick, *The Exegesis of Philip K. Dick,* 4; emphasis mine.

5. Jay Kinney, "The Mysterious Revelations of Philip K. Dick," *Gnosis* 1 (Fall/Winter 1985): 7. A graphically illustrated version of this account can be found in R. Crumb, "The Religious Experience of Philip K. Dick," *Weirdo* 17 (website).

6. An abridged version of this text can be found in Jonas, *The Gnostic Religion,* 112–16. On Egypt as a symbol, see Jonas, 118.

7. Kinney, "The Mysterious Revelations of Philip K. Dick," 6–11. Some brief excerpts from *The Exegesis* are published on pages 12–15 of the same issue.

8. See Casti, *Paradigms Lost,* 25.

9. Nick Herbert, *Quantum Reality: Beyond the New Physics* (Garden City, N.Y.: Doubleday, 1985), 193. For this reference and the previous one I am indebted to Steve Hagen, *How the World Can Be the Way It Is,* 57. Chapter 2 of Hagen's book offers a valuable discussion of these problems.

10. Underhill, *Mysticism,* 9.

11. In James, *The Varieties of Religious Experience,* 397–98. James cites Trevor's 1897 book *My Quest for God* as his source.

12. James, *Varieties,* 380–81.

13. Kline, *Mathematics and the Search for Knowledge,* 21; emphasis added. Again I am indebted to Steve Hagen's book for this reference.

10. CREATING, MAKING, AND THE QUALIA

1. For an extensive discussion of the Four Worlds, see Z'ev ben Shimon Halevi, *Adam and the Kabbalistic Tree.*

2. Thomas Nagel, "What Is It Like to Be a Bat?" in Hofstadter and Dennett, *The Mind's I,* 394. The article originally appeared in *Philosophical Review,* October 1974.

3. Michael Tye, "Qualia," *The Stanford Encyclopedia of Philosophy* (website).

4. Howard Robinson, "The Mind-Body Problem," *The Stanford Encyclopedia of Philosophy* (website).

5. For a brief discussion, see my *How God Became God,* 15–16.

6. Clement of Alexandria, *Stromateis* [Miscellanies], 5.11, in Roberts and Donaldson, *The Ante-Nicene Fathers,* 2:461; emphasis added.

7. The classic account of the Dweller on the Threshold appears in fictional form in Edward Bulwer-Lytton's 1842 novel *Zanoni.*

11. THE SCANDAL OF PARTICULARITY

1. Josipovici, *The Book of God,* 322.

2. Josipovici, *The Book of God,* 323.

3. Couliano, *The Tree of Gnosis,* 15.

4. Couliano, *The Tree of Gnosis,* 18.

5. Barth, *Epistle to the Romans,* 91.

6. See Wood, *In Search of the Trojan War,* 28.

7. Josephus, *The Jewish War,* 5.5.6; translation quoted from Goldhill, *The Temple in Jerusalem,* 71.

8. *Letter of Aristeas* 90; in Charles, *The Apocrypha and Pseudepigrapha,* 2:103.

9. Ullucci, *The Christian Rejection of Animal Sacrifice,* 75.

10. *Faust,* part 1, line 1740; my translation.

11. Homer, *Odyssey,* 11:35–43; my translation.

12. Cicero, *De legibus,* 2.36; my translation and emphasis.

13. Plutarch, *De Iside et Osiride,* 65.1, in Mead, *Thrice-Greatest Hermes,* 240.

14. Ouspensky, *A New Model of the Universe,* 27.

15. In *A Course in Miracles,* ed. Robert Perry, 1882–83.

16. In *A Course in Miracles,* ed. Robert Perry, 1884.

17. See "Reincarnation," His Holiness the 14th Dalai Lama of Tibet (website).

18. *A Course in Miracles,* ed. Robert Perry, 1885.

12. BEING TOWARD DEATH

1. For a summary of Heidegger's view of this subject, see Simon Critchley, "Being and Time, Part 6: Death," *Guardian* (website).

2. Heidegger, *Being and Time,* 239. Emphasis here and in the following quote is in the original. Stambaugh renders Heidegger's term as *Da-sein* rather than the more familiar *Dasein,* pointing out that this was Heidegger's own preference for translations of the book; see her preface, xiv.

3. Heidegger, *Being and Time,* 238.

4. Heidegger, *Being and Time,* 243.

5. Jonathan Swift, *Gulliver's Travels,* chapter 26.

6. Yeats, "Sailing to Byzantium," in *Collected Poems,* 191.

7. Eliot, *Four Quartets,* in *Collected Poems,* 176.

8. Porphyry, *Life of Plotinus,* 1.

9. In Davis, *The Serpent and the Rainbow,* 141; emphasis in the original.

10. *A Course in Miracles,* ed. Robert Perry, 1639n.

11. Skutch, *Journey without Distance,* 27–28.

12. Waddell, *The Desert Fathers,* 112.

13. Josephus, *Jewish War,* 2.8.

14. Longchenpa, *Kindly Bent to Ease Us,* 139.

15. From Richard Smoley, "The Diamond Approach: An Interview with A. H. Almaas," *Gnosis* 25 (Fall 1992), 48.

13. RELATIONSHIPS, SPECIAL AND HOLY

1. Mann, *The Magic Mountain,* 599. Presumably the German *Liebe* extends across the same range of concepts as the English *love.*

2. Smoley, *Conscious Love,* 17.

3. Allen Watson, "What Is a Holy Instant?" Circle of Atonement (website).

4. Skutch, *Journey without Distance,* 33–34; emphasis in the original.

14. CHURCH AND SACRAMENTS

1. *The Catechism of the Catholic Church,* §750.

2. *The Catechism of the Catholic Church,* §752.

3. *The Catechism of the Catholic Church,* §760. The catechism is quoting *The Shepherd of Hermas,* vision 2.4.1.

4. Dostoevsky, *The Brothers Karamazov,* 251.

5. This telling of the myth is adapted from my editorial in "From the Editor's Desk," *Quest: Journal of the Theosophical Society in America* 106, no. 1 (winter 2018): 2.

6. Blavatsky, *Collected Writings,* 8:408.

7. Joyce, *Finnegans Wake,* 4.

8. Joyce, *Ulysses,* 34.

9. Case, *The True and Invisible Rosicrucian Order,* 64. For more about these ideas, see chapter 11, "The Rumor of the Brotherhood," in my *Hidden Wisdom: A Guide to the Western Inner Traditions,* coauthored by Jay Kinney, as well as chapter 11, "The Secret Church," in my *Inner Christianity.*

10. Wapnick, *Love Does Not Condemn,* 484; emphasis in the original.

11. In Wapnick, *Love Does Not Condemn,* 483.

12. Ignatius of Loyola, *The Spiritual Exercises,* 94.

15. THE LADDER OF PRAYER

1. An abundance of literature in English is available on Dzogchen. For a good introduction, see Chögyen Namkhai Norbu, *Dzogchen: The Self-Perfected State.*

2. *A Course in Miracles,* preface, ix.

3. Kaplan, *The Bahir,* 1; bracketed insertion and emphasis in the original.

4. Coton-Alvart, *Les deux lumières,* 22; my translation, emphasis from the original.

5. Turgenev, from "Prayer," in *Poems in Prose,* at Bartleby (website). I have changed the wording to make it more idiomatic.

6. Wittgenstein, *Tractatus,* 7.

7. Climacus, *Ladder of Divine Ascent,* 230. The passage alludes to certain Bible verses: Isaiah 2:3; Psalm 17:33; and Ephesians 4:13.

16. DISPENSATIONS

1. See Ahlstrom, *A Religious History of the American People,* 808–12. For a short but informative account, see Carl E. Olson, "The Twelfth Coming of Less-Than Glorious Fiction," *National Review* (website), April 2, 2004.

2. Booth, *The Course of Time,* 9. Paul and Timothy Loizeaux were late nineteenth-century publishers of material promoting the teachings of the Plymouth Brethren, who were influenced by Darby. Booth's treatise explains the diagram. My source for this book, Books.Logos Free Online Library of Christian Classics (website), does not include the title page or the copyright page.

3. Quoted in McGinn, *Apocalyptic Spirituality,* 99.

4. Joachim of Fiore, *The Book of Concordance,* 2.1.10; in McGinn, *Apocalyptic Spirituality,* 133.

5. McGinn, introduction to Riedl, *A Companion to Joachim of Fiore,* 8.

6. Frances Andrews, "The Influence of Joachim in the Thirteenth Century," in Riedl, *A Companion to Joachim of Fiore,* 241–42.

7. Swedenborg, *True Christianity,* §508; 2:80.

8. Evans, *The New Age and Its Messenger,* 87. An online version is available at Internet Archive: Digital Library of Free and Borrowable Books, Movies, Music & Wayback Machine (website).

9. For a brief survey of Guénon's views, see my article "Waiting for the End of the World: René Guénon and the Kali Yuga," *New Dawn* (website), September 19, 2010.

10. For a history of this concept, see Liz Greene, "The Way of What Is to Come: Jung's Vision of the Aquarian Age," in Stein and Arzt, *Jung's Red Book for Our Time,* 44–84.

11. The original three-volume work is *Gnôsis: Étude et commentaires sur la tradition ésotérique de l'Orthodoxie orientale,* and the English ver-

sion, also in three volumes, is *Gnosis: Study and Commentaries on the Esoteric Tradition of Eastern Orthodoxy.* Citations that follow are from the English edition.

12. For a discussion of this point, see Olivier Santamaria, "Boris Mouravieff et l'ésotérisme chrétien," *Slavica bruxellensia* 3, no. 1 (2009): 48–60, at OpenEdition Journals (website). Santamaria also provides a brief account of Mouravieff's life and ideas.

13. Mouravieff, *Gnosis,* 2:49. Emphasis here and in other quotes from Mouravieff is in the original.

14. Mouravieff, *Gnosis,* 2:37.

15. Mouravieff, *Gnosis,* 2:44.

16. For more on this point, see my book *The Essential Nostradamus,* 295–97.

17. Jaspers, *The Origin and Goal of History,* 2.

18. See, for example, Antony Black, "'The Axial Period': What Was It and What Does It Signify?" *Review of Politics* 70 (2008): 23–39. But even Black concedes, "There was significant mental [*geistlich*] development at that time" (39).

19. For comparable passages, see 1 Samuel 15:22; Psalms 50:8–15; 51:16–18; Isaiah 1:11–12; Jeremiah 7:21–24; and Amos 5:21–24.

20. Ullucci, *Christian Rejection of Animal Sacrifice,* 42–48.

21. On Pythagoras's own views, see Kirk, Raven, and Schofield, *The Presocratic Philosophers,* 230–31. For a useful summary of Pythagorean attitudes toward sacrifice, see Ullucci, *Christian Rejection of Animal Sacrifice,* 59–60; Ullucci cites Diogenes Laertius, 8.12.

22. Hume, *Thirteen Principal Upanishads,* 52–54.

23. Plato, *Laws* 716e–717a; quoted in Ullucci, *Christian Rejection of Animal Sacrifice,* 35. Ullucci is quoting Paul Shorey's translation in the Loeb Classical Library.

24. Graves's translation of this satire is published as an appendix to his novel *Claudius the God,* 514ff. For the quote about Janus, see 522.

25. Jaspers, *Way to Wisdom,* 103.

17. THE AGE OF THE HOLY SPIRIT

1. Cumont, *Les religions orientales,* 291–92; my translation. Available at Internet Archive: Digital Library of Free and Borrowable Books,

Movies, Music & Wayback Machine (website); I am grateful to Wouter J. Hanegraaff for bringing this passage to my attention.

2. See, for example, Justin Martyr, *First Apology for the Christians,* 1.6.

3. Mead, *Echoes of the Gnosis,* 22–23.

4. C. G. Jung, letter to Victor White, April 10, 1954; in Gerhard Adler, ed. *C. G. Jung: Letters,* 2:167. I am taking both the quote and the reference from Liz Greene's article in Stein and Artzt, *Jung's Red Book for Our Time,* 66, 82.

5. Watts, letter to Jim Corsa, January 17, 1947; in *Collected Letters,* 210.

6. Robinson, *Language of Mystery,* 1.

7. *Popper Selections,* 140.

8. Olivia Goldhill, "The Idea That Everything from Spoons to Stones Are Conscious Is Gaining Academic Credibility," Quartz (website), January 27, 2018.

9. Lao-tzu, *Tao Te Ching,* §18.

10. Yu Hua, *China in Ten Words,* 7.

11. For a survey, see Erin O'Connell, "The New Face of Global Christianity: The Emergence of 'Progressive Pentecostalism,'" interview with Donald Miller, Pew Research Center (website), April 12, 2006. See also Pulitzer Center, "Atlas of Pentecostalism: An Expanding Database of the Fastest Growing Religion in the World," Atlas of Pentecostalism (website). Pentecostals usually belong to one of the historical Pentecostal denominations, such as the Assemblies of God or the Church of God in Christ. Charismatic Christians are found in other Protestant denominations as well as in the Catholic Church.

12. Ahlstrom, *Religious History,* 816–22.

13. Quoted in O'Connell interview with Miller, "The New Face of Global Christianity."

14. Horowitz, *One Simple Idea,* 73n.

15. Quoted in Byrne, *The Secret,* 101.

16. Zaleski and Zaleski, *Prayer,* 329.

18. *SUMMA THEOLOGIAE*

1. Shapiro, *Holy Rascals,* 2.

2. See Ouspensky, *In Search of the Miraculous,* 26.

3. Singh, *Commentaries on "A Course in Miracles,"* 75.

4. *Asclepius* 24, in Copenhaver, *Hermetica,* 81. The *Asclepius,* which survives only in a Latin translation, is not always regarded as part of the *Corpus Hermeticum* per se, which is written in Greek, but it is generally acknowledged to be part of the same body of material.

Selected Bibliography

Agrippa, Henry Cornelius. *De occulta philosophia libri tres*. Edited by V. Perrone Compagni. Leiden, The Netherlands: Brill, 1992.

Ahlstrom, Sydney E. *A Religious History of the American People*. New Haven, Conn.: Yale University Press, 1973.

Aland, Kurt, et al., eds. *The Greek New Testament*. 3rd ed. N.p.: United Bible Societies, 1966.

Barfield, Owen. *Saving the Appearances: A Study in Idolatry*. London: Faber & Faber, 1957.

Barker, A. T., Christmas Humphreys, and Elsie Benjamin, eds. *The Mahatma Letters to A. P. Sinnett*. 3rd ed. Adyar, Madras, India: Theosophical Publishing House, 1972.

Barth, Karl. *The Epistle to the Romans*. Translated by Edwyn C. Hoskins. London: Oxford University Press, 1933.

Barker, Margaret. *The Great Angel: A Study of Israel's Second God*. Louisville, Ky.: Westminster/John Knox Press, 1992.

Besant, Annie. *Dharma*. 4th ed. Adyar, Madras, India: Theosophical Publishing House, 1918.

Bishop, Paul. *Jung's Answer to Job: A Commentary*. London: Routledge, 2014.

Blake, William. *The Book of Urizen*. Edited by Kay Parkhurst Easson and Roger R. Easson. Boulder, Colo.: Shambhala, 1978.

Blakney, Raymond, ed. and trans. *Meister Eckhart: A Modern Translation*. New York: Harper & Row, 1941.

Blavatsky, H. P. *Collected Writings*. Edited by Boris de Zirkoff. 15 vols. Wheaton, Ill.: Theosophical Publishing House, 1960–91.

Booth, A. P. *The Course of Time from Eternity to Eternity: Key to a Chart*. N.p: n.d.

Brown, Raymond E., ed. and trans. *The Anchor Bible: The Gospel according to John*. 2 vols. Garden City, N.Y.: Doubleday, 1966.

———. *An Introduction to the New Testament*. New York: Doubleday, 1997.

Byrne, Rhonda. *The Secret*. New York: Atria, 2006.

Campbell, Joseph. *The Masks of God: Creative Mythology*. New York: Viking, 1968.

Case, Paul Foster. *The True and Invisible Rosicrucian Order*. York Beach, Maine: Samuel Weiser, 1985.

Casti, John L. *Paradigms Lost: Tackling the Unanswered Mysteries of Modern Science*. New York: Harper Perennial, 1990.

The Catechism of the Catholic Church. See the Vatican website "Archive" page.

Charles, R. H., ed. *The Apocrypha and Pseudepigrapha of the Old Testament in English*. 2 vols. Oxford: Clarendon Press, 1913.

Charlesworth, James T. *The Good and Evil Serpent: How a Universal Symbol Became Christianized*. New Haven, Conn.: Yale University Press, 2010.

Climacus, John. *The Ladder of Divine Ascent*. Rev. ed. Boston: Holy Transfiguration Monastery, 2001.

Copenhaver, Brian, ed. and trans. *Hermetica: The Greek "Corpus Hermeticum" and the Latin "Asclepius" in a New English Translation with Notes and Introduction*. Cambridge: Cambridge University Press, 1992.

Corbin, Henry. *The Man of Light in Iranian Sufism*. Translated by Nancy Pearson. New Lebanon, N.Y.: Omega, 1994.

Coton-Alvart, Henri. *Les deux lumières: La science de la nature vivante dans ses mutations*. Paris: Dervy, 1996.

Couliano, Ioan P. *The Tree of Gnosis: Gnostic Mythology from Early Christianity to Modern Nihilism*. San Francisco: HarperSanFrancisco, 1992.

A Course in Miracles. 3rd ed. Mill Valley, Calif.: Foundation for Inner Peace, 2007.

A Course in Miracles, Based on the Original Handwritten Notes of Helen Schucman: Complete and Annotated Edition. Edited by Robert Perry. West Sedona, Ariz.: Circle of Atonement, 2017.

Cross, F. L., and E. A. Livingstone, eds. *The Oxford Dictionary of the Christian Church.* 3rd ed. New York: Oxford University Press, 1997.

Cumont, Franz. *Les religions orientales dans le paganisme romain.* Paris: Ernest Leroux, 1909.

Davies, W. G. *The Phoenician Letters.* London: Mowat, 1979.

Davis, Wade. *The Serpent and the Rainbow.* 1985. Reprint, New York: Touchstone, 1997.

Dick, Philip K. *The Exegesis of Philip K. Dick.* Edited by Pamela Jackson and Jonathan Lethem. New York: Houghton Mifflin Harcourt, 2012.

———. *Ubik.* Boston: Houghton Mifflin Harcourt, 2012.

Dostoevsky, Fyodor. *The Brothers Karamazov.* Translated by Richard Pevear and Larissa Volokhonsky. New York: Farrar, Straus, & Giroux, 1990.

Dunn, James D. G. *Jesus Remembered: Christianity in the Making.* Vol. 1. Grand Rapids, Mich.: Eerdmans, 2003.

Eddy, Mary Baker. *Science and Health with Key to the Scriptures.* Boston: Trustees under the Will of Mary Baker G. Eddy, 1908.

Eliade, Mircea. *Myth and Reality.* Translated by Willard R. Trask. New York: Harper & Row, 1963.

Eliot, T. S. *Collected Poems, 1960–1962.* New York: Harcourt, Brace & World, 1963.

Evans, Warren Felt. *The New Age and Its Messenger.* Boston: T. H. Carter, 1864.

[FitzGerald, Edward.] *The Rubáiyát of Omar Khayyám.* London: Macmillan, 1898. This edition was published anonymously.

Freud, Sigmund. *Totem and Taboo: Resemblances between the Psychic Lives of Savages and Neurotics.* Translated by A. A. Brill. Mineola, N.Y.: Dover, 1998.

Friedman, Irving, trans. *The Book of Creation: Sepher Yetzirah.* New York: Samuel Weiser, 1977.

Gay, Peter. *Freud: A Life for Our Time.* New York: Norton, 1988.

Goldhill, Simon. *The Temple in Jerusalem*. Cambridge: Harvard University Press, 2005.

Graves, Robert. *Claudius the God*. 1934. Reprint, New York: Vintage, 1989.

Guénon, René. *The Great Triad*. Translated by Peter Kingsley. Cambridge, U.K.: Quinta Essentia, 1992.

Hagen, Steve. *How the World Can Be the Way It Is: An Inquiry for the New Millennium into Science, Philosophy, and Perception*. Wheaton, Ill.: Quest, 1995.

Halevi, Z'ev ben Shimon. *Adam and the Kabbalistic Tree*. New York: Samuel Weiser, 1974.

Hart, David Bentley. *The New Testament: A Translation*. New Haven, Conn.: Yale University Press, 2017.

Hartman, Louis F., and Alexander A. De Lella. *The Anchor Bible: Daniel*. Garden City, N.Y.: Doubleday, 1978.

Heidegger, Martin. *Being and Time*. Translated by Joan Stambaugh. Albany: State University of New York Press, 1996.

Hoeller, Stephan A. *The Gnostic Jung and the Seven Sermons to the Dead*. Wheaton, Ill.: Quest, 1982.

Hofstadter, Douglas R., and Daniel Dennett, eds. *The Mind's I: Fantasies and Reflections on Self and Soul*. New York: Bantam, 1981.

Homer. *Opera*, vol. III, *Odysseae,* books I–XII. Edited by Thomas W. Allen. 2nd ed. Oxford: Oxford University Press, 1917.

Horowitz, Mitch. *One Simple Idea: How Positive Thinking Reshaped Modern Life*. New York: Crown, 2014.

Hume, Robert Ernest, trans. and ed. *The Thirteen Principal Upanishads*. 2nd ed. Oxford: Oxford University Press, 1931.

Ignatius of Loyola. *The Spiritual Exercises of St. Ignatius*. Translated by Anthony Mottola. New York: Doubleday Image, 1964.

James, William. *The Varieties of Religious Experience*. London: Longmans, Green, & Co., 1910.

Jaspers, Karl. *The Origin and Goal of History*. Translated by Michael Bullock. London: Routledge & Kegan Paul, 1953.

———. *Way to Wisdom: An Introduction to Philosophy*. Translated by Ralph Mannheim. 2nd ed. New Haven, Conn.: Yale University Press, 2003.

Jonas, Hans. *The Gnostic Religion: The Message of the Alien God and the Beginnings of Christianity.* 2nd ed. Boston: Beacon, 1958.

Joseph, Simon J. "Knowledge Is Truth: *A Course in Miracles* as Neo-Gnostic Scripture." *Gnosis: Journal of Gnostic Studies* 2 (2017): 94–125.

Josipovici, Gabriel. *The Book of God: A Response.* New Haven, Conn.: Yale University Press, 1988.

Joyce, James. *Finnegans Wake.* New York: Viking, 1958.

———. *Ulysses.* New York: Random House, 1961.

Jung, C. G. *Collected Letters.* Vol. 2. Translated by Jeffrey Hulen. Princeton, N.J.: Princeton University Press, 1976.

———. *Memories, Dreams, Reflections.* Translated by Richard and Clara Winston. 1973. Rev. ed. New York: Vintage, 1989.

———. *Mysterium Coniunctionis: An Inquiry into the Separation and Synthesis of Psychic Opposites in Alchemy.* 2d ed. Translated by R. F. C. Hull. Princeton, N.J.: Princeton/Bollingen, 1970.

———. *Psychology and Religion.* New Haven, Conn.: Yale University Press, 1938.

———. *Synchronicity: An Acausal Connecting Principle.* Translated by R. F. C. Hull. Princeton, N.J.: Princeton/Bollingen, 1973.

Kant, Immanuel. *Critique of Pure Reason.* Translated by Paul Guyer and Allen W. Wood. Cambridge: Cambridge University Press, 1998.

Kaplan, Aryeh, trans. *The Bahir: An Ancient Kabbalistic Text Attributed to Rabbi Nehuniah ben HaKana.* New York: Samuel Weiser, 1979.

———. *Sefer Yetzirah: The Book of Creation in Theory and Practice.* York Beach, Maine: Samuel Weiser, 1990.

Kirk, G. S., J. E. Raven, and M. Schofield, ed. and trans. *The Presocratic Philosophers.* 2nd ed. Cambridge: Cambridge University Press, 1983.

Kline, Morris. *Mathematics and the Search for Knowledge.* New York: Oxford University Press, 1985.

Longchenpa (Klong-chen rab-'yams-pa). *Kindly Bent to Ease Us, Part One: Mind.* Translated by Herbert V. Guenther. Berkeley, Calif.: Dharma Publishing, 1975.

Mann, Thomas. *The Magic Mountain.* Translated by H. T. Lowe-Porter. 1927. New York: Knopf, 1972.

Marcovich, M., ed. and trans. *Heraclitus: Greek Text with a Short Commentary.* Merida, Venezuela: Los Andes University Press, 1967.

Matt, Daniel C., ed. and trans. *The Essential Kabbalah: The Heart of Jewish Mysticism*. San Francisco: HarperSanFrancisco, 1995.

———. ed. and trans. *The Zohar*. 12 vols. Stanford, Calif.: Stanford University Press, 2004–2018.

McGinn, Bernard, ed. *Apocalyptic Spirituality: Treatises and Letters of Lactantius, Adso of Montier-en-Der, Joachim of Fiore, The Franciscan Spirituals, Savonarola*. New York: Paulist Press, 1979.

Mead, G. R. S. *Echoes of the Gnosis*. Edited by John Algeo. 1906. Reprint, Wheaton, Ill.: Quest, 2006.

———. *Thrice-Greatest Hermes: Studies in Hellenistic Theosophy and Gnosis*. 1906. Reprint, York Beach, Maine: Samuel Weiser, 1992.

Melville, Herman. *Moby-Dick: The Norton Critical Edition*. Edited by Harrison Hayford and Hershel Parker. New York: Norton, 1967.

Miller, D. Patrick. *The Complete Story of the Course: The History, the People, and the Controversies behind "A Course in Miracles."* Berkeley, Calif.: Fearless Books, 1997.

Mouravieff, Boris. *Gnôsis: Étude et commentaires sur la tradition ésotérique de l'Orthodoxie orientale*. 3 vols. Neuchâtel, Switzerland: À la Baconnière, 1969–72.

———. *Gnosis: Study and Commentaries on the Esoteric Tradition of Eastern Orthodoxy*. Translated by S. A. Wissa, Manek d'Oncieu, and Robin Amis. 3 vols. Newbury, Mass.: Praxis Institute Press, 1989–93. A translation of the above-listed work.

Norbu, Chögyen Namkhai. *Dzogchen: The Self-Perfected State*. Translated by John Shane. Ithaca, N.Y.: Snow Lion, 1996.

O'Connell, Erin. "The New Face of Global Christianity: The Emergence of 'Progressive Pentecostalism.'" Interview with Donald Miller, Pew Research Center (website), April 12, 2006.

Origen. *On First Principles*. Translated by G. W. Butterworth. 1936. Reprint, New York: Harper & Row, 1966.

Ouspensky, P. D. *A New Model of the Universe: Principles of the Psychological Method in Its Application in Problems of Science, Religion, and Art*. Translated by R. R. Merton. New York: Knopf, 1931.

———. *In Search of the Miraculous: Fragments of an Unknown Teaching*. New York: Harcourt, Brace, 1949.

Papus. *The Tarot of the Bohemians.* Translated by A. P. Morton. London: Chapman & Hall, 1892.

Philo. *The Works of Philo.* Translated by C. D. Yonge. Peabody, Mass.: Hendrickson, 1993.

Plato. *The Collected Dialogues of Plato, including the Letters.* Edited by Edith Hamilton and Huntington Cairns. Princeton, N.J.: Princeton University Press, 1961.

Popper, Karl. *Popper Selections.* Edited by David Miller. Princeton, N.J.: Princeton University Press, 1985.

Prabhavananda, Swami, and Christopher Isherwood, trans. *Shankara's Crest-Jewel of Discrimination.* Hollywood: Vedanta Press, 1947.

Pulitzer Center. "Atlas of Pentecostalism: An Expanding Database of the Fastest Growing Religion in the World." Atlas of Pentecostalism (website).

Ricoeur, Paul. *The Symbolism of Evil.* Translated by Emerson Buchanan. New York: Harper & Row, 1967.

Riedl, Matthias, ed. *A Companion to Joachim of Fiore.* Leiden, The Netherlands: Brill, 2018.

Riley, Gregory J. *One Jesus, Many Christs: How Jesus Inspired Not One True Christianity, but Many.* San Francisco: HarperSanFrancisco, 1997.

Roberts, Alexander, and James Donaldson, eds. *The Ante-Nicene Fathers: Translations of the Writings of the Fathers Down to AD 325.* 10 vols. Reprint, Edinburgh: T & T Clark, 1994.

Robertson, Robin. *Jungian Archetypes: Jung, Gödel, and the History of Archetypes.* York Beach, Maine: Nicolas-Hays, 1995.

Robinson, Edward. *The Language of Mystery.* London: SCM Press, 1987.

Shapiro, Rami. *Holy Rascals: Advice for Spiritual Revolutionaries.* Boulder, Colo.: Sounds True, 2017.

Singh, Tara. *Commentaries on "A Course in Miracles."* Los Angeles: Life Action, 1986.

Skutch, Robert. *Journey without Distance: The Story behind "A Course in Miracles."* Berkeley, Calif.: Celestial Arts, 1984.

Smoley, Richard. *A Comparison of Miracles: A Concise Study of the Differences between the Early and Standard Versions of "A Course in Miracles."* Berkeley: Fearless Books, 2004.

——. *Conscious Love: Insights from Mystical Christianity.* San Francisco: Jossey-Bass, 2008.

——. *The Dice Game of Shiva: How Consciousness Creates the Universe.* Novato, Calif.: New World Library, 2009.

——. *The Essential Nostradamus.* 3rd ed. New York: Jeremy P. Tarcher/ Penguin, 2010.

——. *Forbidden Faith: The Secret History of Gnosticism.* San Francisco: HarperSanFrancisco, 2006.

——. *How God Became God: What Scholars Are Really Saying about God and the Bible.* New York: Tarcher Perigee, 2016.

——. *Inner Christianity: A Guide to the Esoteric Tradition.* Boston: Shambhala, 2002.

Smoley, Richard, and Jay Kinney. *Hidden Wisdom: A Guide to the Western Inner Traditions.* 2nd ed. Wheaton, Ill.: Quest, 2006.

Stein, Murray, and Thomas Arzt, eds. *Jung's Red Book for Our Time: Searching for Soul under Postmodern Conditions.* Asheville, N.C.: Chiron, 2017.

Sudman, Natalie. *Application of Impossible Things: My Near Death Experience in Iraq.* Huntsville, Ark.: Ozark Mountain Press, 2012.

Swedenborg, Emanuel. *True Christianity.* Translated by Jonathan S. Rose. Vol. 2. West Chester, Pa.: Swedenborg Foundation, 2012.

[Tomberg, Valentin]. *Meditations on the Tarot: A Journey into Christian Hermeticism.* Translated by Robert A. Powell. Amity, N.Y.: Amity House, 1985.

Ullucci, Daniel C. *The Christian Rejection of Animal Sacrifice.* Oxford: Oxford University Press, 2012.

Underhill, Evelyn. *Mysticism.* 12th ed. New York: Dutton, n.d.

Van den Broeck, R., and M. J. Vermaseren, eds. *Studies in Gnosticism and Hellenistic Religions: Presented to Gilles Quispel on the Occasion of His Sixty-Fifth Birthday.* Leiden, The Netherlands: E. J. Brill, 1981.

Van der Post, Laurens. *The Lost World of the Kalahari.* New York: William Morrow, 1958.

Waddell, Helen, trans. *The Desert Fathers.* 1936. Reprint, Ann Arbor: University of Michigan Press, 1957.

Wapnick, Kenneth R. *Absence from Felicity: The Story of Helen Schucman and Her Scribing of "A Course in Miracles."* Temecula, Calif.: Foundation for *A Course in Miracles,* 1991.

———. ed. *Concordance of A "Course in Miracles": A Complete Index.* New York: Viking, 1997.

———. *Love Does Not Condemn: The World, the Flesh, and the Devil according to Platonism, Christianity, Gnosticism, and "A Course in Miracles."* Roscoe, N.Y.: Foundation for *A Course in Miracles,* 1989.

Watts, Alan. *The Collected Letters of Alan Watts.* Edited by Joan Watts and Anne Watts. Novato, Calif.: New World Library, 2017.

Wei, Henry. *The Guiding Light of Lao Tzu: A New Translation and Commentary on the Tao Teh Ching.* Wheaton, Ill.: Quest, 1982.

Wink, Walter. *The Human Being: Jesus and the Enigma of the Son of Man.* Minneapolis, Minn.: Fortress, 2002.

Wittgenstein, Ludwig. *Tractatus Logico-Philosophicus.* Translated by D. F. Pears and B. F. McGuiness. 2d ed. London: Routledge and Kegan Paul, 1971.

Wood, Michael. *In Search of the Trojan War.* 2d ed. Berkeley: University of California Press, 1998.

Yeats, W. B. *The Collected Poems of W. B. Yeats.* 2nd ed. New York: Macmillan, 1950.

Yu Hua. *China in Ten Words.* Translated by Allan H. Barr. New York: Anchor, 2012.

Zaleski, Philip, and Carol Zaleski. *Prayer: A History.* Boston: Houghton Mifflin, 2005.

Zur, G., and W. G. Davies, ed. and trans. *Sepher HaBahir: Book of Enlightenment; Sepher Yetzirah: Book of Formation; Two Kabbalistic Classics.* Unpublished ms., London, 1976.

Index

afterlife, 124, 190

Age of the Holy Spirit
  flexible use of ritual, 176
  humanistic ethics, 177
  inner experience, 174
  internalization of divine and, 173–74
  limits of science, 178
  resilient worldviews, 178
  restoration of beauty, 176–77
  rigorous theology, 177–78
  scripture for advice and inspiration, 174
  transformed clergy, 174–75
  transition, 171
  universal truths, 177

Agrippa, Henry Cornelius, 50

Ahab, from *Moby Dick,* 62–63

Ain Sof, 12–13, 14, 17, 24, 33, 51

Ali, Hameed, 129

altar, 142

apotheosis, 170

Application of Impossible Things (Sudman), 26

Assiah, 97–98, 100, 103, 104

Atonement
  complete acceptance of, 128
  concept, 70–71, 110
  crusade and, 192
  defined, 188
  forgiveness in, 86
  full awareness of, 87
  as interlocking chain of forgiveness, 75
  principle of, 71
  separation and, 71
  time frame, 184
  as universal process, 128
  whole, at time's end, 89

Atziluth, 99, 100, 103

avatars, 109

axiom of Maria, 39

Azriel of Gerona, 12–13

Bahir, 153

beauty, restoration to religion, 176–77

"beginning," 14, 15

bereshith ("in the beginning"), 15, 32

Besant, Annie, 73

black light, 33, 35
Blake, William, 54–55
Blavatsky, H. P., 19, 143
body
    Christianity and, 123
    Course and, 84–85, 117, 123–24
    as death, 121
    defense of, 124
    ego and, 84–85
    insistence that we are the, 122
    as learning device, 125
Boehme, Jacob, 153
Book of Urizen (Blake), 54–55
Booth, A. P., 161
brain-wave levels, 36–37
Briah, 99, 100, 103
Brotherhood, 144–45
Buddhism, 9–10, 16, 19, 35, 118, 127,
    149–50

Cantor, Georg, 33
Case, Paul Foster, 145
Casti, John L., 93
Catholic Church, 139–40, 147, 169
Centering Prayer, 151
change
    dimension of, 22–23
    of mind, 76
    movement and, 22
    time as measurement of, 23
Charlesworth, James T., 3–4
Christ
    coming of, 108
    death of, as sacrifice, 112–13
    debate over nature of, 108
    human versus divine nature of, 107

nature and person of, 119
passion, death, and resurrection of,
    115–16
redemptive action of, 114
within, 164
Christian, definition of a, 8
Christian belief, 2
Christianity
    birth of, 107
    conventional doctrine of, 113–14
    evangelical, 7–8
    hermeneutics, 2–3
    as our background, 9
Christian theology, 7, 60, 106, 108
Christian Trinity, 17–18, 39–40
Christocentrism, 110–19
Christology, 189–90
church
    Course and, 141–42, 191
    defined, 139
    evangelical denominations, 140
    liberal denominations, 140–41
    as organization, 139–40
    purpose of, beyond own survival, 143
Clement of Alexandria, 104
clergy, transformed, 174–75
Climacus, John, 158–59
cloud of oblivion, 32–37, 38, 58, 104,
    150, 152–53
Cloud of Unknowing, The, 34–35, 36,
    151, 152
collective memory, 166
*Conscious Love: Insights from Mystical
    Christianity,* 131
consciousness
    dark, 51

doorway behind, 105
loss of, 35, 58
meditation and, 37
shifting levels of, 73
waking state of, 36
correspondence, 50
Coton-Alvart, Henri, 153–54
Couliano, Ioan P., 107–8
Course in Miracles, A
in answering questions, 10
authorship of, 60
as Christocentric, 110–19
events leading to writing of, 136
history of, 59
importance of, 58–59
Kabbalah system and, 102–3
mainstream Christianity and, 60
major parts of, 197
masculine pronouns, 70
studying, 197–98
Teacher's Manual, 197–98
Text, 197, 198
theology of, 58, 59, 61, 186
Workbook, 197–98
world characterization, 67–68
craziness, 63
creation, 187
creativity, of action, 27
cross, 114, 147–48
crucifixion, message of, 114
Cumont, Franz, 172–73
Cycle of the Holy Spirit, 163–65

darkness, 33, 34, 35
Deal: A Guide to Radical and Complete Forgiveness, The, 86

death
being toward, 120–21
of the body, 121
facing, 120–22
imagery, 123
soul after, 126–27
de la Torre, Miguel, 7–8
Demiurge, 47, 49, 53
desire, 80
devil, as ego, 66
dharma, 19, 73
Dice Game of Shiva: How Consciousness Creates the Universe, The, 179
Dick, Philip K., 88–90, 91
Diogenes, 167
directions, 23
dispensationalism, 161
dispensations, 160–71
divine
as having no personal aspect, 19
human longing for, 195
internalization of, 173–74, 184
man as, 108
as nature of Christ, 107, 119
wisdom, 64
divine justice, 188
divine order, 73
divine realm, 99, 100
dogmatism, 185
Dweller on the Threshold, 105

Eckhart, Meister, 17–18
Economist, The, 5
ego
arising of, 81–82
defined, 85

as the devil, 66
evolution and, 64–65
as fear, 65, 82
God perception of, 65
as primordial disassociation, 85
relationships and, 133
emanation body, 118
enlightenment, 127–28
eschatology, 127–29, 191
Essential Nostradamus, The, 165
ethics, humanistic, 177
evil, 7, 22–24, 27, 28, 68, 145, 157.
    See also good and evil
evolution
    ego and, 64–65
    inner nature of a given stage and,
      73
existentialists, 80

faith, 2, 8, 79, 158, 162
Fall, the
    Atonement and, 70
    cause of, 58
    Course and, 62
    Genesis myth, 28
    nature and, 68
    world of, 51, 54, 103
    Yetzirah as locus of, 103
Father
    as infinite light and love, 61
    separation and, 71
    Son and, 61, 64
fear
    circle of, 66–67
    ego, 65, 82, 84
first-person pronoun, 53

five-dimensional box, 21–31, 38, 53,
    57–58
five-dimensional reality, 34, 49, 84, 85
forgiveness
    in Atonement, 86
    importance of, 134–35
    in letting go of grievances, 85
    personal redemption through, 59
    true, 86
forgiveness-for-salvation, 86
forgiveness-to-destroy, 85–86
Forster, E. M., 7
fourth, the, 38–39
fourth force, 40
Four Worlds
    Assiah, 97–98, 100, 103, 104
    Atziluth, 99, 100, 103
    Bible obscurities and, 100
    Briah, 99, 100, 103
    Course correlation, 103
    defined, 97
    interlocking diagram, 101
    Yetzirah, 98, 99, 100, 102, 103, 104

general judgment, 126–27
Genesis, dual accounts of, 100
Genesis myth, 28, 54, 58, 65, 66
Gichtel, Johann George, 51, 52
Gnosis, 57
Gnosticism, 47, 53
God. *See also* Father
    Ain Sof as, 17, 18
    as angry, 67
    behind Christian Trinity, 17–18
    as beyond the gates of death, 37
    direct experience of, 193

ego perception of, 65
ego revolt against, 82, 83
Final Judgment, 71
as infinite love, 61
laws of, 74
personal, 18
question of, 10
Son of, 61, 62, 63
teachers of, 191–92
Godhead, 17
Goldhill, Olivia, 179
good and evil, 28, 49, 56, 58, 68, 187
Gospels, 107, 126, 127, 131
Great Rays, 125
Great Triad, The (Guénon), 19
grievances, 85, 86, 87, 152
Ground of Being, 10
Guénon, René, 19
guilt, 132–33
Gurdjieff, G. I., 6–7, 72–73

hamartiology, 187
heaven, 23–24, 61, 124, 190
Heidegger, Martin, 120
Hell, 124, 190
Herbert, Nick, 93
hermeneutics, 2–3
Hinduism, 9, 19, 109
Hoeller, Stephan A., 53
holy instant, 135
holy relationships
    defined, 131
    transmutation of special
        relationships into, 137–38
Holy Spirit, 71, 84, 138, 181–82, 183–84
Huxley, Aldous, 95

I Ching, 51
inferior function, 39
Infinite, the, 12–13, 14, 17, 24, 33
infinite darkness, 13–14
infinite light, 14
Inner Christianity: A Guide to the
    Esoteric Tradition, 9, 193–94,
    195–96
"in the beginning," 15, 32–33

James, William, 94–95
Jaspers, Karl, 166–67, 171
Joachim of Fiore, 161–62, 166
Josipovici, Gabriel, 106
Jung, C. G., 24–25, 26, 30, 39–40, 44,
    45, 174

Kabbalah
    Ain Sof and, 12
    Course system and, 102–3
    Four Worlds, 97–105
    ten sefirot, 50
    veils of negative existence, 13
Kant, Immanuel, 42–43
Karadjeri myth, 82, 83
Kline, Morris, 95
Koot Hoomi, 19

Ladder of Ascent, The (Climacus),
    158–59
Lahiri, Sheikh, 35
Lao-tzu, 17, 119, 180
Last Judgment, 127, 128–29
laws
    of physical world, 73
    of physics, 118

of time, 75
transcending, 74
levels
defined, 70
grounded in reality and, 105
laws of, 74
life
as having no meaning, 80
meaning of, 78–81
purpose of, 81
loss of consciousness, 35, 58
love
Course and, 142–43
relationships, 131–33
transactional, 131
unconditional, 131, 133–34
luminous darkness, 33

madness, 57
Mahayana Buddhism, 127
manifestation, levels of, 41
man in a mirrored box analogy, 47–49,
    71, 83–84, 145–46
Mann, Thomas, 130
Maria Prophetissa, 39
materialism, 8, 93, 94, 95–96, 99, 179
mathematics, 45
Matrix, The, 86–87
meaningless world, 81, 86
meaning of life
common answers to, 79–80
concept, 78–79
desire for, 80
expression of, 80
as within life, 79
question of, 81

mediator, 71
meditation
to access unconditional self, 51, 150
Christian, 150–51
cloud of oblivion and, 35–36, 150
consciousness and, 37
effects of, 150
forms of, 149
spiritual practice as, 149
time devoted to, 150
Meditations on the Tarot (Tomberg),
    64
Miller, Donald, 181
mind
body and, 84
change of, 76
defense of body and, 124
training, 151
mindfulness meditation, 149
miracles
in correcting false thinking, 75
defined, 72–73
dysentery story and, 75–76
as expression of inner awareness, 75
as learning device, 75
Moore, Thomas, 50
moral theology, 190
Mosaic Law, 74
Mouravieff, Boris, 163–65, 166, 173
movement, 22

Nagel, Thomas, 98–99
nature and humanity relationship, 165
near-death experiences (NDEs)
Jung account of, 24–25
not wanting to come back and, 25

Plato's account, 27
Sudman account, 26–30
nothing, 15
numbers
    as archetypes, 45
    levels of manifestation and, 41
    low counting, 44
    three, 42
    twelve, 41–43

Oedipus complex, 83
other. See self and other
Ouspensky, P. D., 115–16

Papus, 16
particular judgment, 126–27
Patanjali, 37
Pentecostalism, 181–83, 184
physical life, view of, 26
physical world, 72, 73, 92, 93
planets in the body, 51, 52
Plato, 27, 30, 39, 47, 51, 109, 167
pneumatology, 188
prayer
    arising out of problems, 155, 156–57
    conflict and confusion and, 154
    Course and, 154–55
    for enemies, 157
    to escape consequences, 154
    motives for, 154
    prosperity gospel and, 183
predestination, 72
problem, 34, 35, 156–57
projection, 134
prosperity gospel, 182, 183
Protestantism, 6, 8

Pythagoras, 167

quantum theory, 94
Queen of the Sciences, 1

reality
    coordinates of, 21–22
    creation of, 21
    five-dimensional, 34, 49, 84, 85
    physical level of, 29, 72
    ten-directional schema as structure
        of, 24
    in truest sense, 73
real world, 85, 91–92, 125
reincarnation, 124–25
relation. *See also* self, other, and relation
    defined, 16
    as primary force, 24
    in various traditions, 18
relationships. *See* holy relationships;
        special relationships
religious development
    age of world religions, 168–69
    first phase, 166–68, 169
    prehistory, 166, 169
religious experience
    emotions and, 6–7
    example, 5–6
    as free of conceptual content, 6
    problem of, 5
    theology and, 4–5
reshit, 14, 15
resilient worldviews, 178
resurrection, meaning of, 116–18
revelation, 192–93
Ricoeur, Paul, 2

Riscajche, Mariano, 5–6
ritual, flexible use of, 176
Robertson, Robin, 44

sacraments, 145–48
sacred ternary, 18
sacrifice, 111–12
salvation, 86, 188–89
samadhi, 51
Sarajevo War Hostel, 29–30
Schopenhauer, Arthur, 48
Schucman, Helen, 59, 60, 117, 198
science, 4, 8, 45, 92, 93, 178–79
scientism, 179
scripture for advice and inspiration, 174
Sefer Yetzirah ("Book of Formation"),
    24, 41–42, 43, 49, 51, 103
Self, 26, 30, 35, 116, 164, 174
self, other, and relation
  defined, 16
  as extending outward from the
    primal point, 42
  Infinite as giving rise to, 24
  Kant's categories related to, 43
  as relative stances, 16
self and other
  Absolute and, 16
  concept, 15
  distinction between, 15–16
  Ego and Non-Ego as, 16
  fourth entity and, 38
  as primary forces, 24
  as relative stances, 16–17
  Tao and, 17
  in various traditions, 18
seminaries, 3

separation
  fall as, 143
  Father, as not aware of, 71
  idea of, 62
  imagined, 156
  as never occurred, 87
  "sin" of, 187
seven planets, 49
Shankara, 48
Shapiro, Rami, 185
six directions, 21, 38, 42
Skutch, Robert, 125–26, 135–36
Smith, Huston, 3
Song of Prayer, The, 155, 158
Sonship, 61, 134, 135
Sons of God, 61, 62, 63, 129, 132, 134
soteriology, 188–89
special relationships
  defined, 131
  hate, 134
  holy relationships versus, 131, 137,
    138
  love, 131–33
  transcending, 135
  transmuting into holy relationships,
    137
spiritual experience
  as center of religion, 174
  Gurdjieff on, 6–7
  in ordinary people, 8
  theology and, 8
  unbalanced, 7
spiritual practice, 149, 151
Sudman, Natalie, 26–30
Swedenborg, Emanuel, 162
Symbolism of Evil, The (Ricoeur), 2

Tao, 17

Tao Te Ching, 17

teachers of God, 191–92

ten-directional schema, 23–24

Tetragrammaton, 18, 24, 40

theodicy, 188

theology

    Christian, 7, 60, 106, 108

    A Course in Miracles, 58, 59, 61, 186

    current times and, 194–95

    expression of, 195

    guidance in spiritual matters and, 7

    moral, 190

    more rigorous, 177

    as Queen of the Sciences, 1

    religious experience and, 4–5

    rethinking, 4

Thetford, Bill, 59, 117, 198

thoughts, 84

three forces, 42

"thrownness," 73

Tibetan Buddhism, 118, 149

Tomberg, Valentin, 64

transactional love, 131

Transcendental Meditation (TM), 149

tulku, 118

twelve, number, 41–43

twelve signs of the zodiac, 41, 43,
    49–50

Tyson, Neil deGrasse, 46

Ubik (Dick), 88–89

unconditional love, 131, 133–34

unconditioned, 51

Underhill, Evelyn, 94, 95

universal truths, 177

universe

    beginning of, 109

    creation of, 21

    Gnostic view of, 47

    as simulation, 46

unknowing, 35, 36

Upanishads, 167

van der Post, Laurens, 28

veils of negative existence, 13

vibration, 16

vipassana meditation, 149, 150

Virgin Mary, 39, 40

Vitale, Joe, 183

Voice, 117, 141, 146–47

Wapnick, Kenneth R., 146

Watts, Alan, 175–76

Whole Self, 29, 30

willpower, 77

world

    Course characterization of, 67–68

    of ego, 72

    as ending in joy, 129

    of God, 72

    as good and evil, 68

    illusory nature of, 94

    meaningless, 81, 86

    physical, 92, 93

    real, 85, 91–92, 125

Yetzirah, 98, 99, 100, 102, 103, 104

yoga nidra, 36

Yoga Sutras, 37

Yu Hua, 180

Zohar, 14, 33

BOOKS OF RELATED INTEREST

The Gospel of Thomas
The Gnostic Wisdom of Jesus
by Jean-Yves Leloup
Foreword By Jacob Needleman

Jung, Buddhism, and the Incarnation of Sophia
Unpublished Writings from the Philosopher of the Soul
by Henry Corbin

The Woman with the Alabaster Jar
Mary Magdalen and the Holy Grail
by Margaret Starbird

Learning to Love
by Eileen Caddy and David Earl Platts, PhD

Instructions for Spiritual Living
by Paul Brunton

Breathing as Spiritual Practice
Experiencing the Presence of God
by Will Johnson

Christian Mythology
Revelations of Pagan Origins
by Philippe Walter
Foreword by Claude Lecouteux

The Miracle Club
How Thoughts Become Reality
by Mitch Horowitz

INNER TRADITIONS • BEAR & COMPANY
P.O. Box 388
Rochester, VT 05767
1-800-246-8648
www.InnerTraditions.com

Or contact your local bookseller